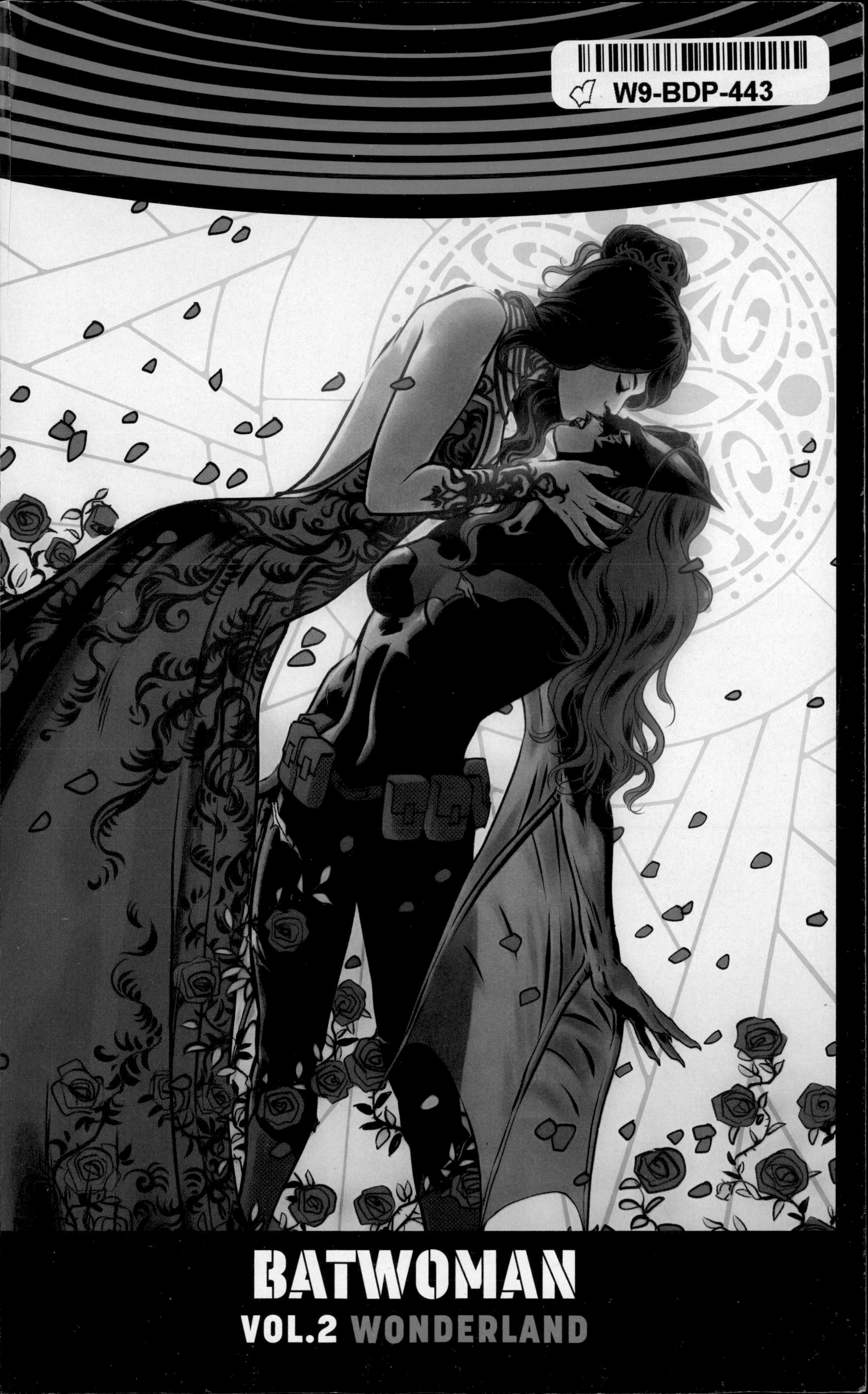

BATWOMAN

VOL.2 WONDERLAND

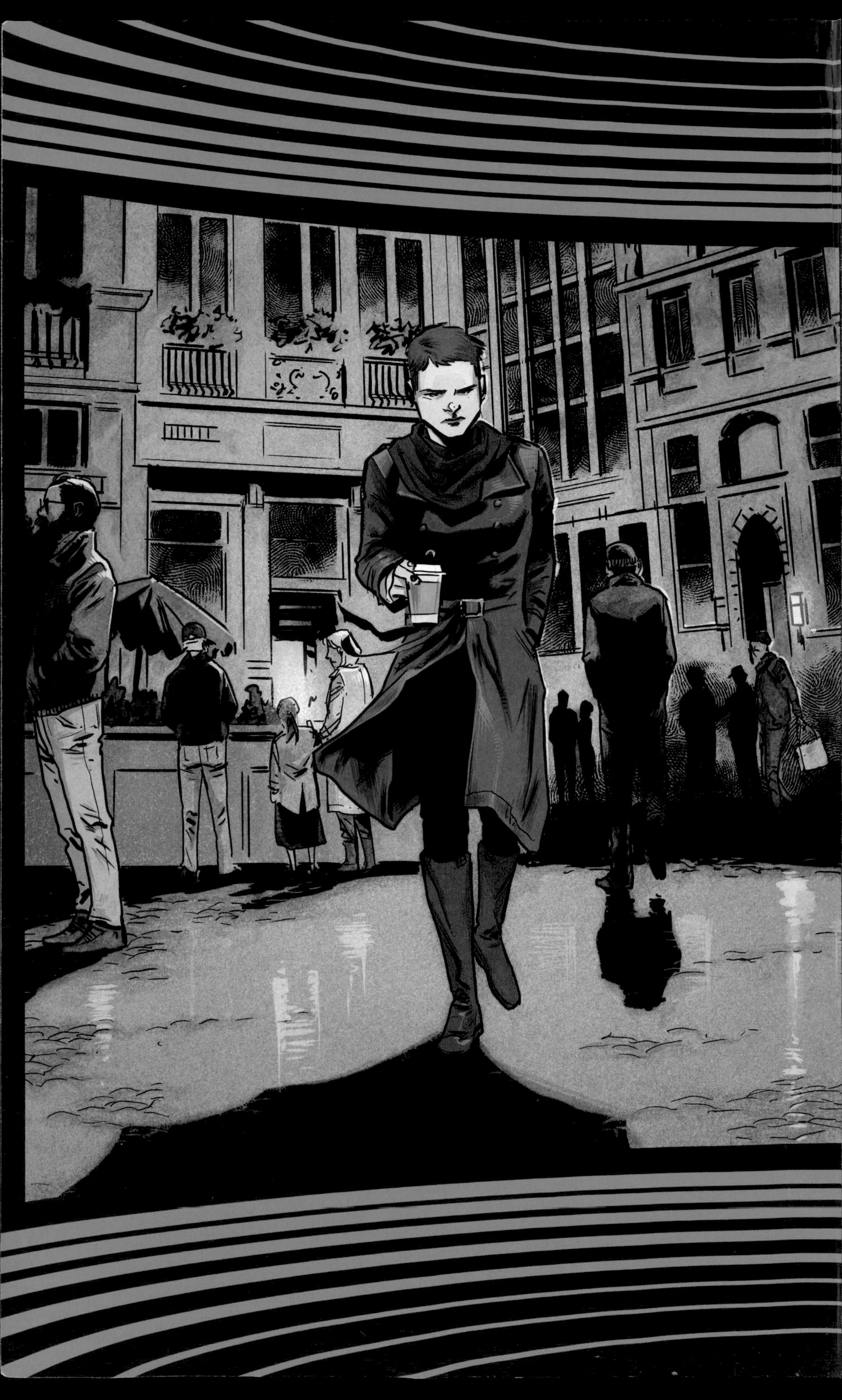

BATWOMAN
VOL.2 WONDERLAND

MARGUERITE BENNETT
K. PERKINS
writers

FERNANDO BLANCO
SCOTT GODLEWSKI
MARC LAMING
artists

JOHN RAUCH
colorist

DERON BENNETT
letterer

MICHAEL CHO
collection cover artist

PROFESSOR PYG created by **GRANT MORRISON, ANDY KUBERT** and **FRANK QUITELY**

MIKE COTTON KATIE KUBERT Editors - Original Series ⁕ **BRITTANY HOLZHERR** Associate Editor - Original Series
JEB WOODARD Group Editor - Collected Editions ⁕ **ROBIN WILDMAN** Editor - Collected Edition
STEVE COOK Design Director - Books ⁕ **MEGEN BELLERSEN** Publication Design

BOB HARRAS Senior VP - Editor-in-Chief, DC Comics
PAT McCALLUM Executive Editor, DC Comics

DIANE NELSON President ⁕ **DAN DiDIO** Publisher ⁕ **JIM LEE** Publisher ⁕ **GEOFF JOHNS** President & Chief Creative Officer
AMIT DESAI Executive VP - Business & Marketing Strategy, Direct to Consumer & Global Franchise Management
SAM ADES Senior VP & General Manager, Digital Services ⁕ **BOBBIE CHASE** VP & Executive Editor, Young Reader & Talent Development
MARK CHIARELLO Senior VP - Art, Design & Collected Editions ⁕ **JOHN CUNNINGHAM** Senior VP - Sales & Trade Marketing
ANNE DePIES Senior VP - Business Strategy, Finance & Administration ⁕ **DON FALLETTI** VP - Manufacturing Operations
LAWRENCE GANEM VP - Editorial Administration & Talent Relations ⁕ **ALISON GILL** Senior VP - Manufacturing & Operations
HANK KANALZ Senior VP - Editorial Strategy & Administration ⁕ **JAY KOGAN** VP - Legal Affairs ⁕ **JACK MAHAN** VP - Business Affairs
NICK J. NAPOLITANO VP - Manufacturing Administration ⁕ **EDDIE SCANNELL** VP - Consumer Marketing
COURTNEY SIMMONS Senior VP - Publicity & Communications ⁕ **JIM (SKI) SOKOLOWSKI** VP - Comic Book Specialty Sales & Trade Marketing
NANCY SPEARS VP - Mass, Book, Digital Sales & Trade Marketing ⁕ **MICHELE R. WELLS** VP - Content Strategy

BATWOMAN VOL.2: WONDERLAND

Published by DC Comics. Compilation and all new material Copyright © 2018 DC Comics. All Rights Reserved.
Originally published in single magazine form in BATWOMAN 7-11. Copyright 2017, 2018 DC Comics. All Rights Reserved.
All characters, their distinctive likenesses and related elements featured in this publication are trademarks of DC Comics.
The stories, characters and incidents featured in this publication are entirely fictional.
DC Comics does not read or accept unsolicited submissions of ideas, stories or artwork.

DC Comics, 2900 West Alameda Ave., Burbank, CA 91505
Printed by LSC Communications, Kendallville, IN, USA. 4/27/18. First Printing.
ISBN: 978-1-4012-7871-7

Library of Congress Cataloging-in-Publication Data is available.

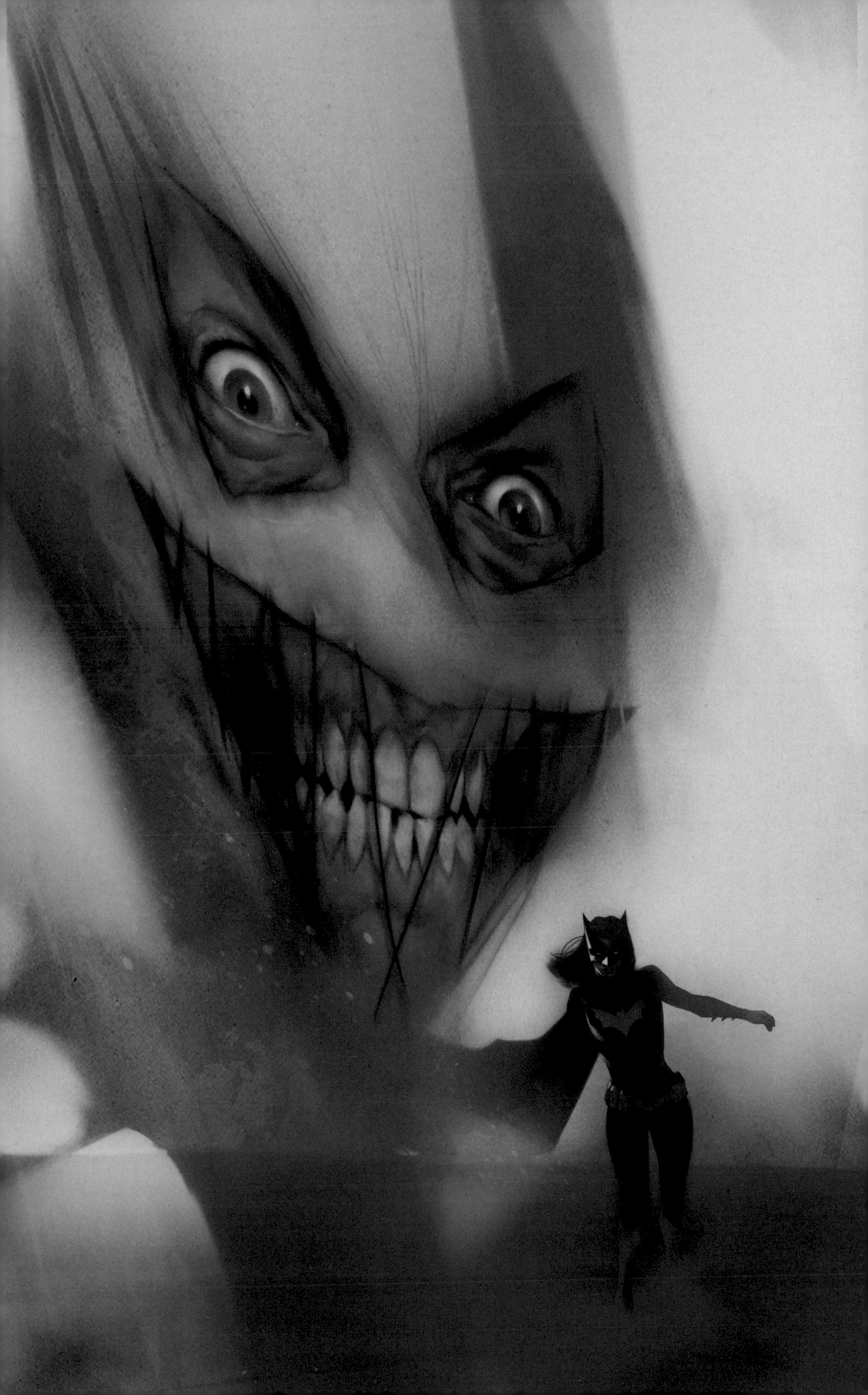

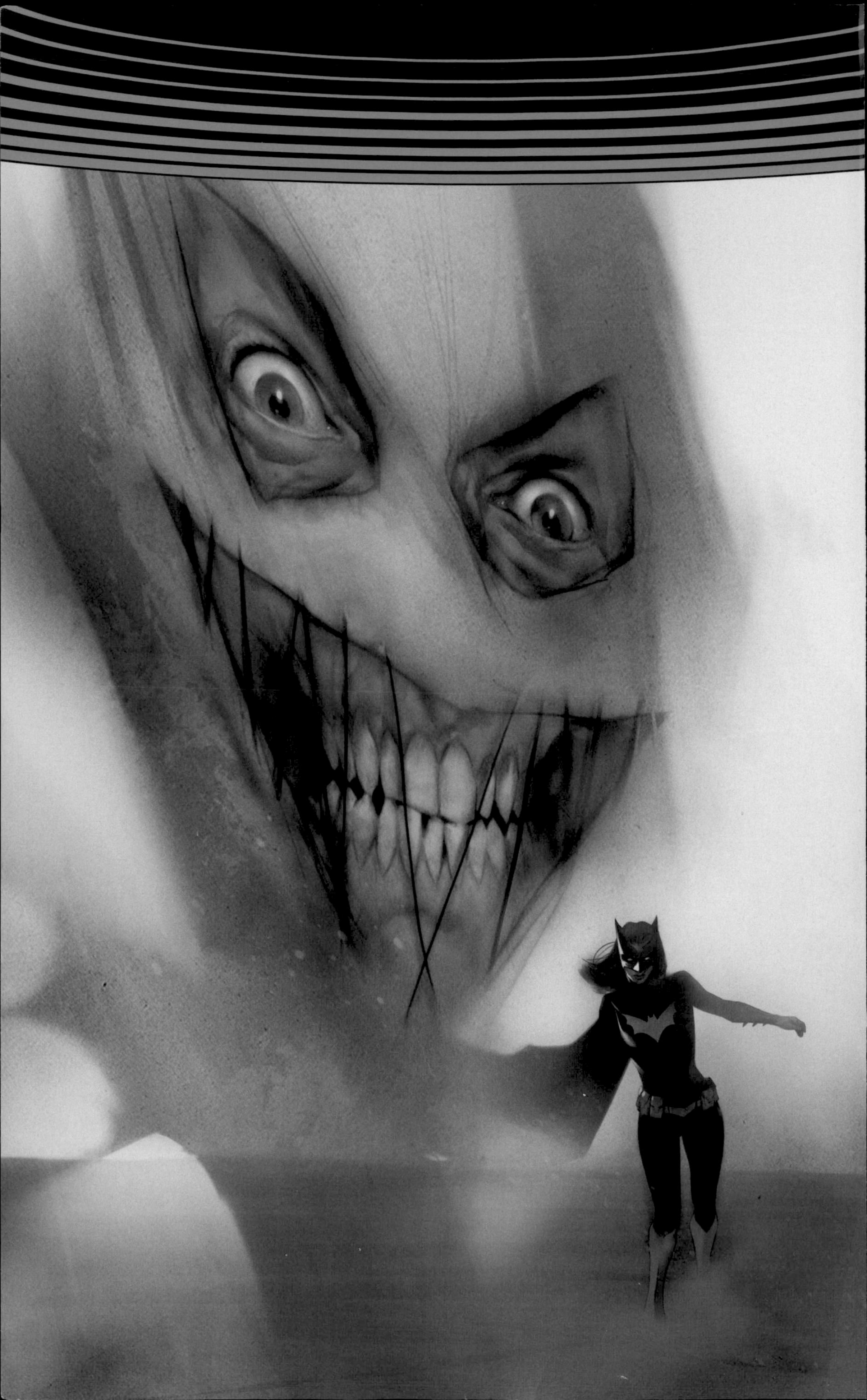

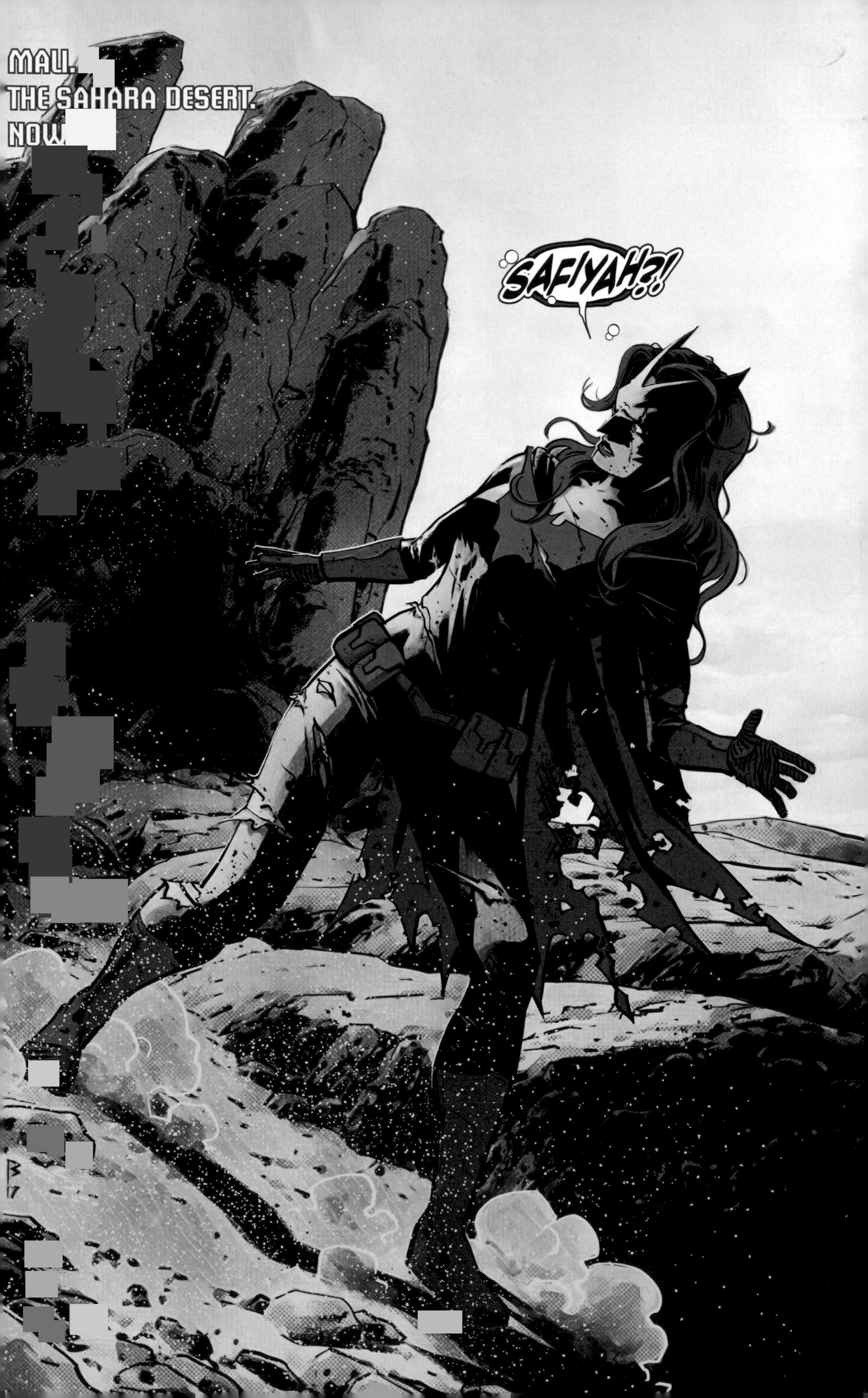
MALI.
THE SAHARA DESERT.
NOW
SAFIYAH?!

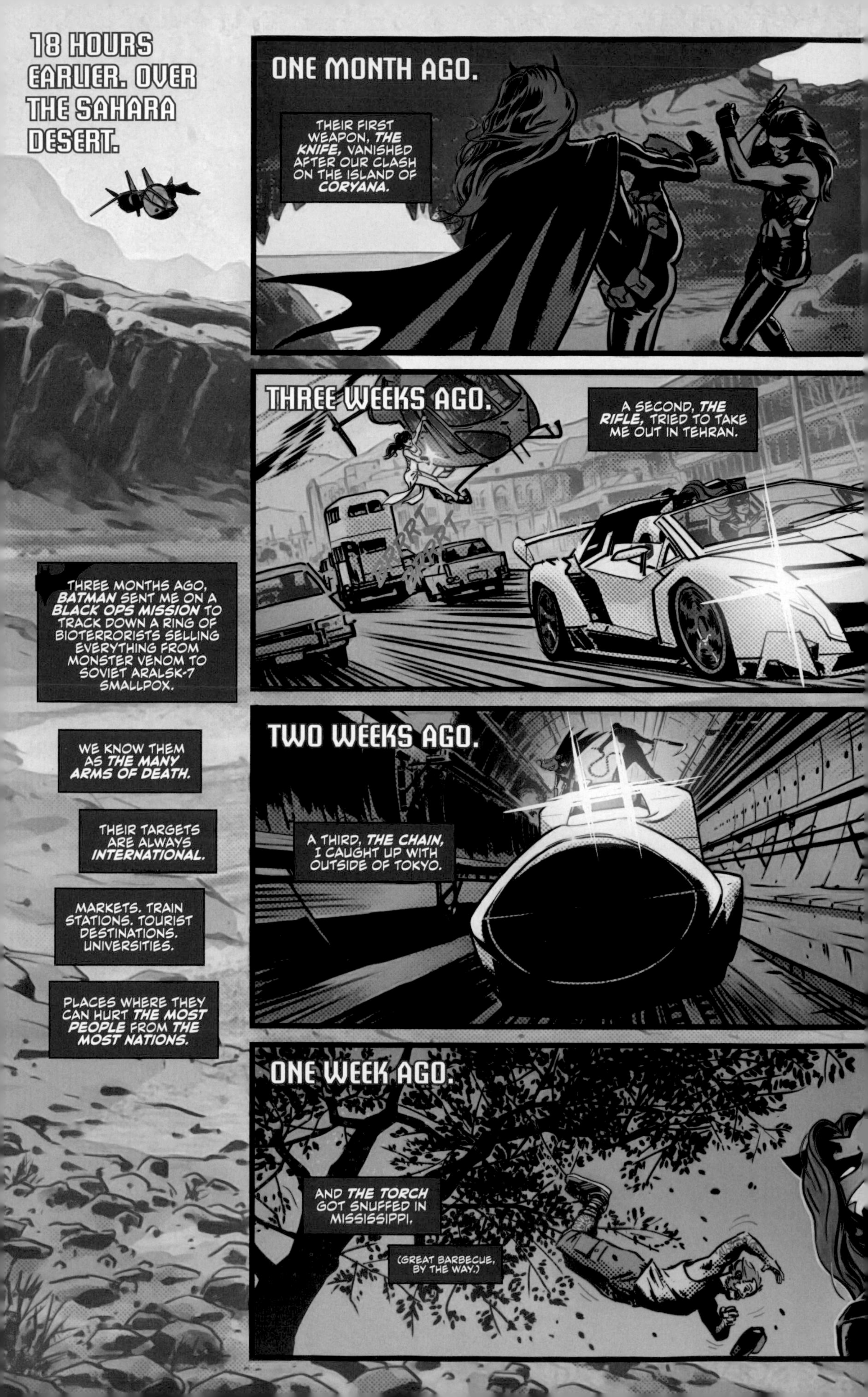
18 HOURS EARLIER. OVER THE SAHARA DESERT.
ONE MONTH AGO.
THEIR FIRST WEAPON, THE KNIFE, VANISHED AFTER OUR CLASH ON THE ISLAND OF CORYANA.
THREE WEEKS AGO.
A SECOND, THE RIFLE, TRIED TO TAKE ME OUT IN TEHRAN.
BRRRT
BRRRT
THREE MONTHS AGO, BATMAN SENT ME ON A BLACK OPS MISSION TO TRACK DOWN A RING OF BIOTERRORISTS SELLING EVERYTHING FROM MONSTER VENOM TO SOVIET ARALSK-7 SMALLPOX.
WE KNOW THEM AS THE MANY ARMS OF DEATH.
THEIR TARGETS ARE ALWAYS INTERNATIONAL.
MARKETS. TRAIN STATIONS. TOURIST DESTINATIONS. UNIVERSITIES.
PLACES WHERE THEY CAN HURT THE MOST PEOPLE FROM THE MOST NATIONS.
TWO WEEKS AGO.
A THIRD, THE CHAIN, I CAUGHT UP WITH OUTSIDE OF TOKYO.
ONE WEEK AGO.
AND THE TORCH GOT SNUFFED IN MISSISSIPPI.
(GREAT BARBECUE, BY THE WAY.)

NOW I'M HUNTING A MAN THEY'RE CALLING *THE NEEDLE*.

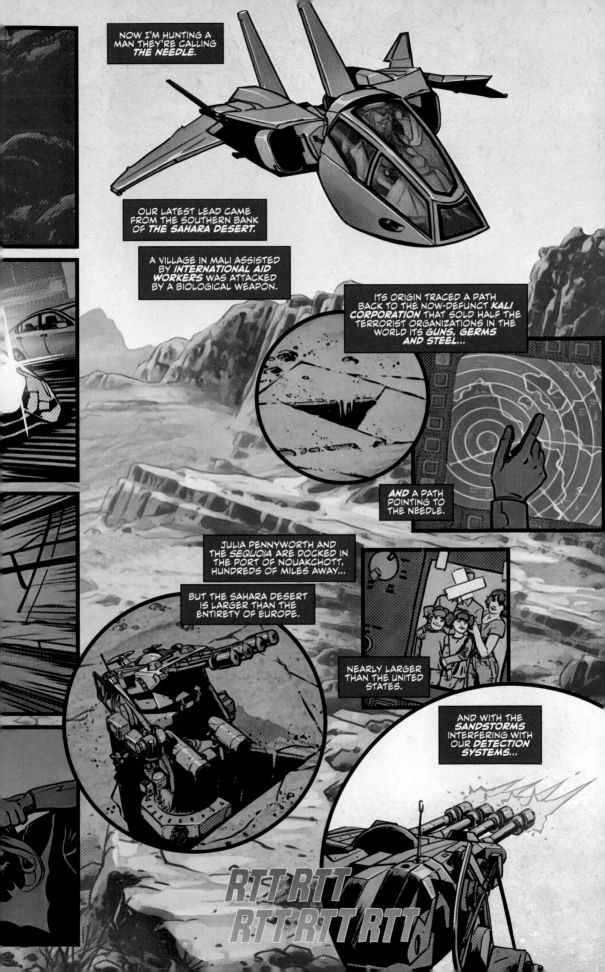

OUR LATEST LEAD CAME FROM THE SOUTHERN BANK OF *THE SAHARA DESERT*.

A VILLAGE IN MALI ASSISTED BY *INTERNATIONAL AID WORKERS* WAS ATTACKED BY A BIOLOGICAL WEAPON.

ITS ORIGIN TRACED A PATH BACK TO THE NOW-DEFUNCT *KALI CORPORATION* THAT SOLD HALF THE TERRORIST ORGANIZATIONS IN THE WORLD ITS *GUNS, GERMS AND STEEL...*

AND A PATH POINTING TO THE NEEDLE.

JULIA PENNYWORTH AND THE *SEQUOIA* ARE DOCKED IN THE PORT OF NOUAKCHOTT, HUNDREDS OF MILES AWAY...

BUT THE SAHARA DESERT IS LARGER THAN THE ENTIRETY OF EUROPE.

NEARLY LARGER THAN THE UNITED STATES.

AND WITH THE *SANDSTORMS* INTERFERING WITH OUR *DETECTION SYSTEMS...*

RTT RTT
RTT RTT RTT

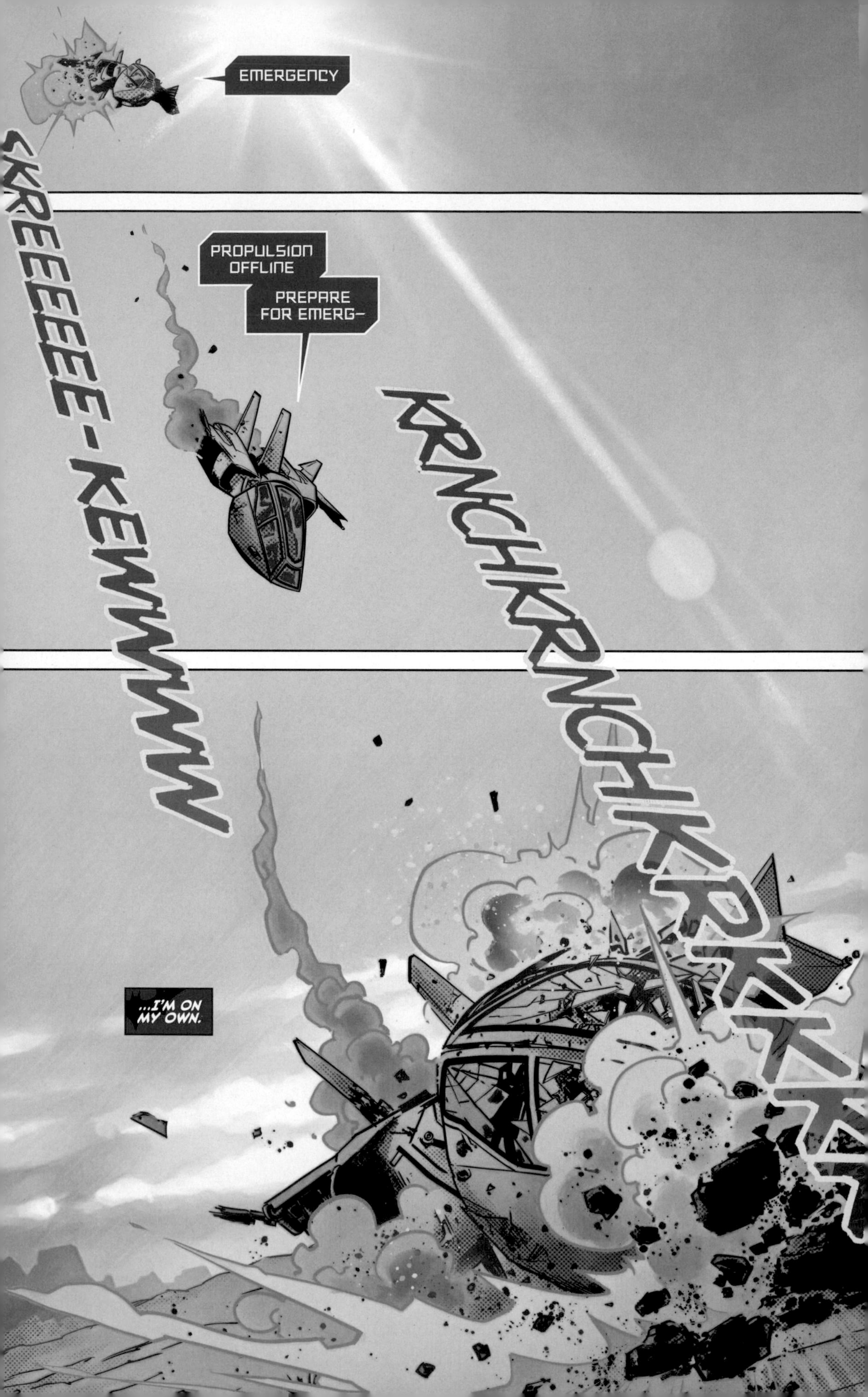
EMERGENCY
SKREEEEEEE-KEWWWWW
PROPULSION OFFLINE
PREPARE FOR EMERG–
KRNCHKRNCHKRKRKKK
...I'M ON MY OWN.

THE ISLAND OF CORYANA.

MHMM...?

THE LOST YEAR.

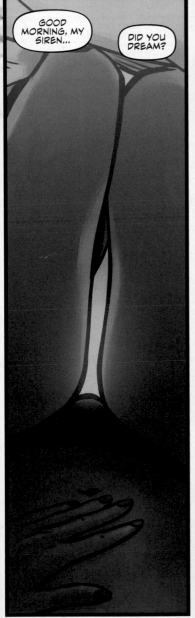

GOOD MORNING, MY SIREN...

DID YOU DREAM?

SAFIYAH.

MY LADY OF THE ISLAND.

¿AHEM¿?

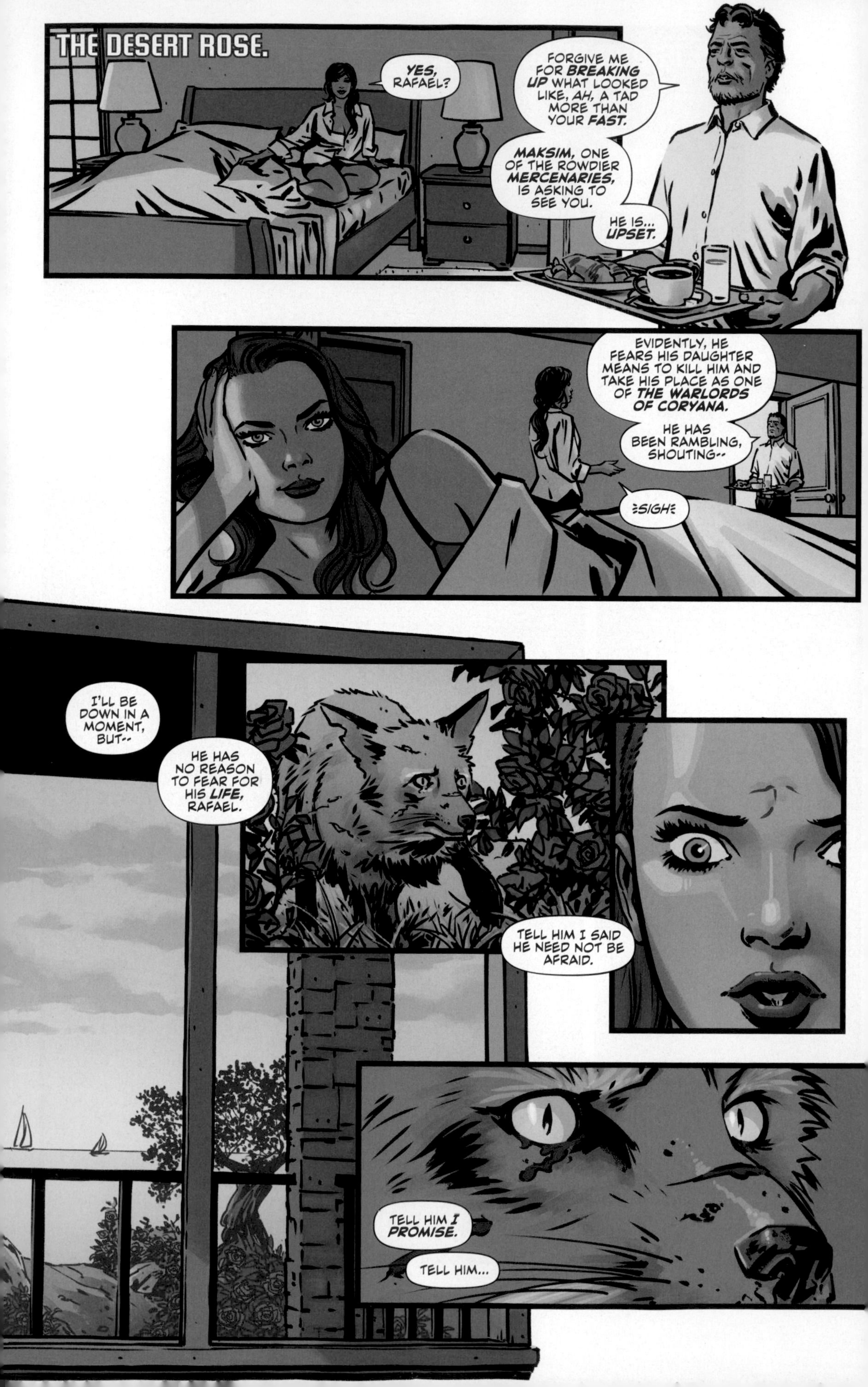
THE DESERT ROSE.
YES, RAFAEL?
FORGIVE ME FOR BREAKING UP WHAT LOOKED LIKE, AH, A TAD MORE THAN YOUR FAST.
MAKSIM, ONE OF THE ROWDIER MERCENARIES, IS ASKING TO SEE YOU.
HE IS... UPSET.
EVIDENTLY, HE FEARS HIS DAUGHTER MEANS TO KILL HIM AND TAKE HIS PLACE AS ONE OF THE WARLORDS OF CORYANA.
HE HAS BEEN RAMBLING, SHOUTING--
SIGH
I'LL BE DOWN IN A MOMENT, BUT--
HE HAS NO REASON TO FEAR FOR HIS LIFE, RAFAEL.
TELL HIM I SAID HE NEED NOT BE AFRAID.
TELL HIM I PROMISE.
TELL HIM...

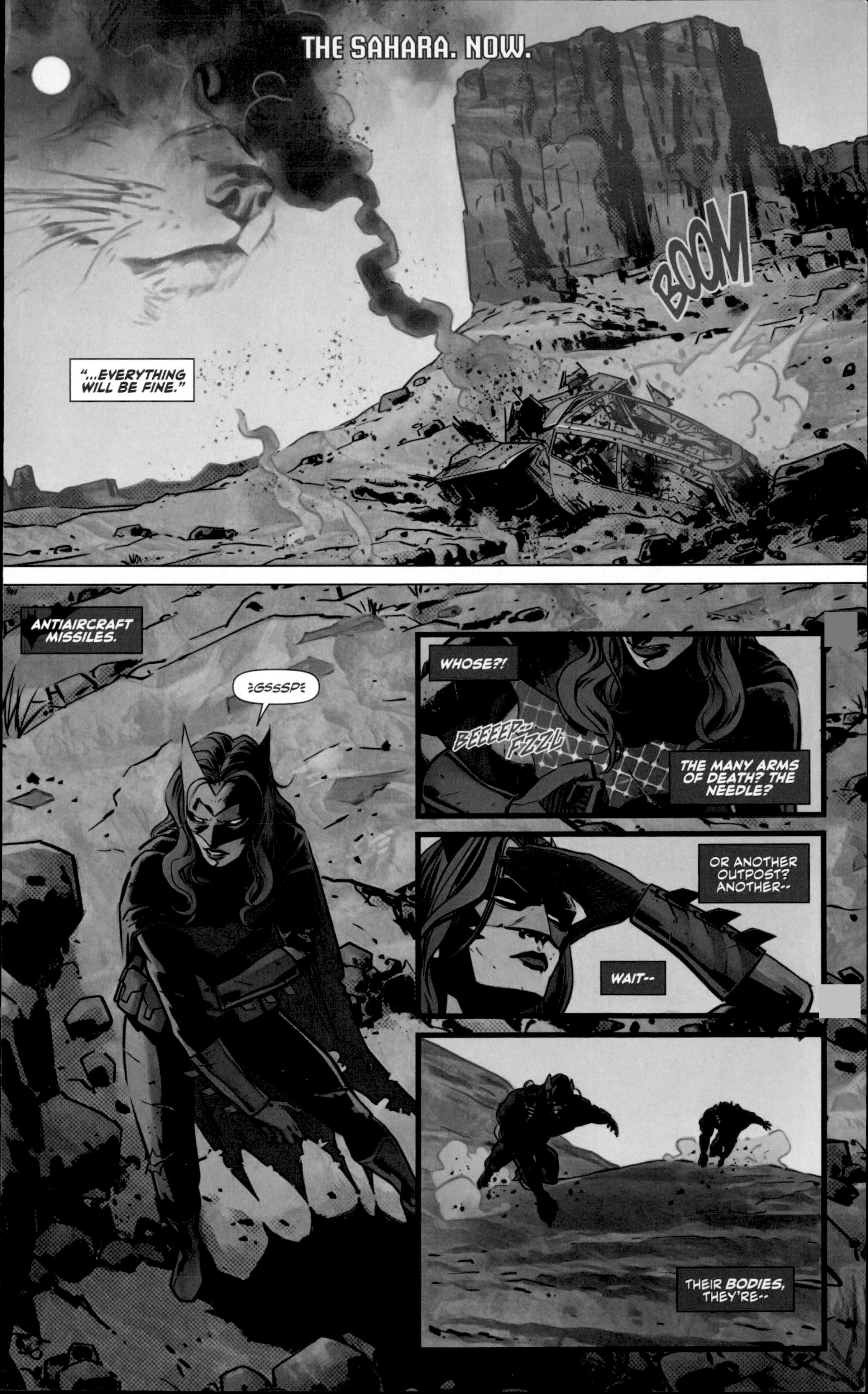
THE SAHARA. NOW.
BOOM
"...EVERYTHING WILL BE FINE."
ANTIAIRCRAFT MISSILES.
GSSSP
WHOSE?!
BEEEEP-- FZZL
THE MANY ARMS OF DEATH? THE NEEDLE?
OR ANOTHER OUTPOST? ANOTHER--
WAIT--
THEIR BODIES, THEY'RE--

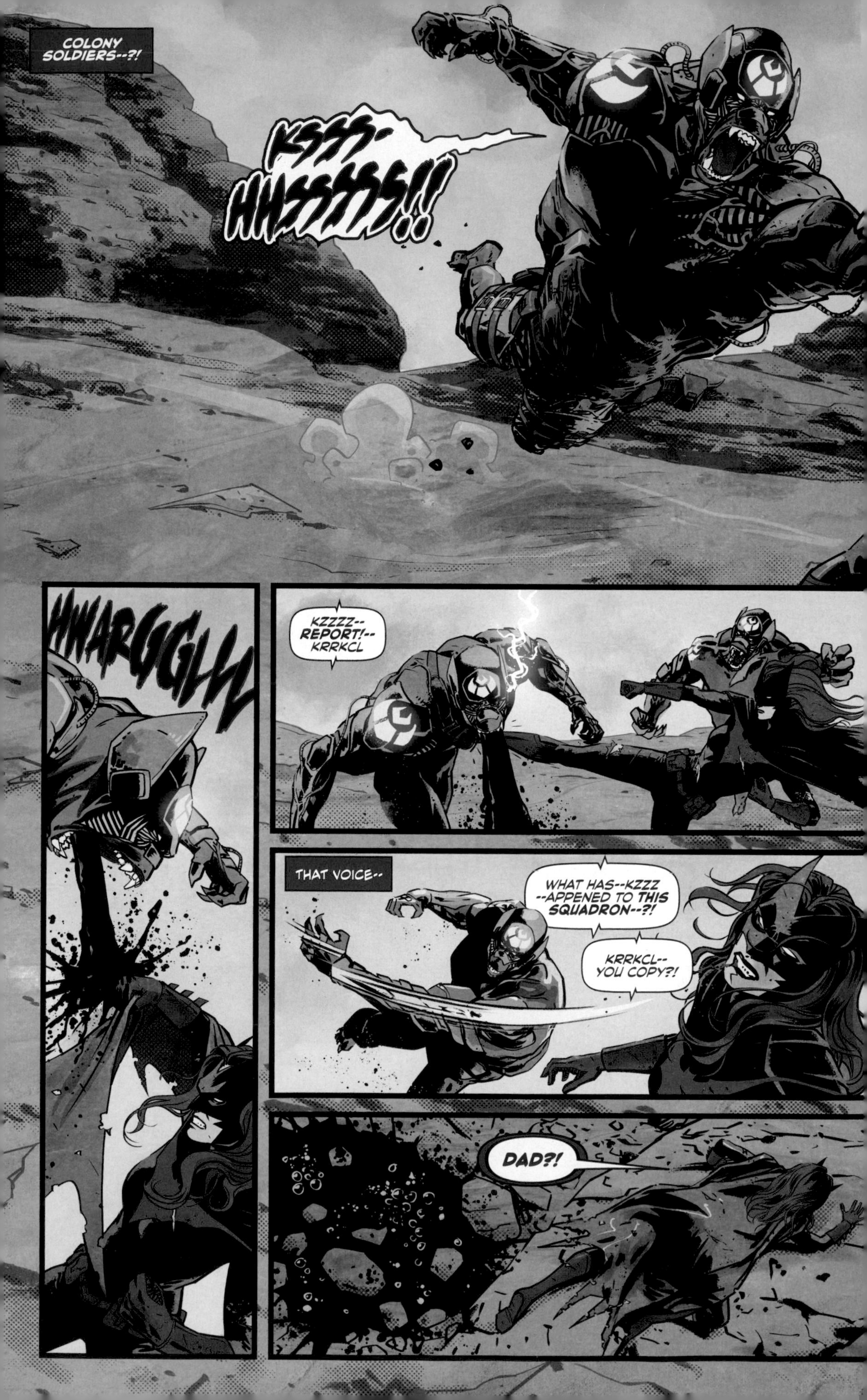
COLONY SOLDIERS--?!
KSSSS-HHSSSSSS!!
HWARGGLW
KZZZZ-- REPORT!-- KRRKCL
THAT VOICE--
WHAT HAS--KZZZ --APPENED TO THIS SQUADRON--?!
KRRKCL-- YOU COPY?!
DAD?!

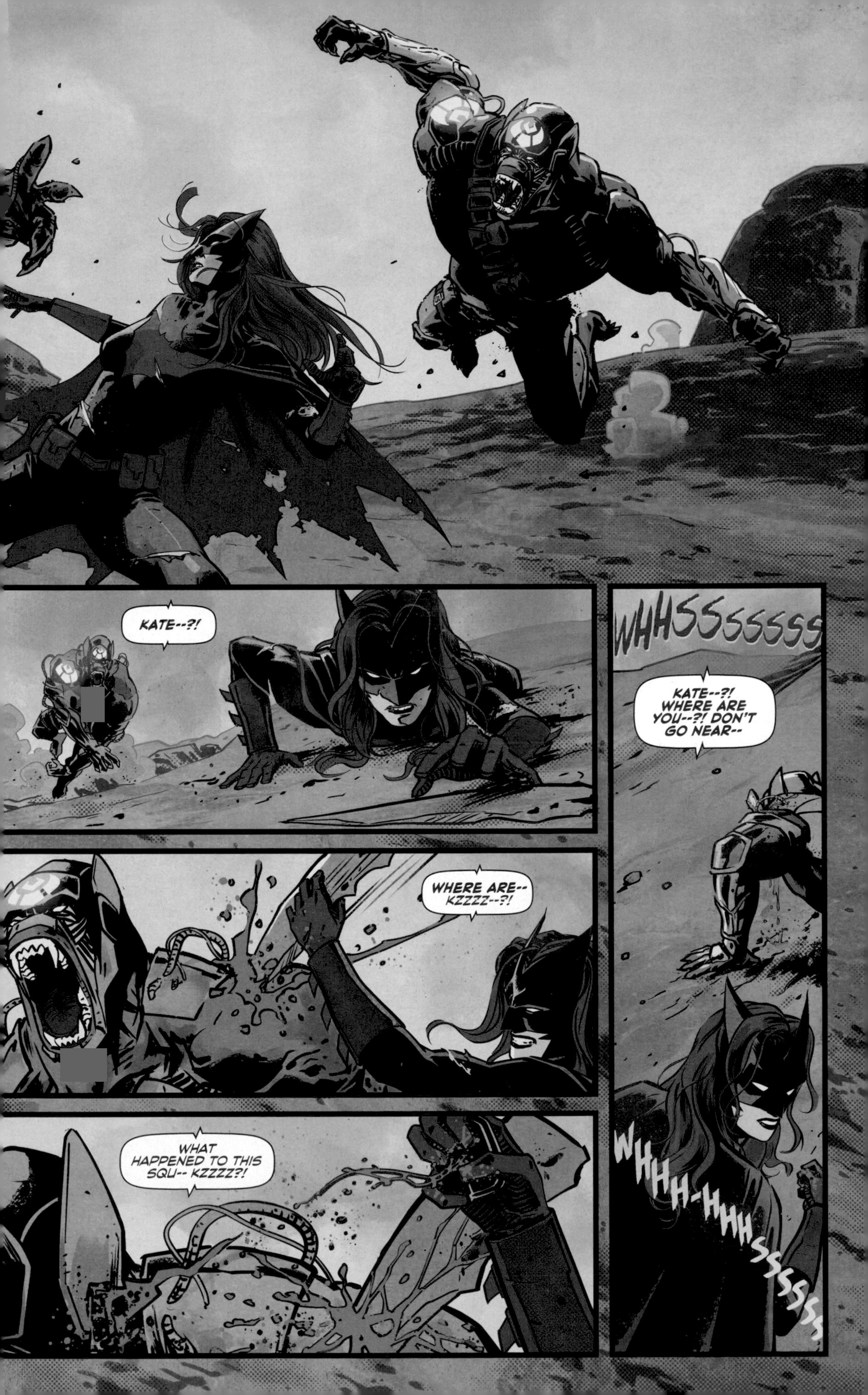
KATE--?!
WHERE ARE-- KZZZZ--?!
WHAT HAPPENED TO THIS SQU-- KZZZZ?!
WHHSSSSSSS
KATE--?! WHERE ARE YOU--?! DON'T GO NEAR--
WHHH-HHHSSSSSSS

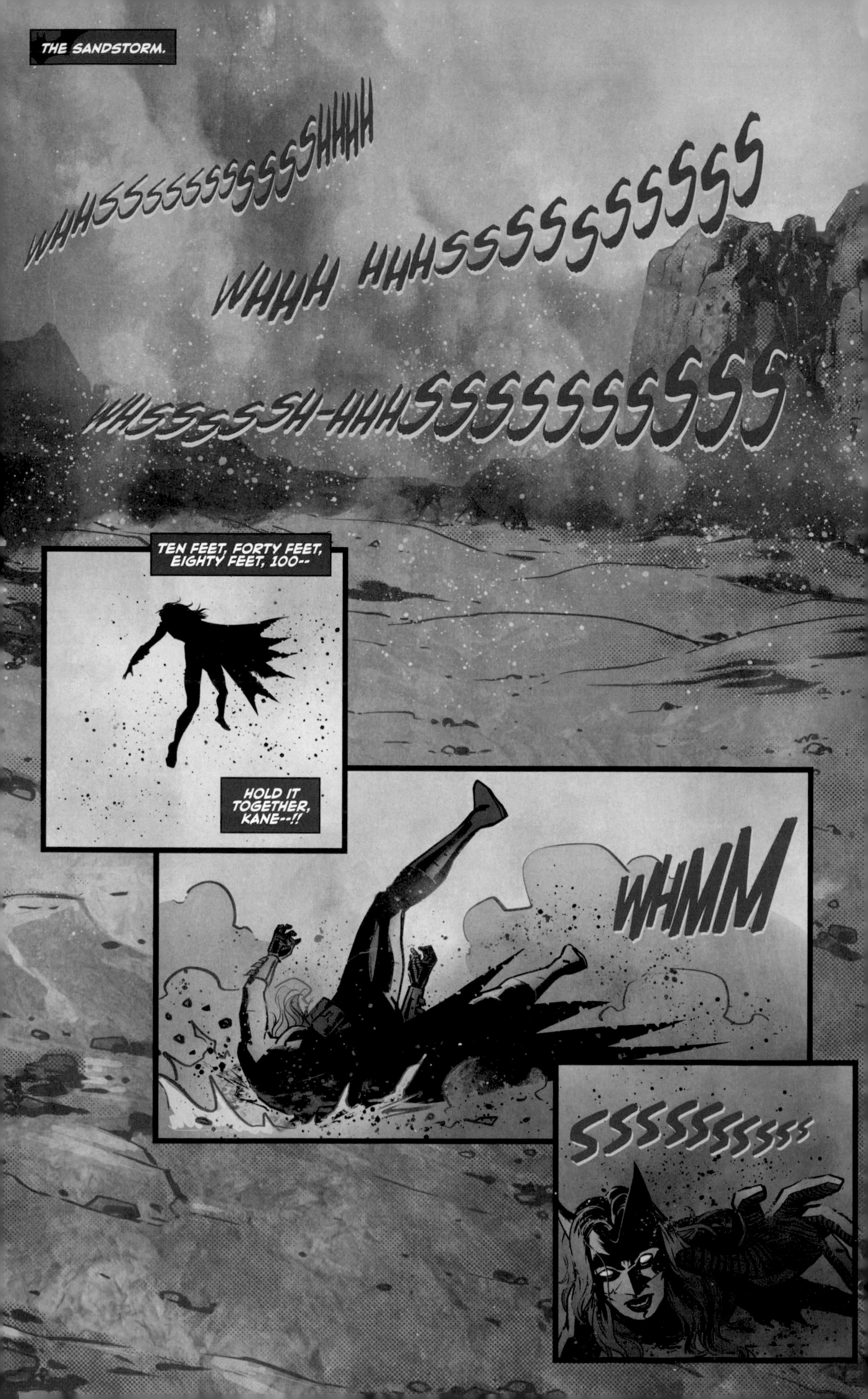
THE SANDSTORM.
WHHSSSSSSSSSSSHHHH
WHHH HHHSSSSSSSSSSS
WHSSSSSSH-HHHSSSSSSSSSSS
TEN FEET, FORTY FEET, EIGHTY FEET, 100--
HOLD IT TOGETHER, KANE--!!
WHMM
SSSSSSSSSSS

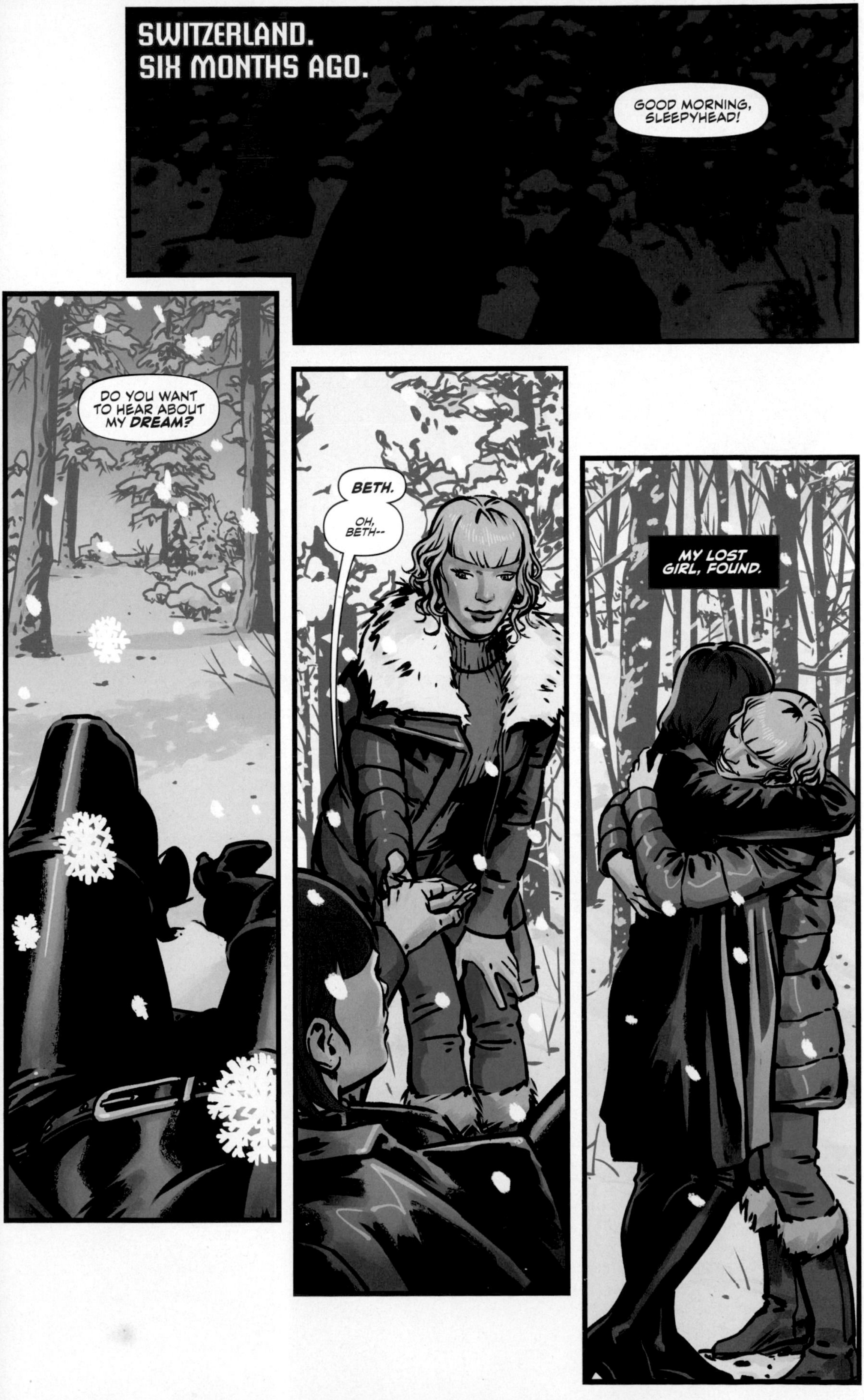
SWITZERLAND.
SIX MONTHS AGO.
GOOD MORNING, SLEEPYHEAD!
DO YOU WANT TO HEAR ABOUT MY DREAM?
BETH.
OH, BETH--
MY LOST GIRL, FOUND.

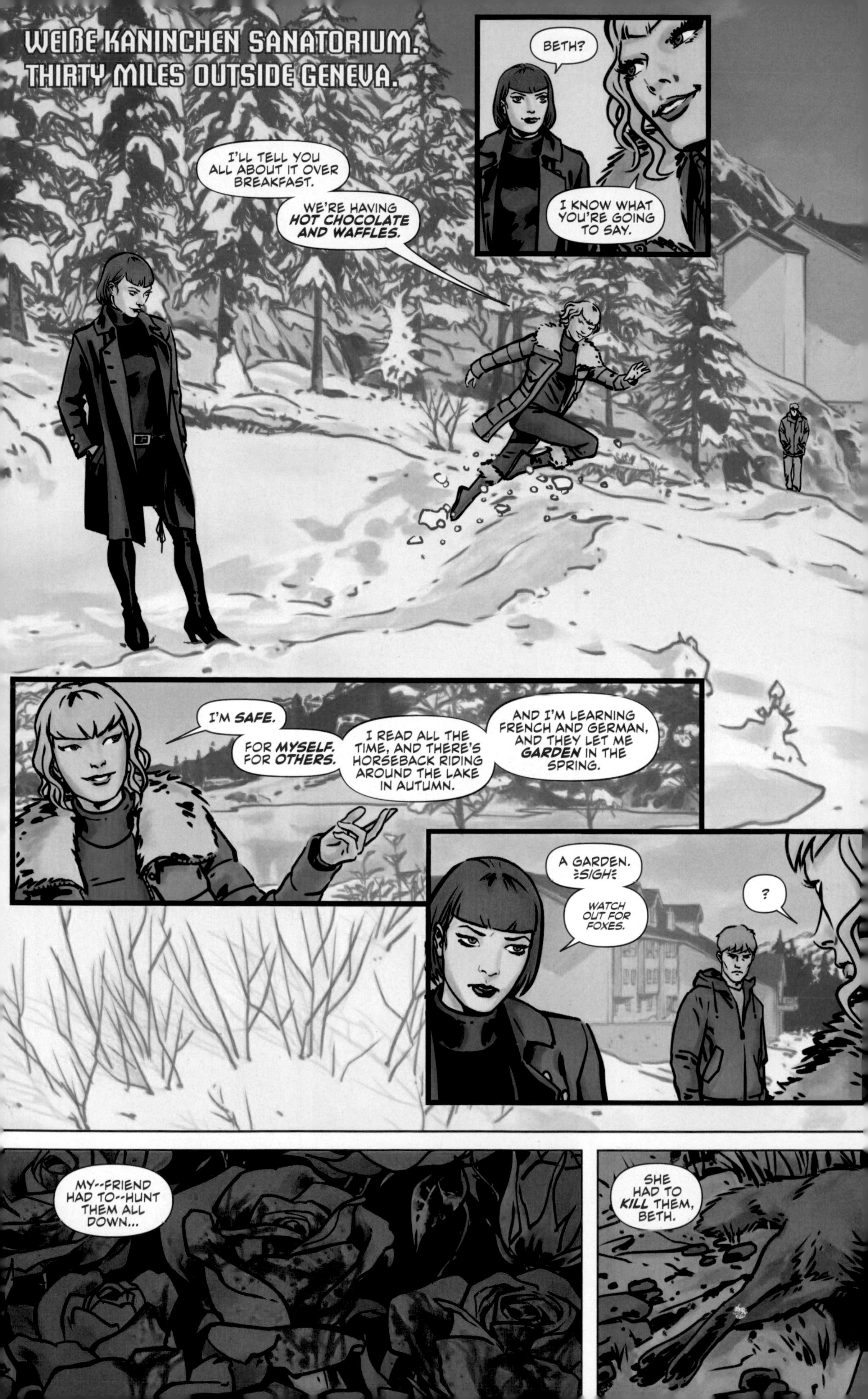

WEIßE KANINCHEN SANATORIUM. THIRTY MILES OUTSIDE GENEVA.
BETH?
I KNOW WHAT YOU'RE GOING TO SAY.
I'LL TELL YOU ALL ABOUT IT OVER BREAKFAST.
WE'RE HAVING HOT CHOCOLATE AND WAFFLES.
I'M SAFE.
FOR MYSELF. FOR OTHERS.
I READ ALL THE TIME, AND THERE'S HORSEBACK RIDING AROUND THE LAKE IN AUTUMN.
AND I'M LEARNING FRENCH AND GERMAN, AND THEY LET ME GARDEN IN THE SPRING.
A GARDEN. SIGH
WATCH OUT FOR FOXES.
?
MY--FRIEND HAD TO--HUNT THEM ALL DOWN...
SHE HAD TO KILL THEM, BETH.

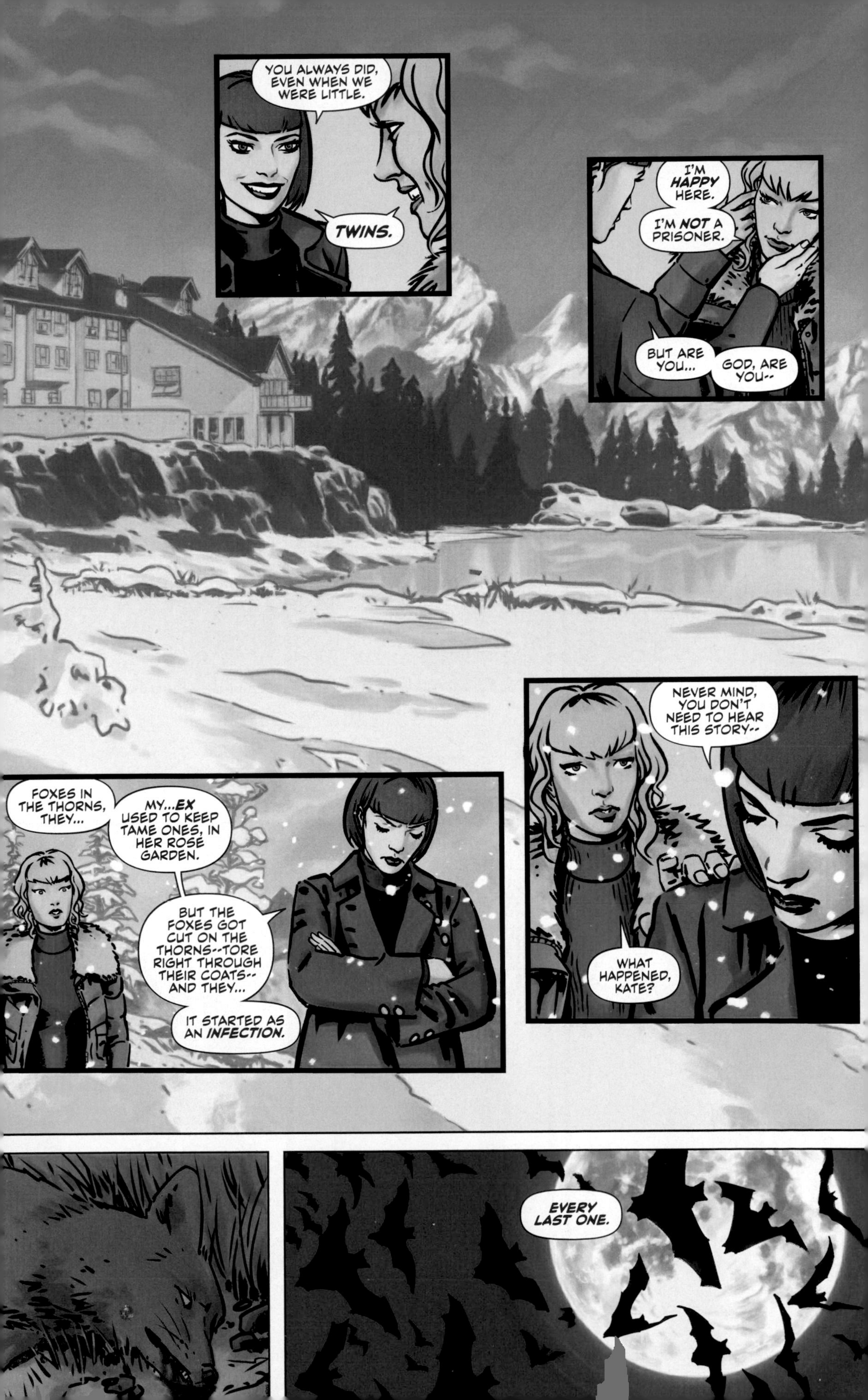
YOU ALWAYS DID, EVEN WHEN WE WERE LITTLE.
TWINS.
I'M HAPPY HERE.
I'M NOT A PRISONER.
BUT ARE YOU...
GOD, ARE YOU--
NEVER MIND, YOU DON'T NEED TO HEAR THIS STORY--
WHAT HAPPENED, KATE?
FOXES IN THE THORNS, THEY...
MY...EX USED TO KEEP TAME ONES, IN HER ROSE GARDEN.
BUT THE FOXES GOT CUT ON THE THORNS--TORE RIGHT THROUGH THEIR COATS--AND THEY...
IT STARTED AS AN INFECTION.
EVERY LAST ONE.

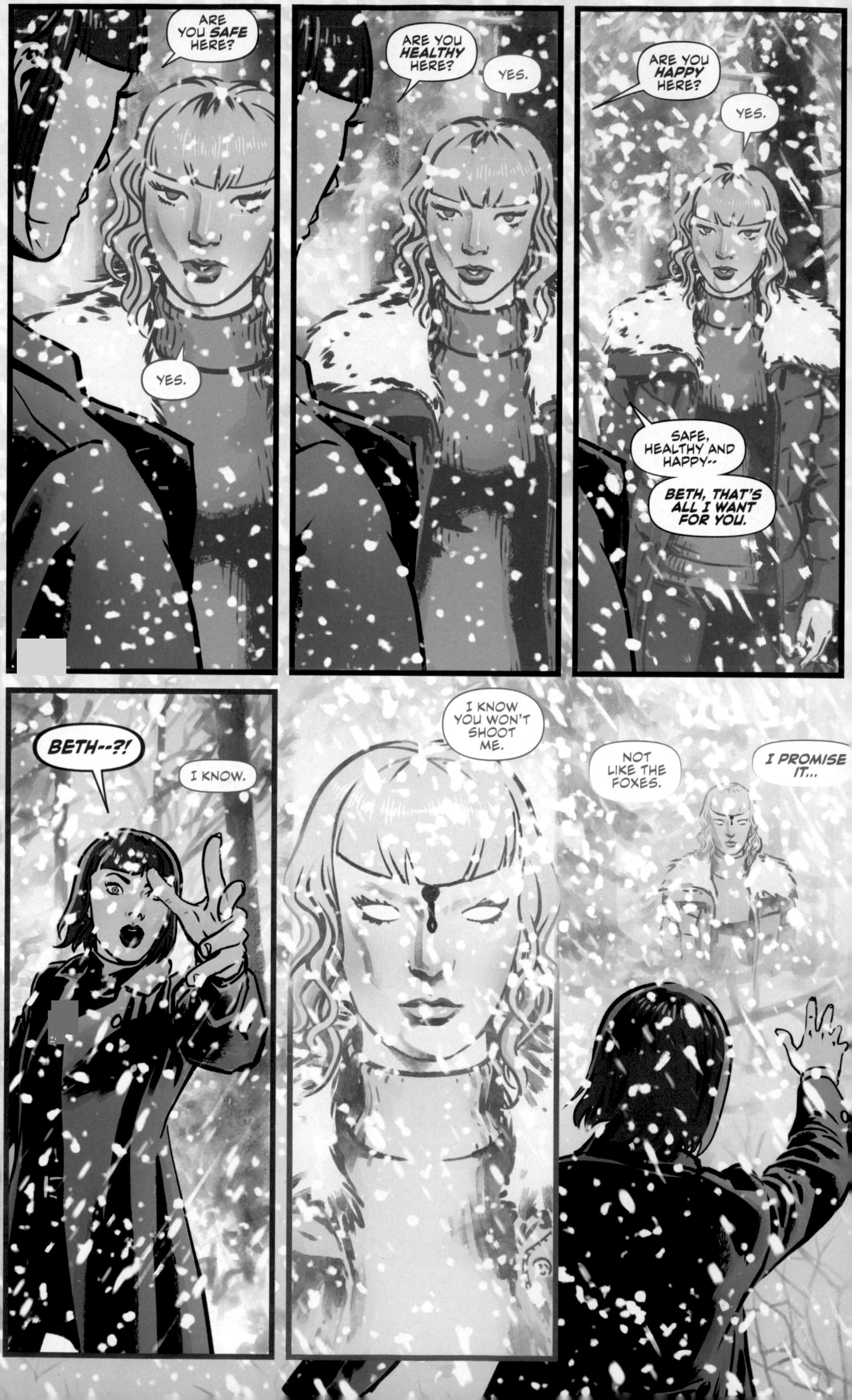
ARE YOU SAFE HERE?
YES.
ARE YOU HEALTHY HERE?
YES.
ARE YOU HAPPY HERE?
YES.
SAFE, HEALTHY AND HAPPY--
BETH, THAT'S ALL I WANT FOR YOU.
BETH--?!
I KNOW.
I KNOW YOU WON'T SHOOT ME.
NOT LIKE THE FOXES.
I PROMISE IT...

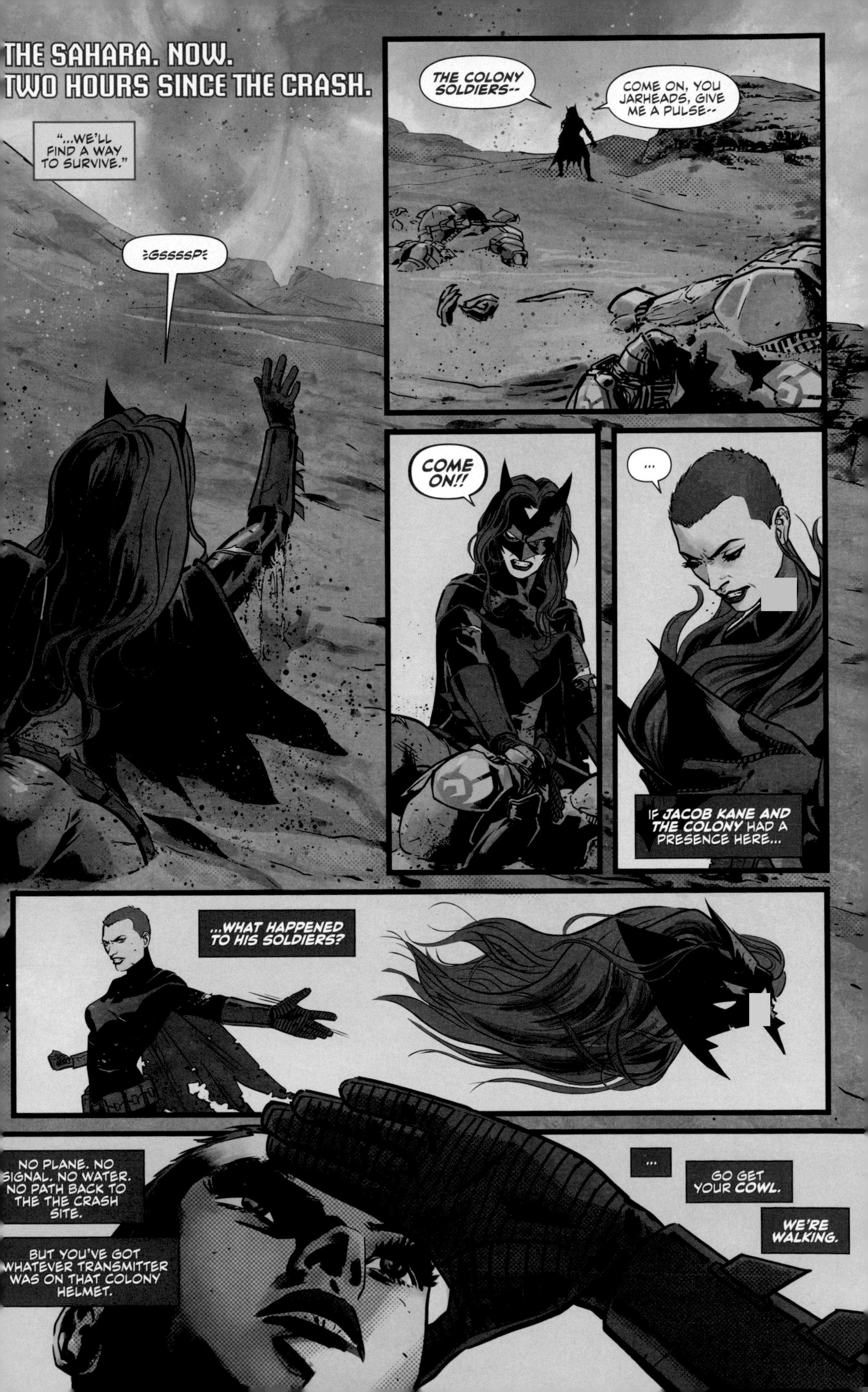
THE SAHARA. NOW.
TWO HOURS SINCE THE CRASH.
"...WE'LL FIND A WAY TO SURVIVE."
GSSSSP
THE COLONY SOLDIERS--
COME ON, YOU JARHEADS, GIVE ME A PULSE--
COME ON!!
...
IF JACOB KANE AND THE COLONY HAD A PRESENCE HERE...
...WHAT HAPPENED TO HIS SOLDIERS?
NO PLANE. NO SIGNAL. NO WATER. NO PATH BACK TO THE THE CRASH SITE.
BUT YOU'VE GOT WHATEVER TRANSMITTER WAS ON THAT COLONY HELMET.
...
GO GET YOUR COWL.
WE'RE WALKING.

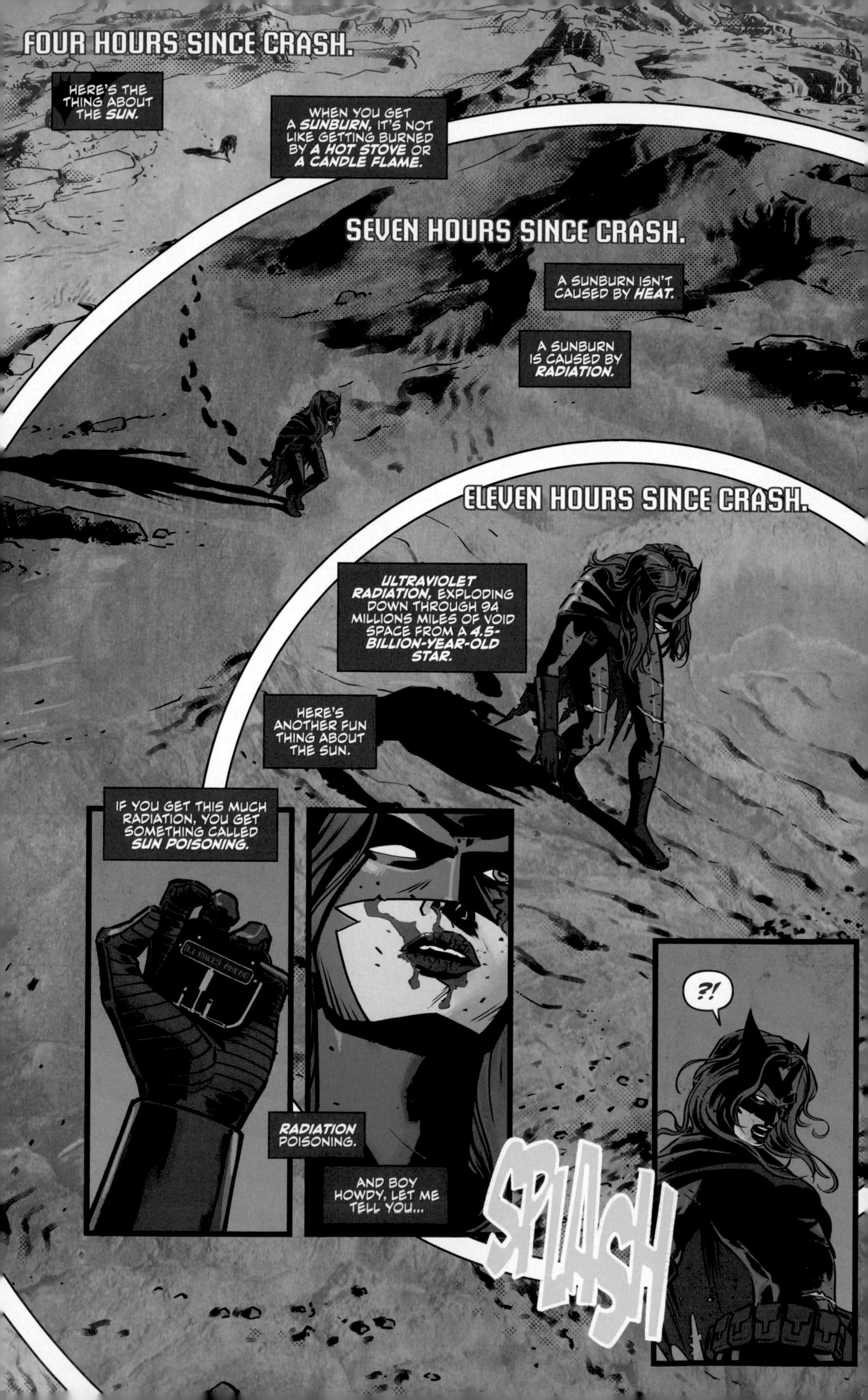

FOUR HOURS SINCE CRASH.
HERE'S THE THING ABOUT THE SUN.
WHEN YOU GET A SUNBURN, IT'S NOT LIKE GETTING BURNED BY A HOT STOVE OR A CANDLE FLAME.
SEVEN HOURS SINCE CRASH.
A SUNBURN ISN'T CAUSED BY HEAT.
A SUNBURN IS CAUSED BY RADIATION.
ELEVEN HOURS SINCE CRASH.
ULTRAVIOLET RADIATION, EXPLODING DOWN THROUGH 94 MILLIONS MILES OF VOID SPACE FROM A 4.5-BILLION-YEAR-OLD STAR.
HERE'S ANOTHER FUN THING ABOUT THE SUN.
IF YOU GET THIS MUCH RADIATION, YOU GET SOMETHING CALLED SUN POISONING.
RADIATION POISONING.
AND BOY HOWDY, LET ME TELL YOU...
?!
SPLASH

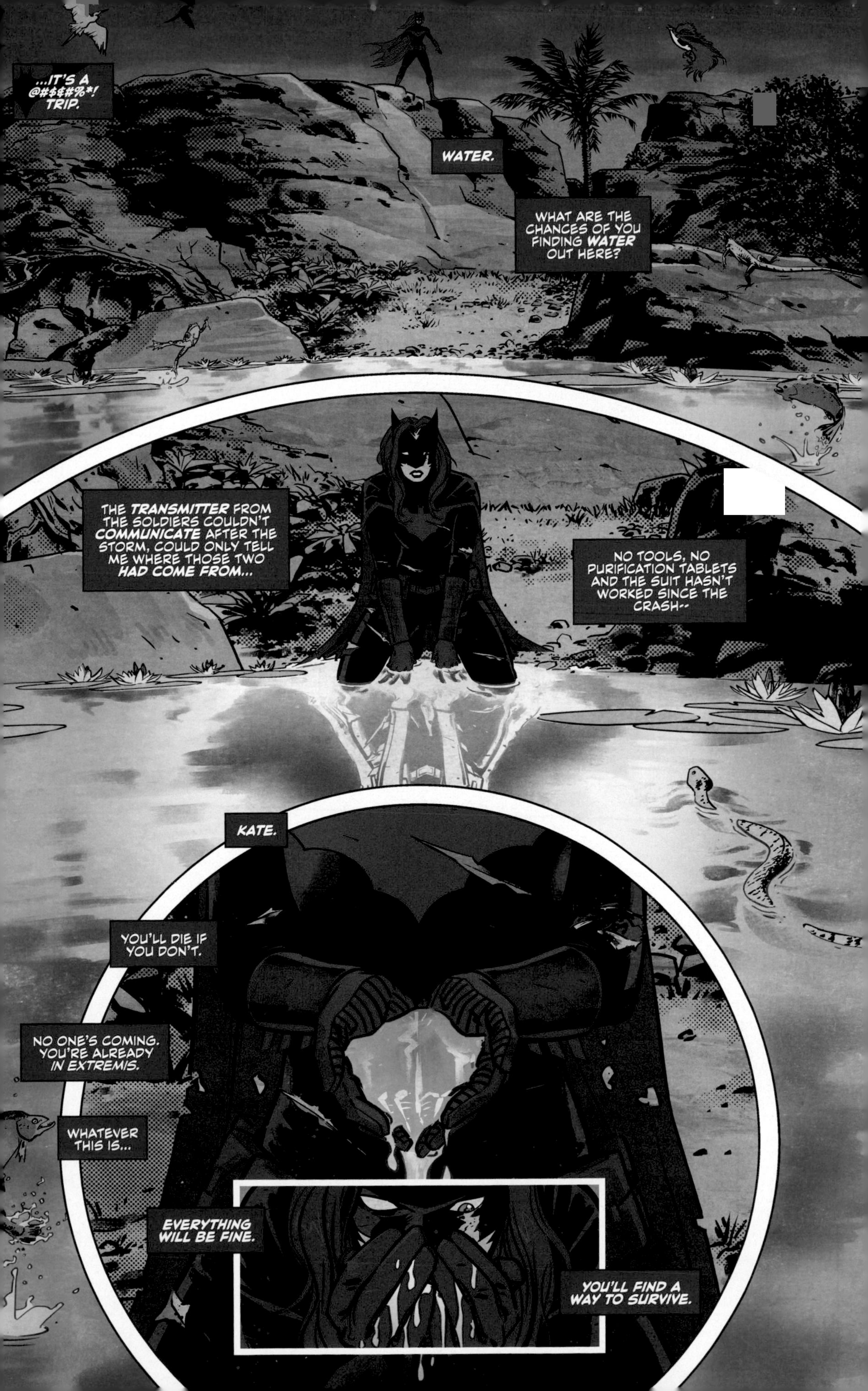
...IT'S A @#$¢#%*! TRIP.
WATER.
WHAT ARE THE CHANCES OF YOU FINDING WATER OUT HERE?
THE TRANSMITTER FROM THE SOLDIERS COULDN'T COMMUNICATE AFTER THE STORM, COULD ONLY TELL ME WHERE THOSE TWO HAD COME FROM...
NO TOOLS, NO PURIFICATION TABLETS AND THE SUIT HASN'T WORKED SINCE THE CRASH--
KATE.
YOU'LL DIE IF YOU DON'T.
NO ONE'S COMING. YOU'RE ALREADY IN EXTREMIS.
WHATEVER THIS IS...
EVERYTHING WILL BE FINE.
YOU'LL FIND A WAY TO SURVIVE.

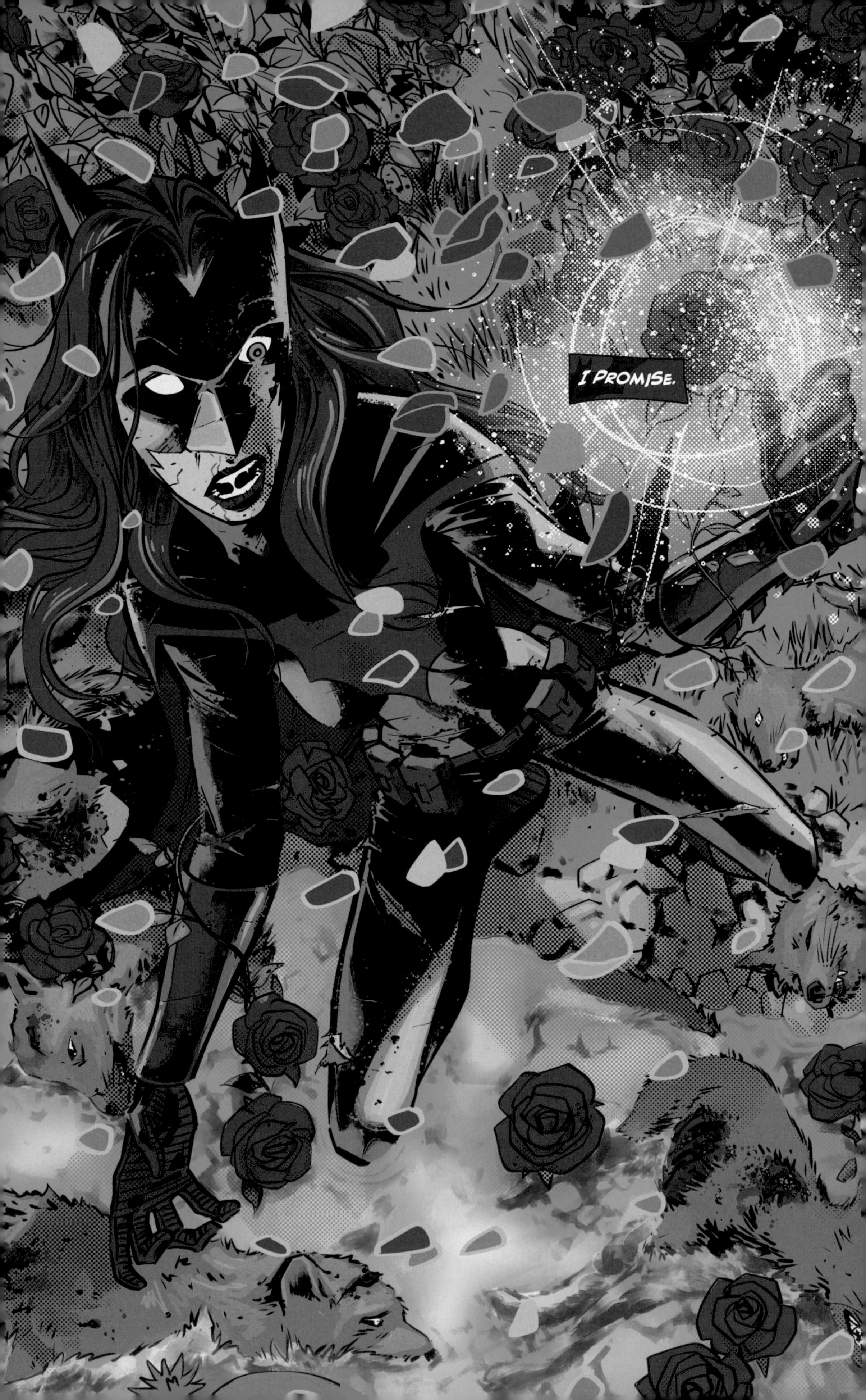
I PROMISE.

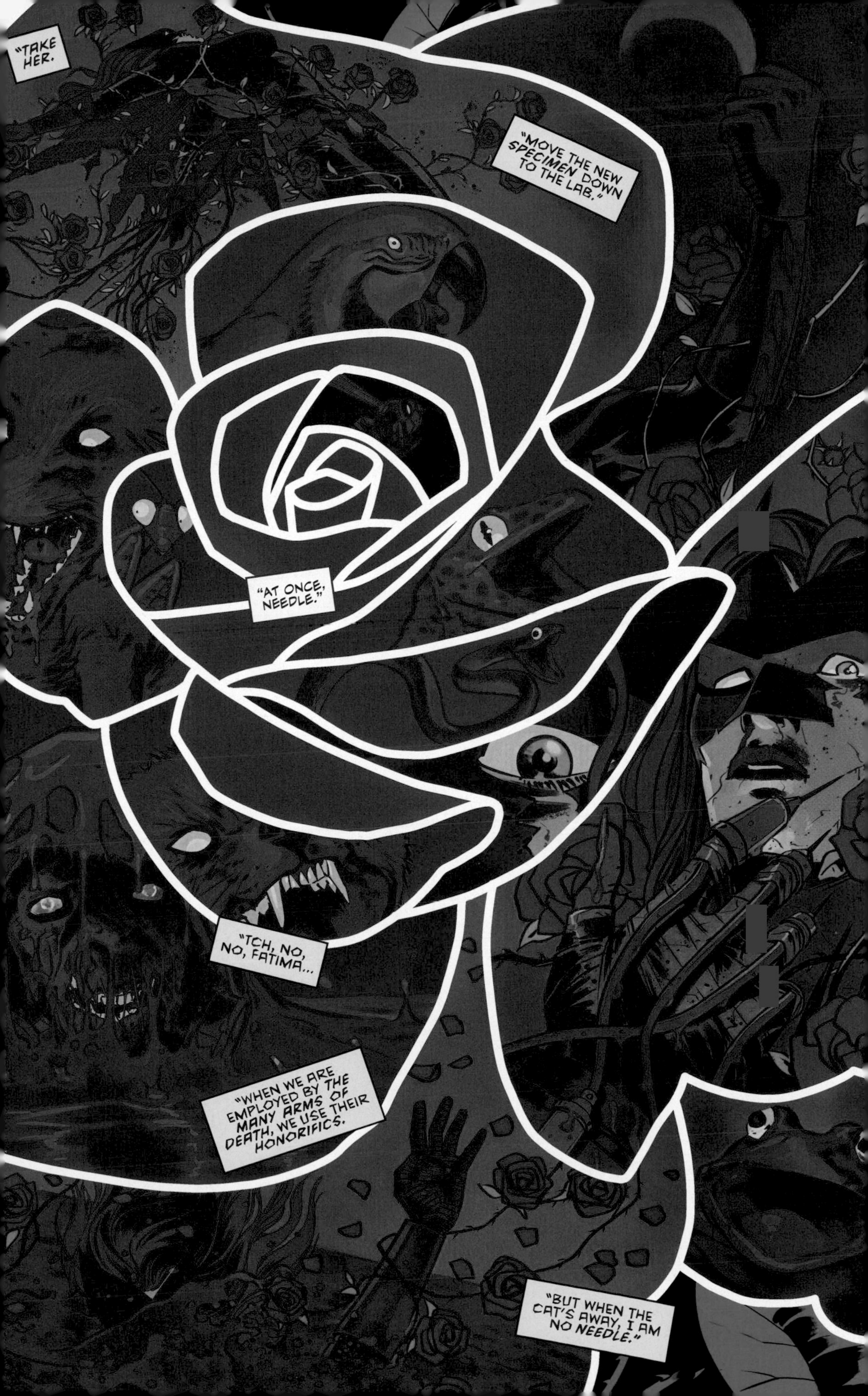
"TAKE HER.
"MOVE THE NEW SPECIMEN DOWN TO THE LAB."
"AT ONCE, NEEDLE."
"TCH, NO, NO, FATIMA...
"WHEN WE ARE EMPLOYED BY THE MANY ARMS OF DEATH, WE USE THEIR HONORIFICS.
"BUT WHEN THE CAT'S AWAY, I AM NO NEEDLE."

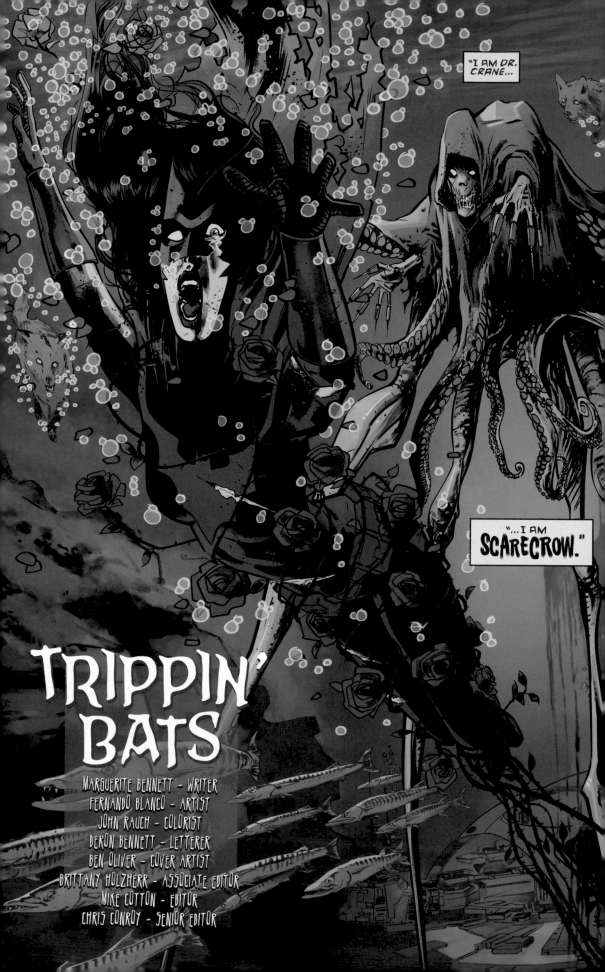

"I AM DR. CRANE...

"...I AM SCARECROW."

TRIPPIN' BATS

MARGUERITE BENNETT — WRITER
FERNANDO BLANCO — ARTIST
JOHN RAUCH — COLORIST
DERON BENNETT — LETTERER
BEN OLIVER — COVER ARTIST
BRITTANY HOLZHERR — ASSOCIATE EDITOR
MIKE COTTON — EDITOR
CHRIS CONROY — SENIOR EDITOR

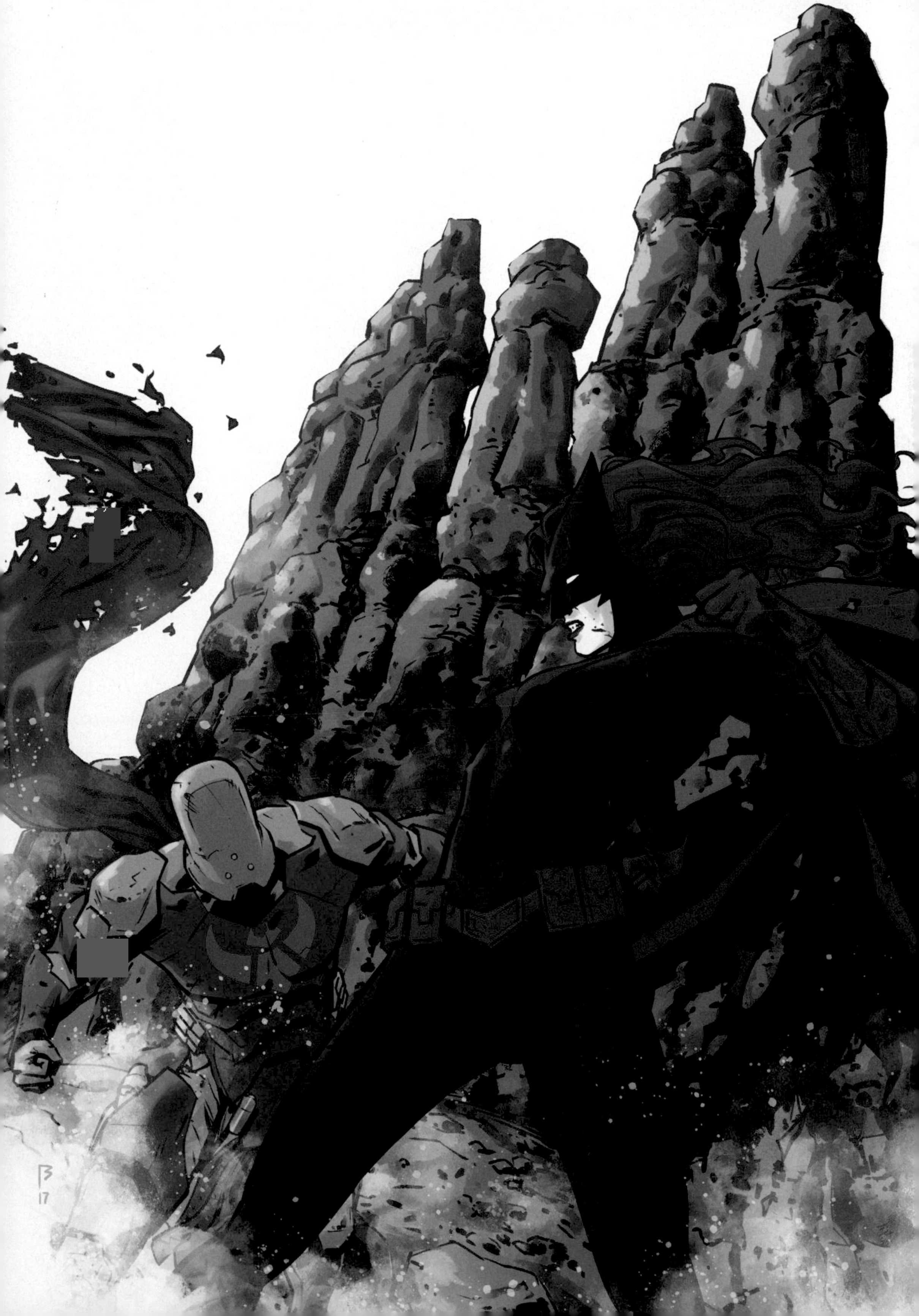

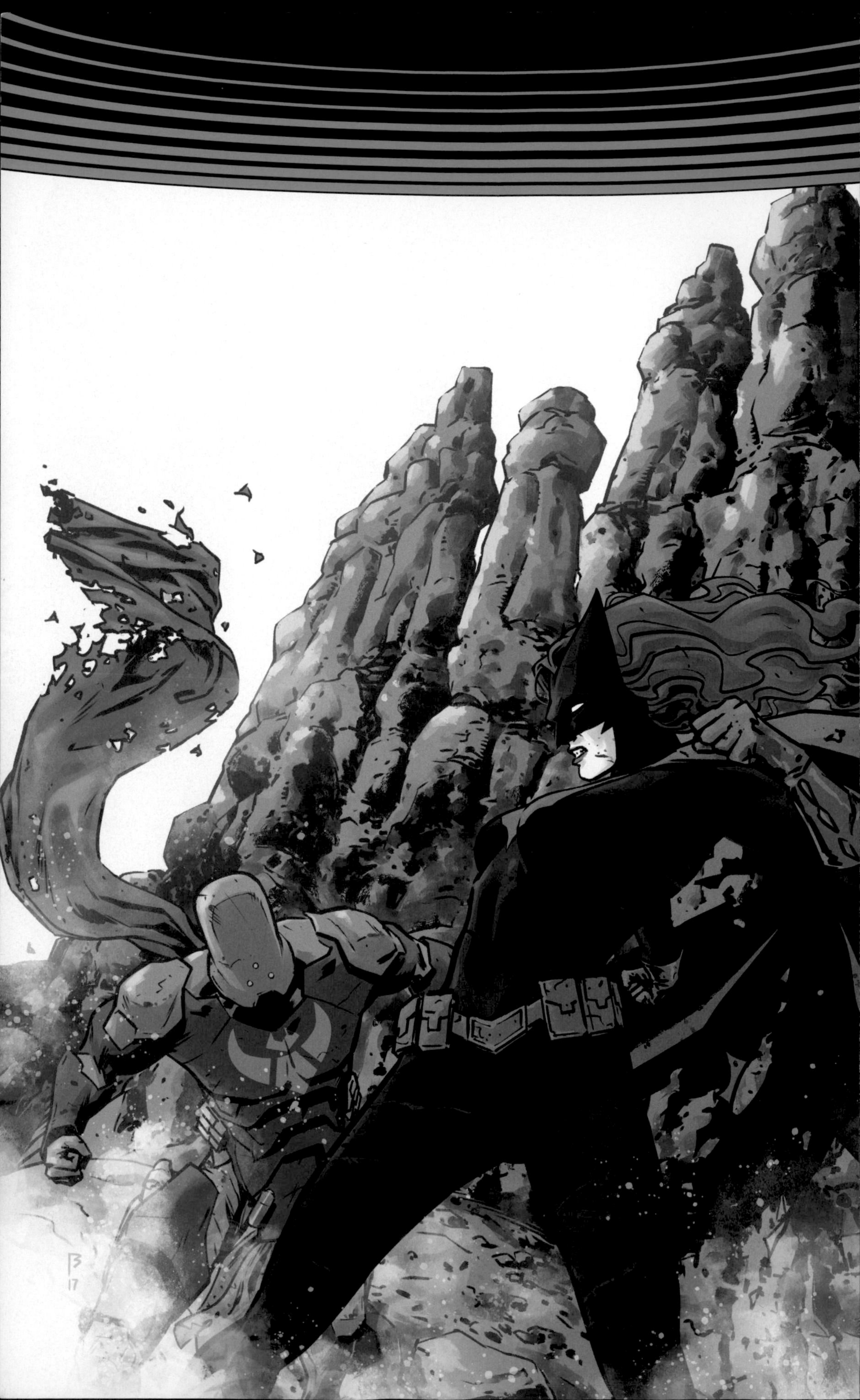

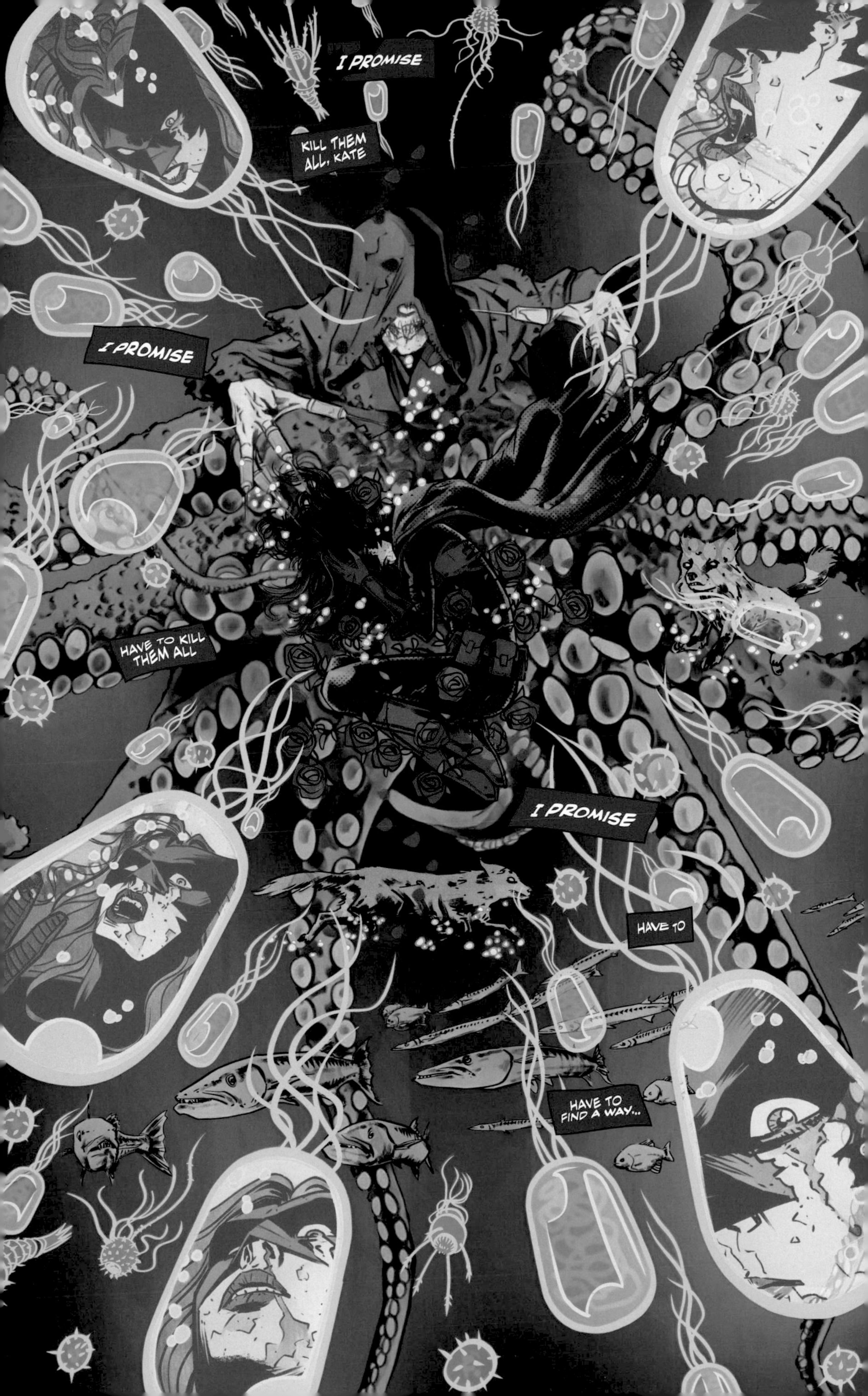
I PROMISE
KILL THEM ALL, KATE
I PROMISE
HAVE TO KILL THEM ALL
I PROMISE
HAVE TO
HAVE TO FIND A WAY...

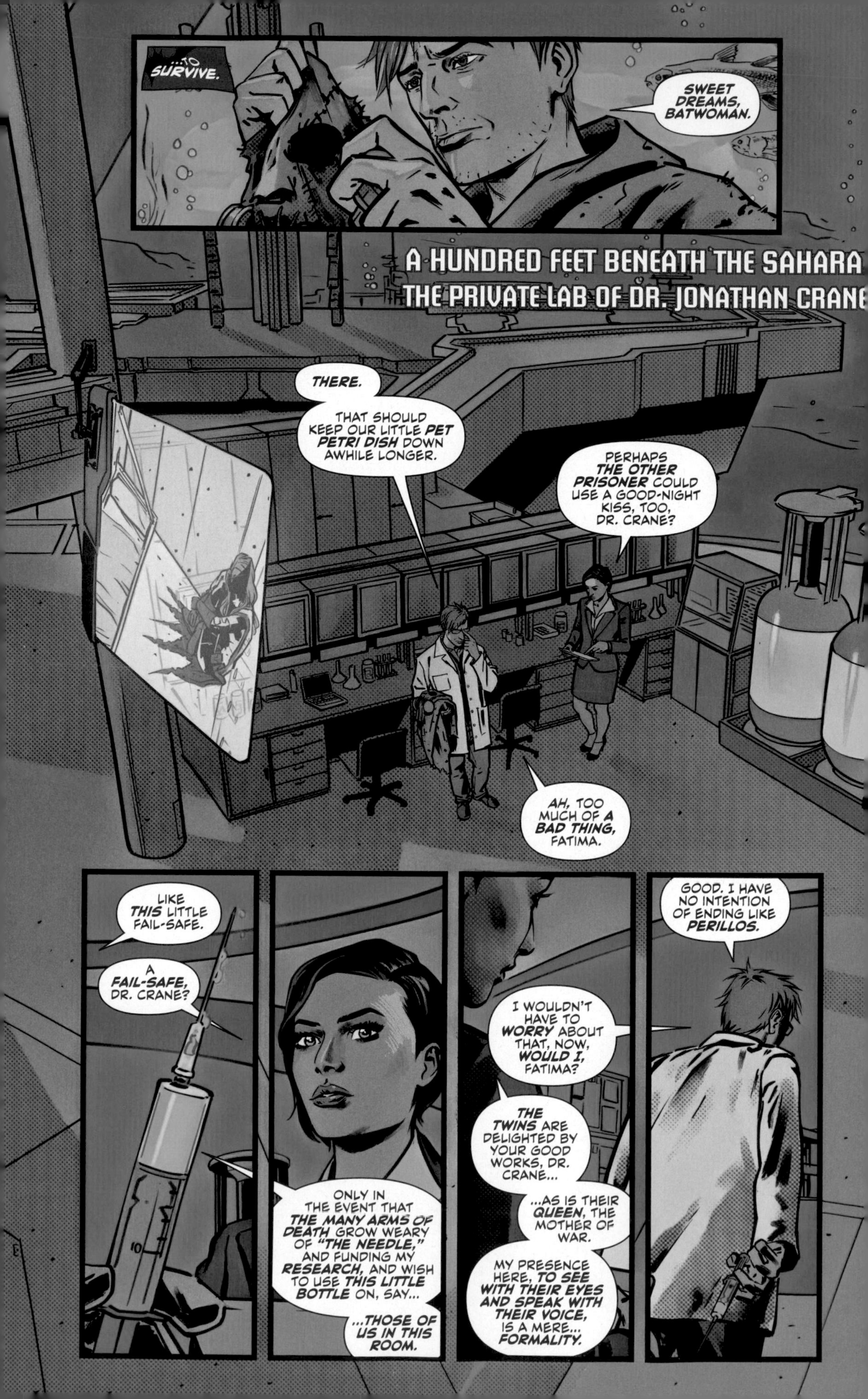
...TO SURVIVE.
SWEET DREAMS, BATWOMAN.
A HUNDRED FEET BENEATH THE SAHARA
THE PRIVATE LAB OF DR. JONATHAN CRANE
THERE.
THAT SHOULD KEEP OUR LITTLE PET PETRI DISH DOWN AWHILE LONGER.
PERHAPS THE OTHER PRISONER COULD USE A GOOD-NIGHT KISS, TOO, DR. CRANE?
AH, TOO MUCH OF A BAD THING, FATIMA.
LIKE THIS LITTLE FAIL-SAFE.
A FAIL-SAFE, DR. CRANE?
ONLY IN THE EVENT THAT THE MANY ARMS OF DEATH GROW WEARY OF "THE NEEDLE," AND FUNDING MY RESEARCH, AND WISH TO USE THIS LITTLE BOTTLE ON, SAY...
...THOSE OF US IN THIS ROOM.
I WOULDN'T HAVE TO WORRY ABOUT THAT, NOW, WOULD I, FATIMA?
THE TWINS ARE DELIGHTED BY YOUR GOOD WORKS, DR. CRANE...
...AS IS THEIR QUEEN, THE MOTHER OF WAR.
MY PRESENCE HERE, TO SEE WITH THEIR EYES AND SPEAK WITH THEIR VOICE, IS A MERE... FORMALITY.
GOOD. I HAVE NO INTENTION OF ENDING LIKE PERILLOS.

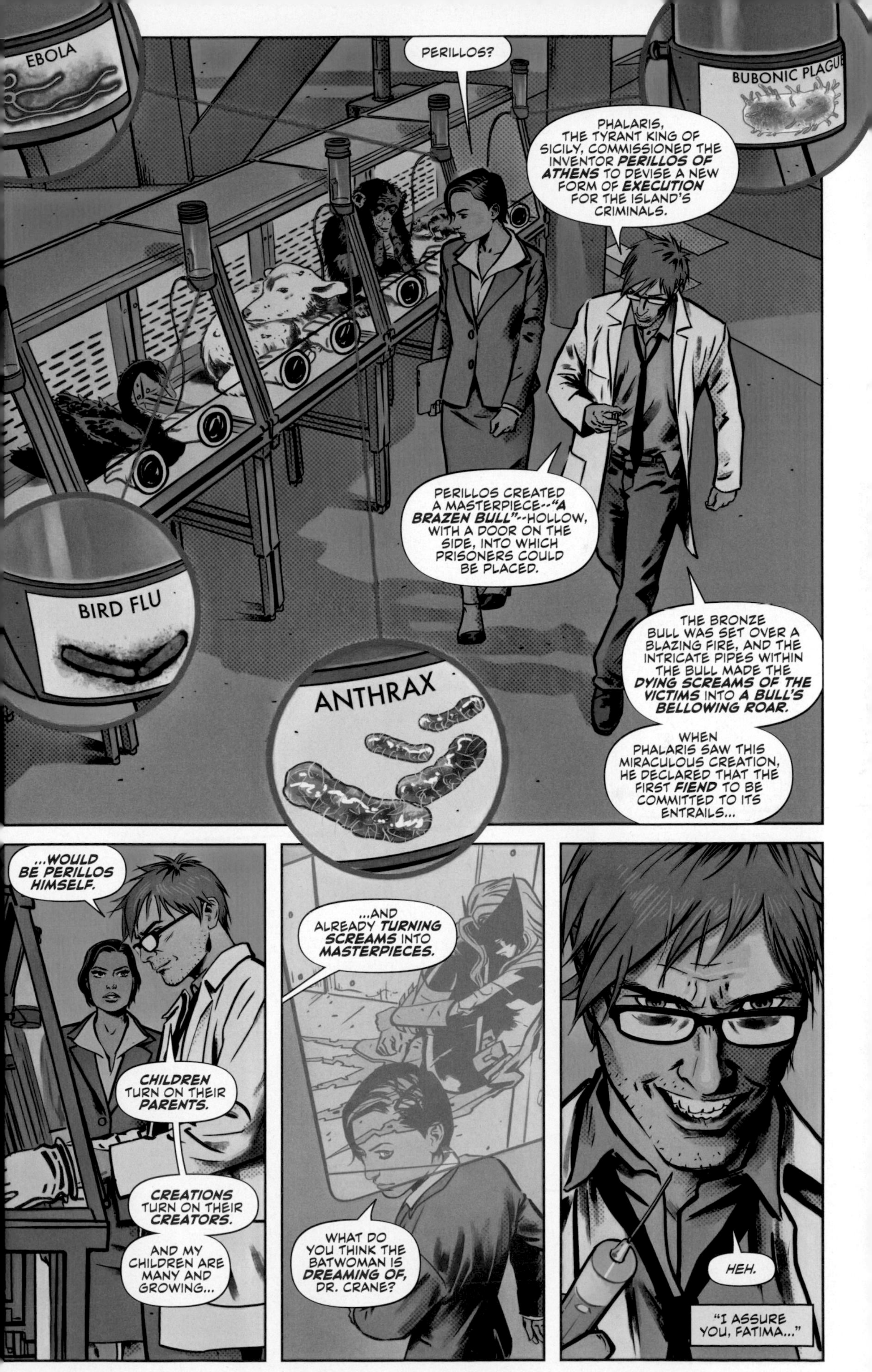
EBOLA
BUBONIC PLAGUE
PERILLOS?
PHALARIS, THE TYRANT KING OF SICILY, COMMISSIONED THE INVENTOR PERILLOS OF ATHENS TO DEVISE A NEW FORM OF EXECUTION FOR THE ISLAND'S CRIMINALS.
PERILLOS CREATED A MASTERPIECE--"A BRAZEN BULL"--HOLLOW, WITH A DOOR ON THE SIDE, INTO WHICH PRISONERS COULD BE PLACED.
BIRD FLU
THE BRONZE BULL WAS SET OVER A BLAZING FIRE, AND THE INTRICATE PIPES WITHIN THE BULL MADE THE DYING SCREAMS OF THE VICTIMS INTO A BULL'S BELLOWING ROAR.
ANTHRAX
WHEN PHALARIS SAW THIS MIRACULOUS CREATION, HE DECLARED THAT THE FIRST FIEND TO BE COMMITTED TO ITS ENTRAILS...
...WOULD BE PERILLOS HIMSELF.
CHILDREN TURN ON THEIR PARENTS.
CREATIONS TURN ON THEIR CREATORS.
AND MY CHILDREN ARE MANY AND GROWING...
...AND ALREADY TURNING SCREAMS INTO MASTERPIECES.
WHAT DO YOU THINK THE BATWOMAN IS DREAMING OF, DR. CRANE?
HEH.
"I ASSURE YOU, FATIMA..."

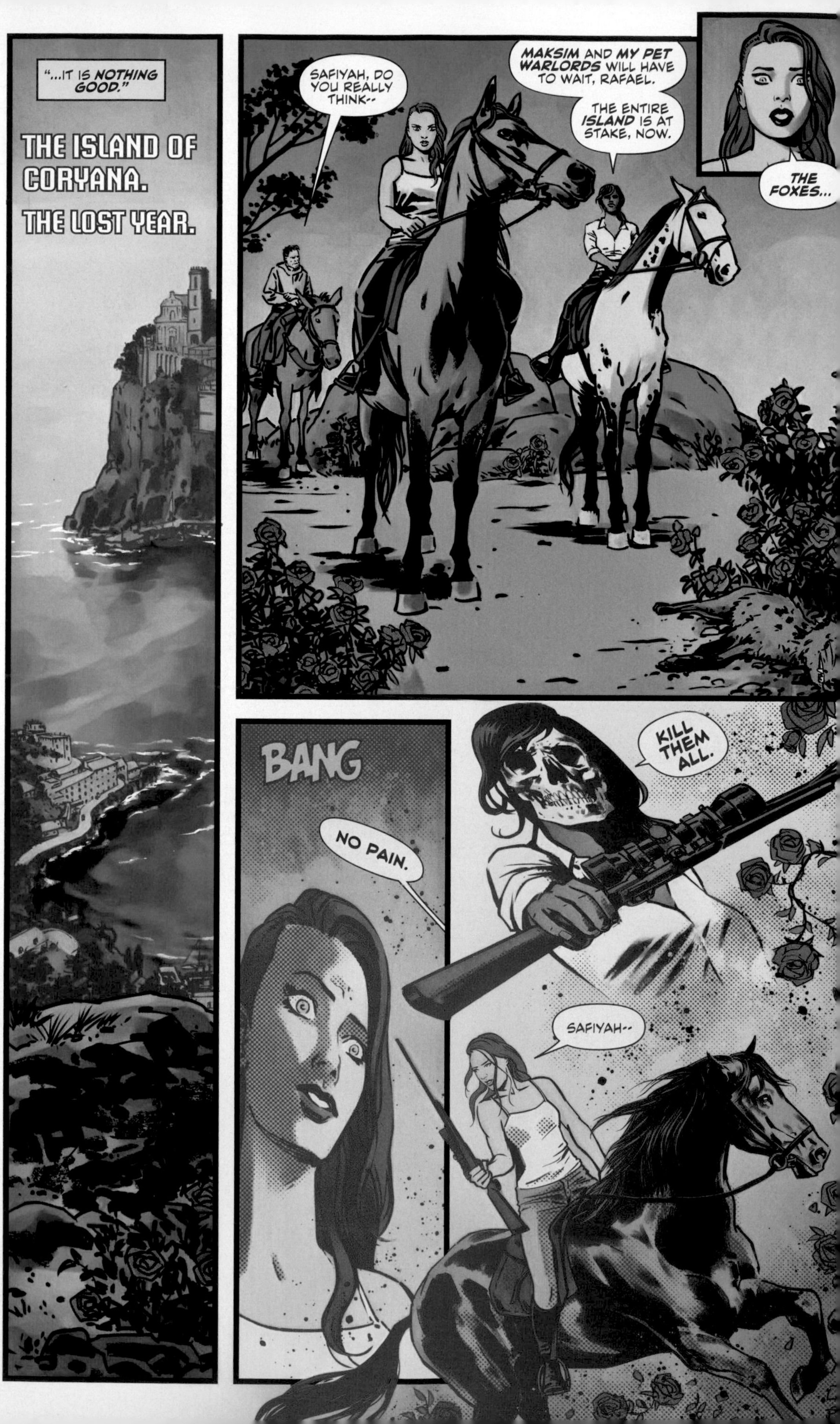
"...IT IS NOTHING GOOD."
THE ISLAND OF CORYANA.
THE LOST YEAR.
SAFIYAH, DO YOU REALLY THINK--
MAKSIM AND MY PET WARLORDS WILL HAVE TO WAIT, RAFAEL.
THE ENTIRE ISLAND IS AT STAKE, NOW.
THE FOXES...
BANG
NO PAIN.
KILL THEM ALL.
SAFIYAH--

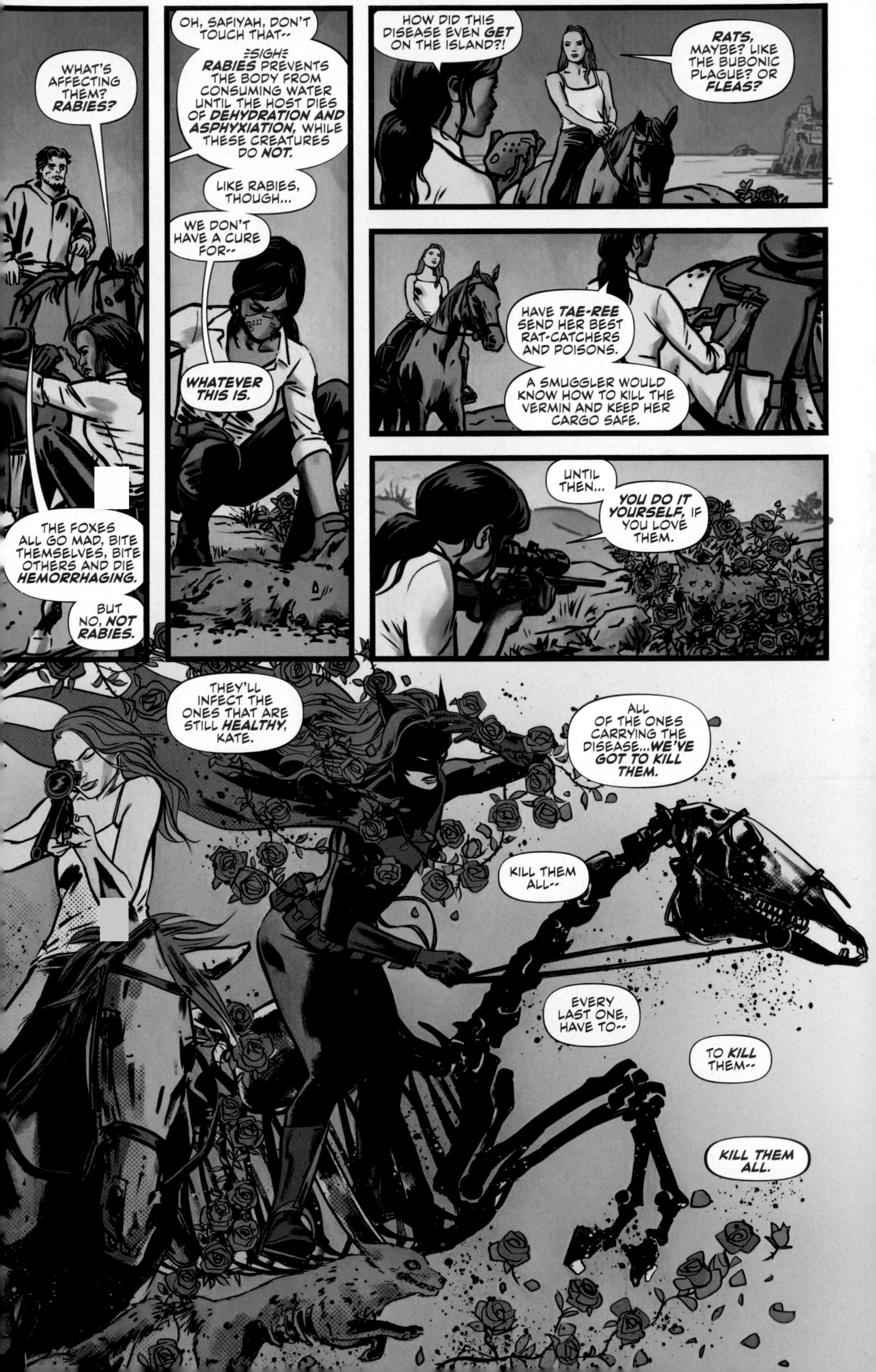
WHAT'S AFFECTING THEM? RABIES?
THE FOXES ALL GO MAD, BITE THEMSELVES, BITE OTHERS AND DIE HEMORRHAGING.
BUT NO, NOT RABIES.
OH, SAFIYAH, DON'T TOUCH THAT--
≡SIGH≡ RABIES PREVENTS THE BODY FROM CONSUMING WATER UNTIL THE HOST DIES OF DEHYDRATION AND ASPHYXIATION, WHILE THESE CREATURES DO NOT.
LIKE RABIES, THOUGH...
WE DON'T HAVE A CURE FOR--
WHATEVER THIS IS.
HOW DID THIS DISEASE EVEN GET ON THE ISLAND?!
RATS, MAYBE? LIKE THE BUBONIC PLAGUE? OR FLEAS?
HAVE TAE-REE SEND HER BEST RAT-CATCHERS AND POISONS.
A SMUGGLER WOULD KNOW HOW TO KILL THE VERMIN AND KEEP HER CARGO SAFE.
UNTIL THEN...
YOU DO IT YOURSELF, IF YOU LOVE THEM.
THEY'LL INFECT THE ONES THAT ARE STILL HEALTHY, KATE.
ALL OF THE ONES CARRYING THE DISEASE...WE'VE GOT TO KILL THEM.
KILL THEM ALL--
EVERY LAST ONE, HAVE TO--
TO KILL THEM--
KILL THEM ALL.

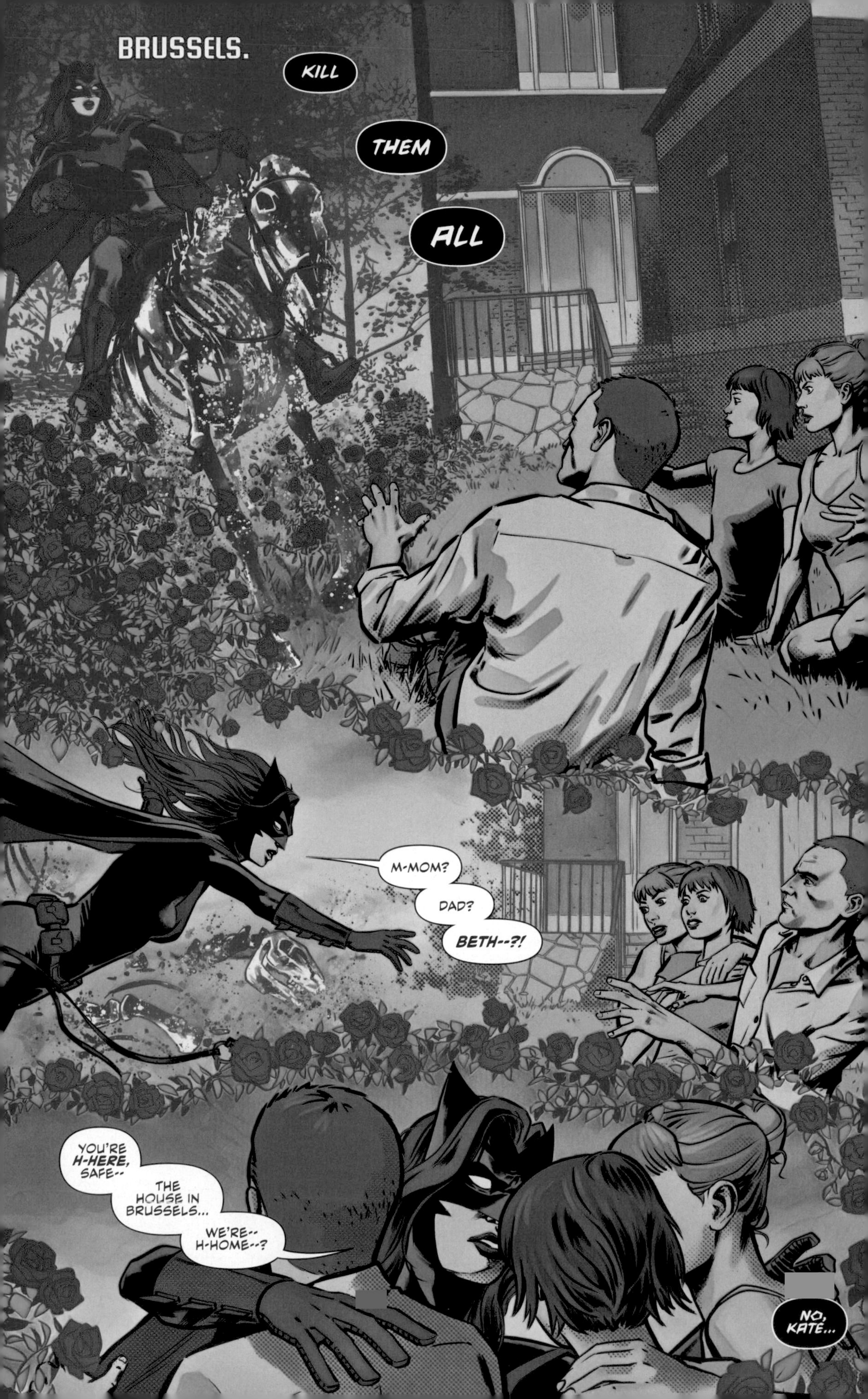
BRUSSELS.
KILL
THEM
ALL
M-MOM?
DAD?
BETH--?!
YOU'RE H-HERE, SAFE--
THE HOUSE IN BRUSSELS...
WE'RE-- H-HOME--?
NO, KATE...

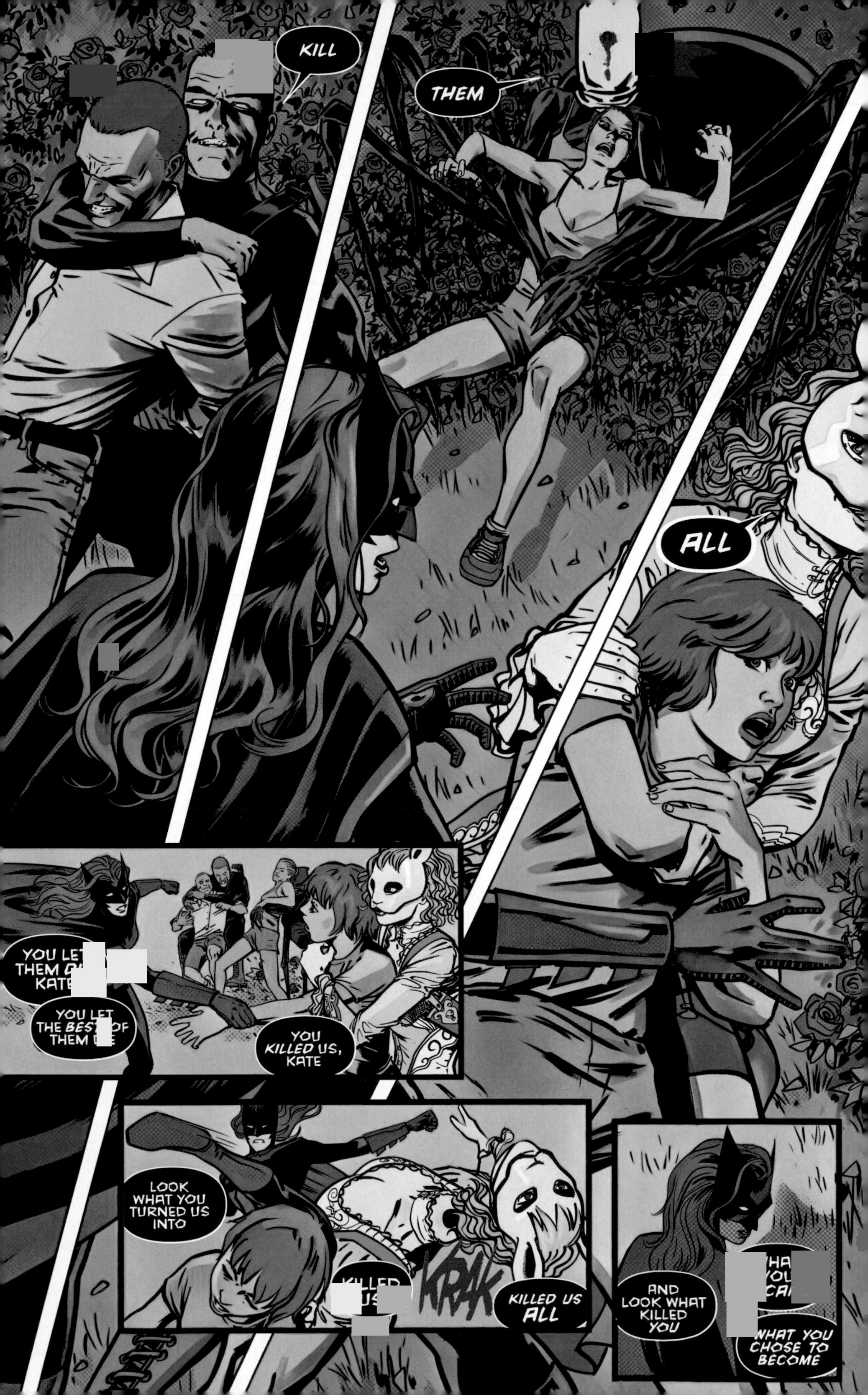
KILL
THEM
ALL
YOU LET
KATE
YOU LET
THEM
YOU KILLED US, KATE
LOOK WHAT YOU TURNED US INTO
KILLED
KRAK
KILLED US ALL
AND LOOK WHAT KILLED YOU
WHAT YOU CHOSE TO BECOME

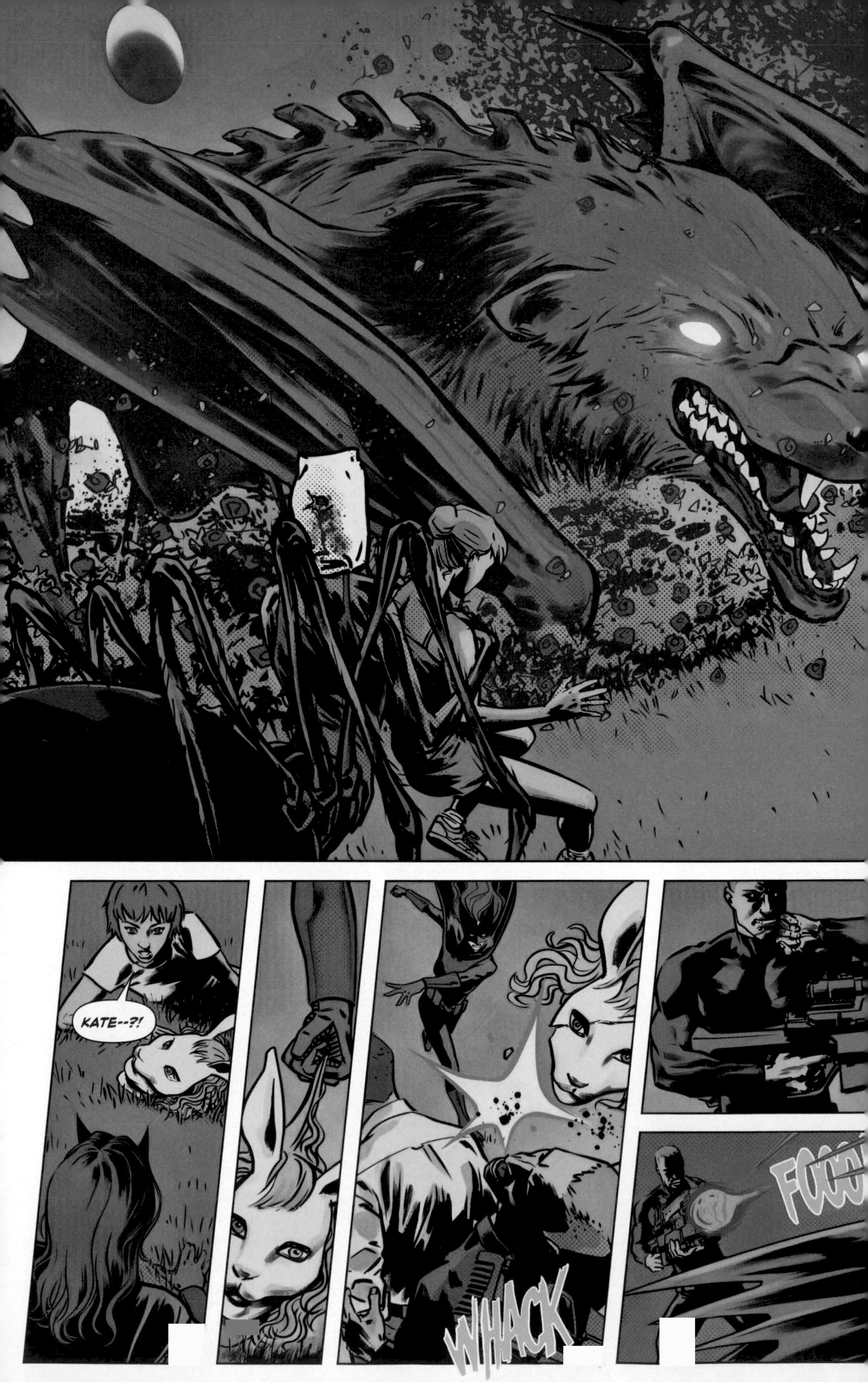
KATE--?!
WHACK

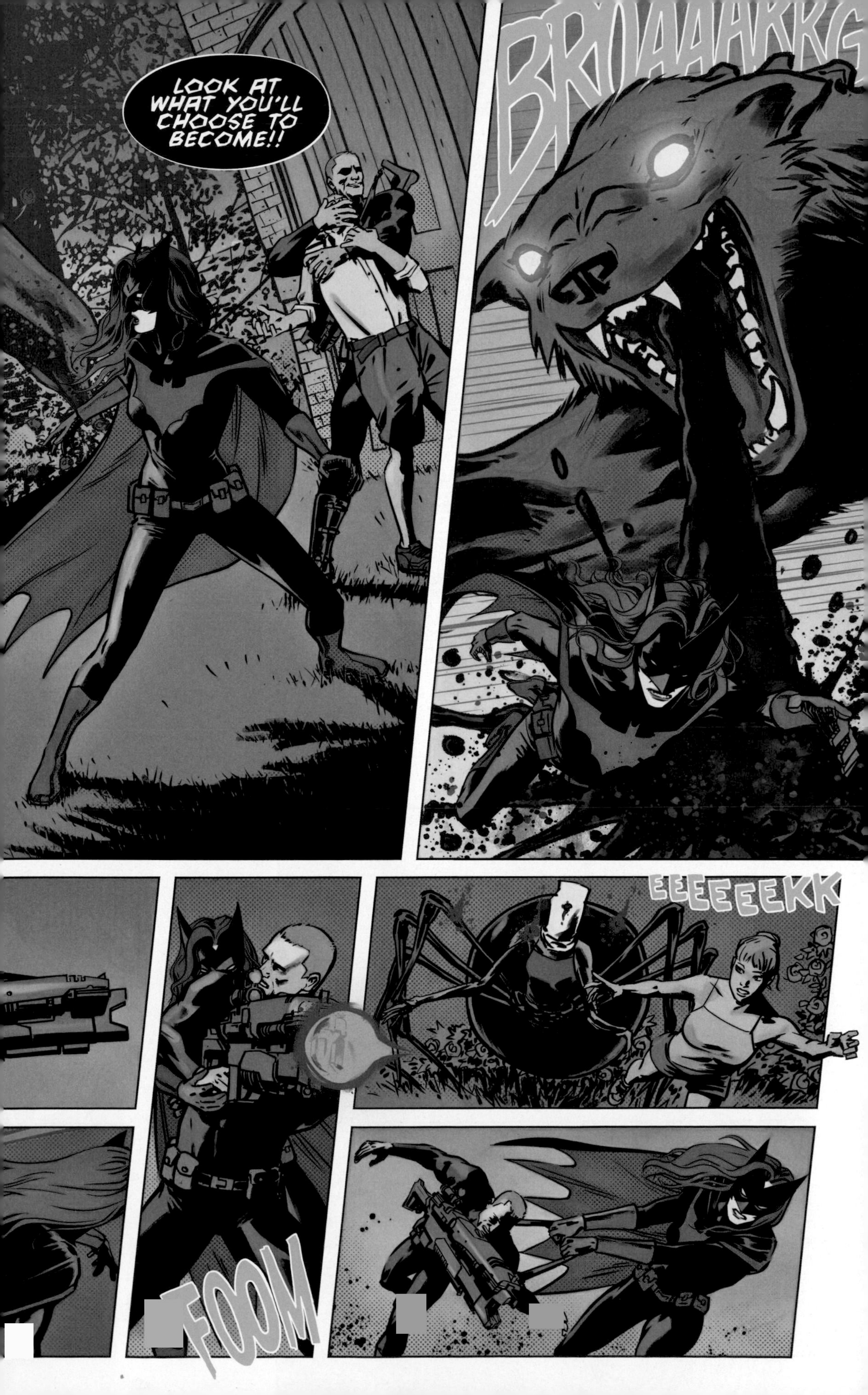
LOOK AT WHAT YOU'LL CHOOSE TO BECOME!!
BRRAAAKKG
FOOM
EEEEEEKK

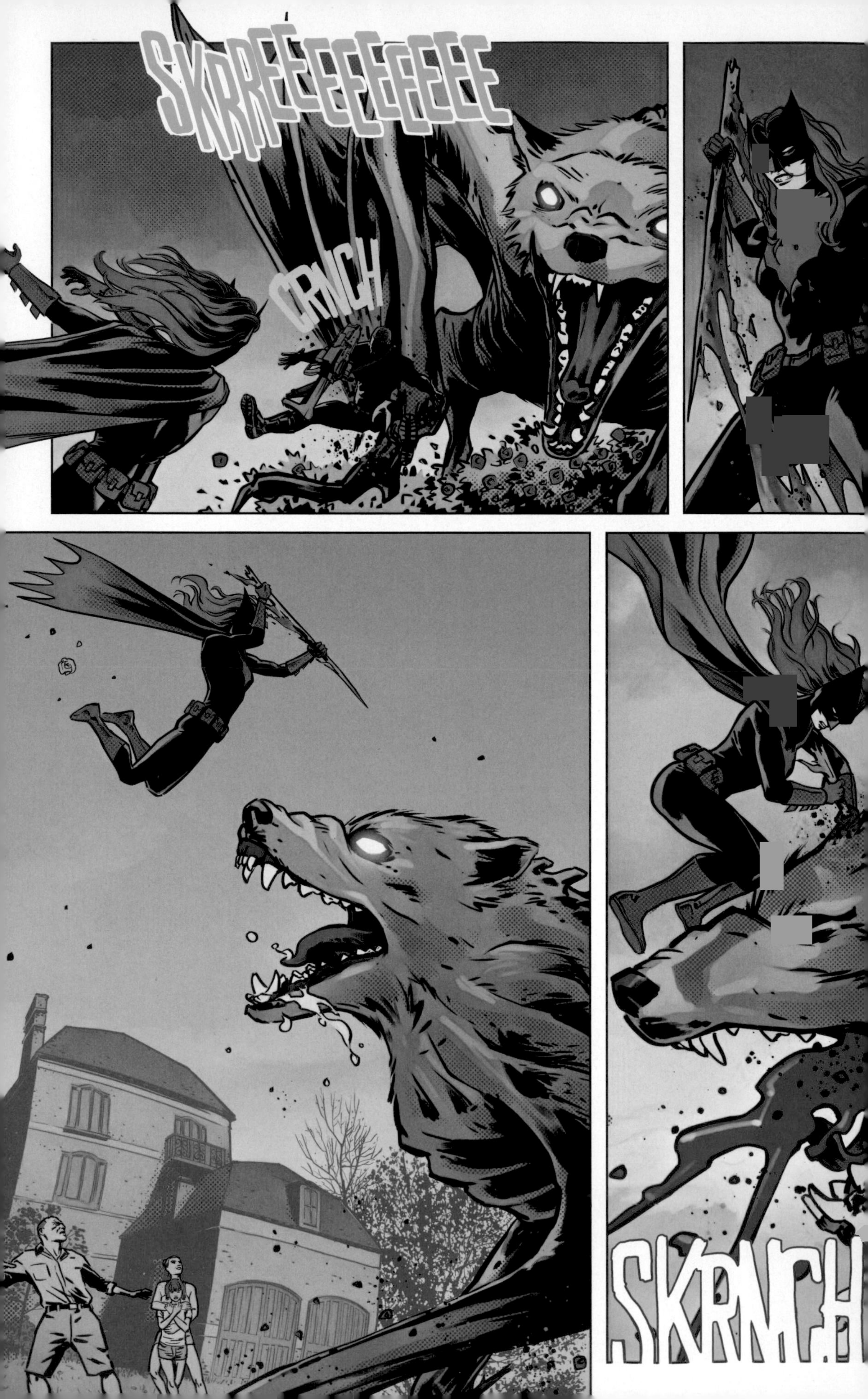
SKRREEEEEEEE
CRNCH
SKRNCH

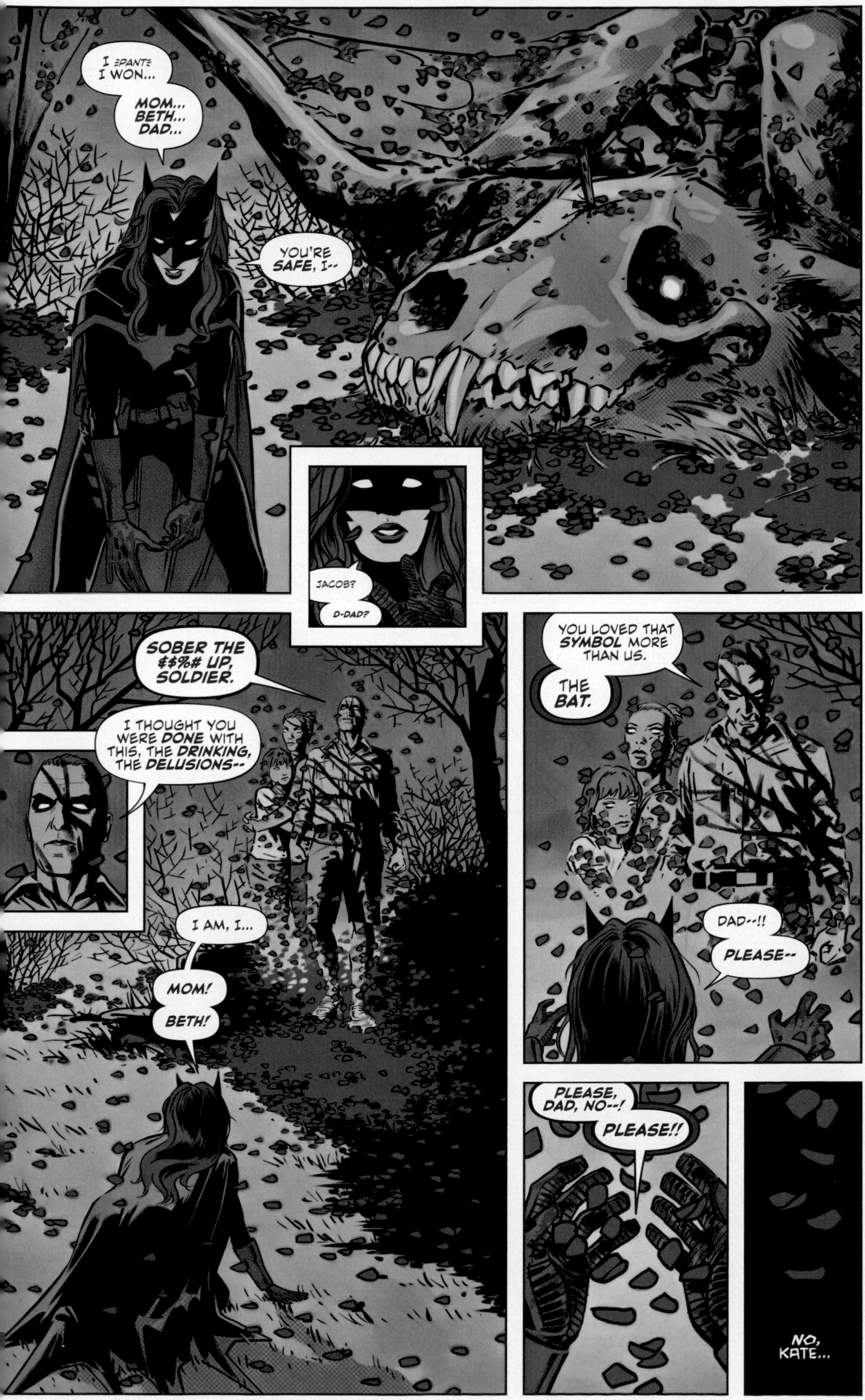
I =PANT= I WON...
MOM... BETH... DAD...
YOU'RE SAFE, I--
JACOB?
D-DAD?
SOBER THE $$%# UP, SOLDIER.
I THOUGHT YOU WERE DONE WITH THIS, THE DRINKING, THE DELUSIONS--
I AM, I...
MOM!
BETH!
YOU LOVED THAT SYMBOL MORE THAN US.
THE BAT.
DAD--!!
PLEASE--
PLEASE, DAD, NO--!
PLEASE!!
NO, KATE...

NO...

...NOT *DADDY*.

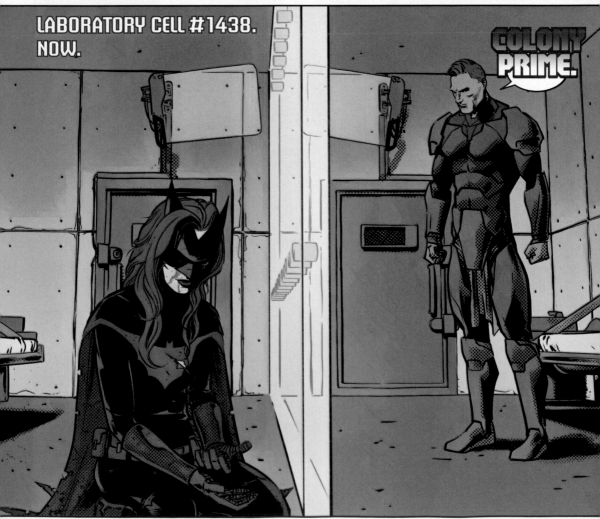

LABORATORY CELL #1438.
NOW.

COLONY PRIME.

SO, WHO'S *SAFIYAH?*

DON'T YOU HAVE ANYTHING *BETTER* TO DO THAN LOOM OVER SLEEPING *WOMEN?!*

WHAT DID SHE DO? YOU KEPT *BEGGING* HER NOT TO *KILL*--

WHERE IS JACOB KANE?!

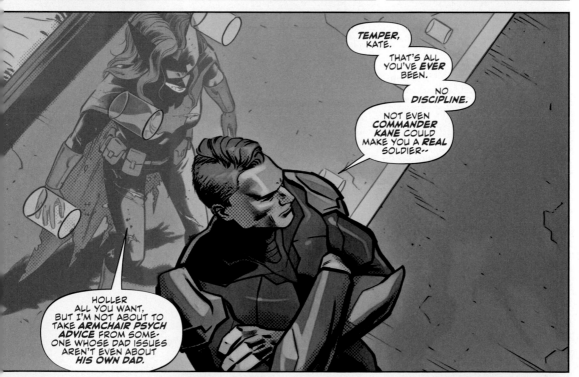

TEMPER, KATE.

THAT'S ALL YOU'VE *EVER* BEEN.

NO *DISCIPLINE.*

NOT EVEN *COMMANDER KANE* COULD MAKE YOU A *REAL* SOLDIER--

HOLLER ALL YOU WANT, BUT I'M NOT ABOUT TO TAKE *ARMCHAIR PSYCH ADVICE* FROM SOMEONE WHOSE DAD ISSUES AREN'T EVEN ABOUT *HIS OWN DAD.*

I'M GUESSING THE *TRACKER* I TOOK FROM THOSE COLONY SOLDIERS WAS LEADING ME TO *YOU.*

OR TO THE *TRACER* IN *MY HELMET,* WHICH THAT *WOMAN* HELPING SCARECROW-- *FATIMA,* I THINK SHE'S CALLED--TOOK FROM ME.

HOW THE HELL DID YOUR *COLONY JACKBOOTS* EVEN WIND UP HERE?

≡HMPH≡

BLIP

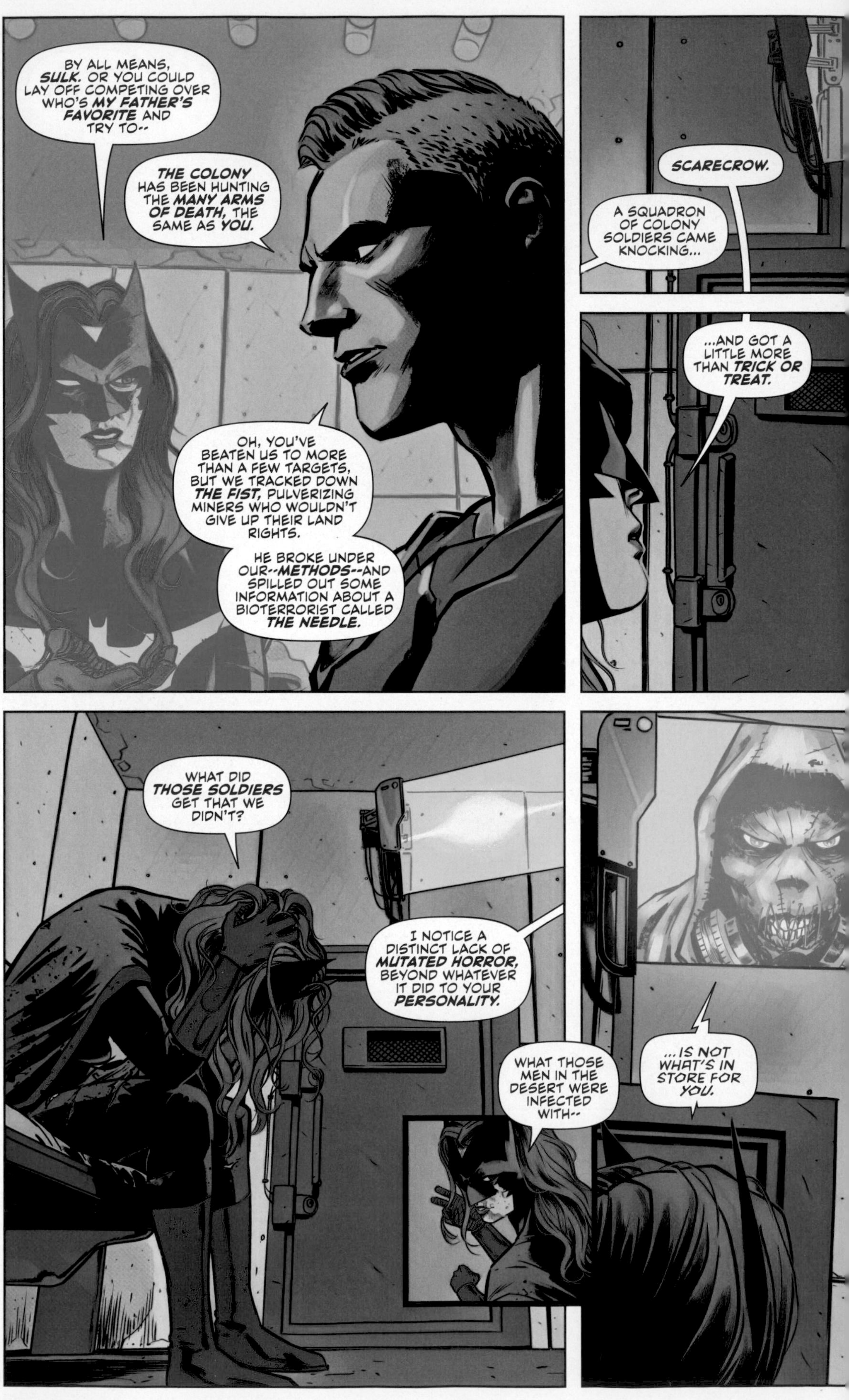
BY ALL MEANS, SULK. OR YOU COULD LAY OFF COMPETING OVER WHO'S MY FATHER'S FAVORITE AND TRY TO--
THE COLONY HAS BEEN HUNTING THE MANY ARMS OF DEATH, THE SAME AS YOU.
OH, YOU'VE BEATEN US TO MORE THAN A FEW TARGETS, BUT WE TRACKED DOWN THE FIST, PULVERIZING MINERS WHO WOULDN'T GIVE UP THEIR LAND RIGHTS.
HE BROKE UNDER OUR--METHODS--AND SPILLED OUT SOME INFORMATION ABOUT A BIOTERRORIST CALLED THE NEEDLE.
SCARECROW.
A SQUADRON OF COLONY SOLDIERS CAME KNOCKING...
...AND GOT A LITTLE MORE THAN TRICK OR TREAT.
WHAT DID THOSE SOLDIERS GET THAT WE DIDN'T?
I NOTICE A DISTINCT LACK OF MUTATED HORROR, BEYOND WHATEVER IT DID TO YOUR PERSONALITY.
WHAT THOSE MEN IN THE DESERT WERE INFECTED WITH--
...IS NOT WHAT'S IN STORE FOR YOU.

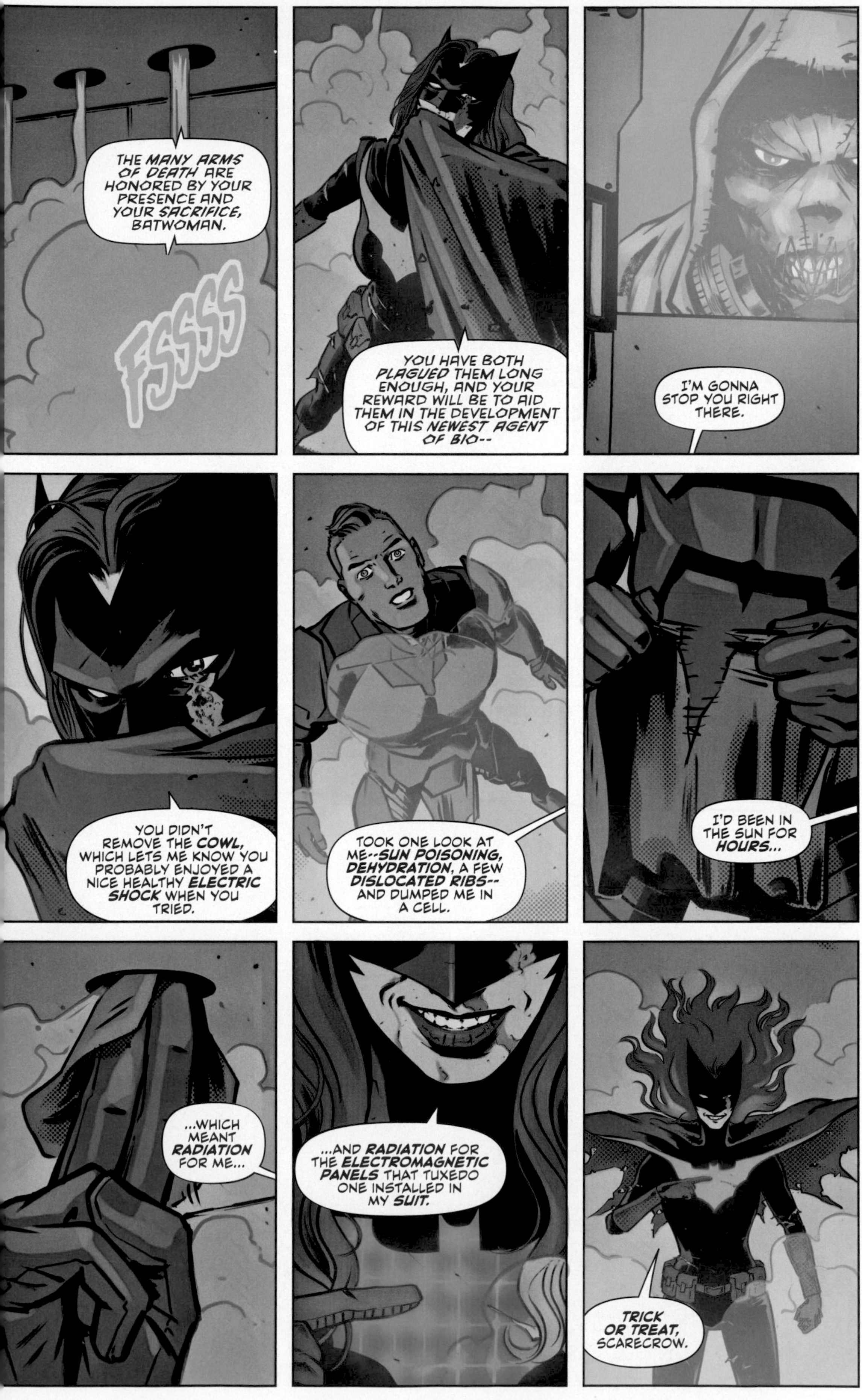
THE MANY ARMS OF DEATH ARE HONORED BY YOUR PRESENCE AND YOUR SACRIFICE, BATWOMAN.
FSSSS
YOU HAVE BOTH PLAGUED THEM LONG ENOUGH, AND YOUR REWARD WILL BE TO AID THEM IN THE DEVELOPMENT OF THIS NEWEST AGENT OF BIO--
I'M GONNA STOP YOU RIGHT THERE.
YOU DIDN'T REMOVE THE COWL, WHICH LETS ME KNOW YOU PROBABLY ENJOYED A NICE HEALTHY ELECTRIC SHOCK WHEN YOU TRIED.
TOOK ONE LOOK AT ME--SUN POISONING, DEHYDRATION, A FEW DISLOCATED RIBS--AND DUMPED ME IN A CELL.
I'D BEEN IN THE SUN FOR HOURS...
...WHICH MEANT RADIATION FOR ME...
...AND RADIATION FOR THE ELECTROMAGNETIC PANELS THAT TUXEDO ONE INSTALLED IN MY SUIT.
TRICK OR TREAT, SCARECROW.

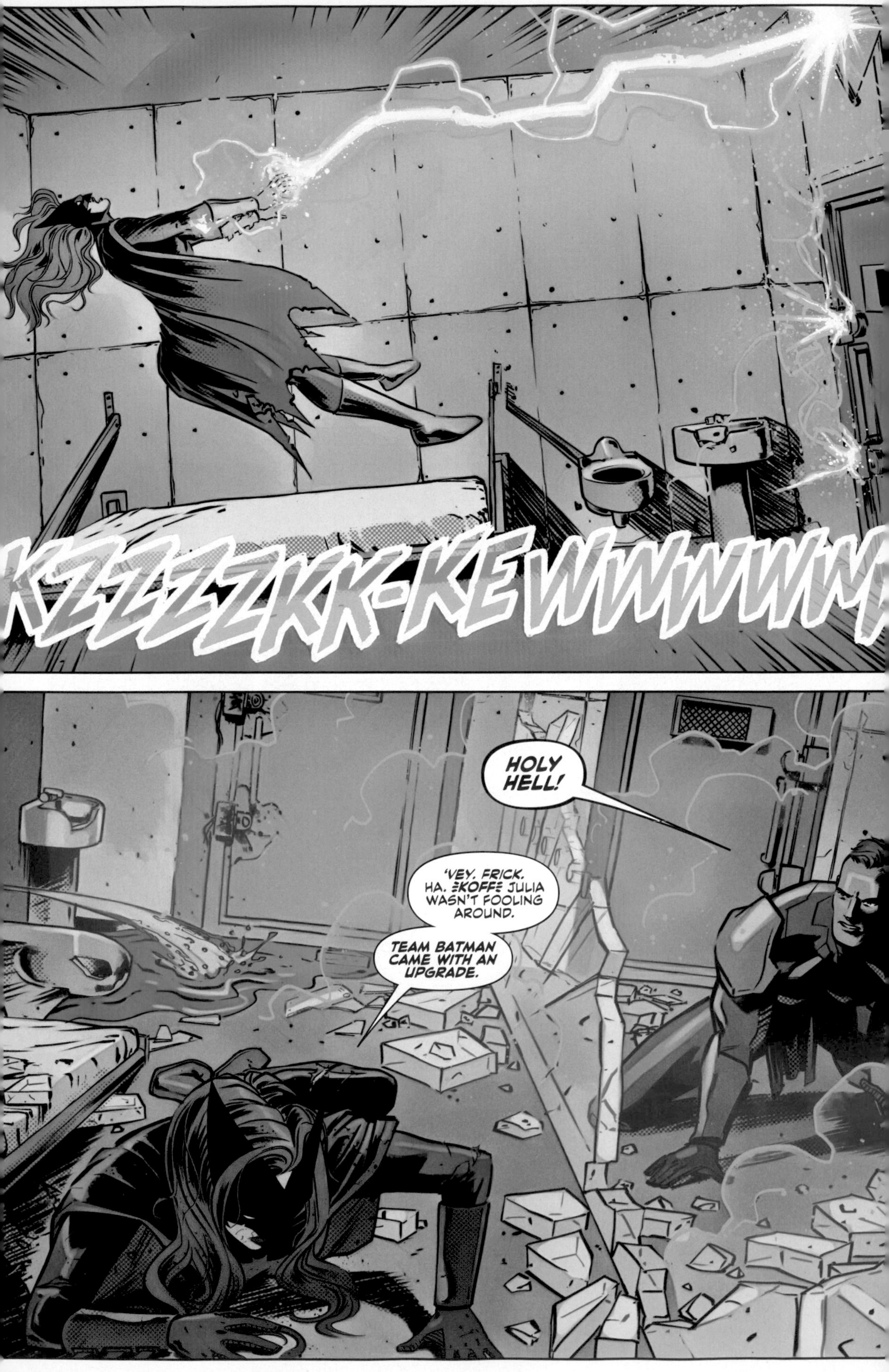
KZZZZKK-KEWWWWW
HOLY HELL!
'VEY. FRICK. HA. ≡KOFF≡ JULIA WASN'T FOOLING AROUND.
TEAM BATMAN CAME WITH AN UPGRADE.

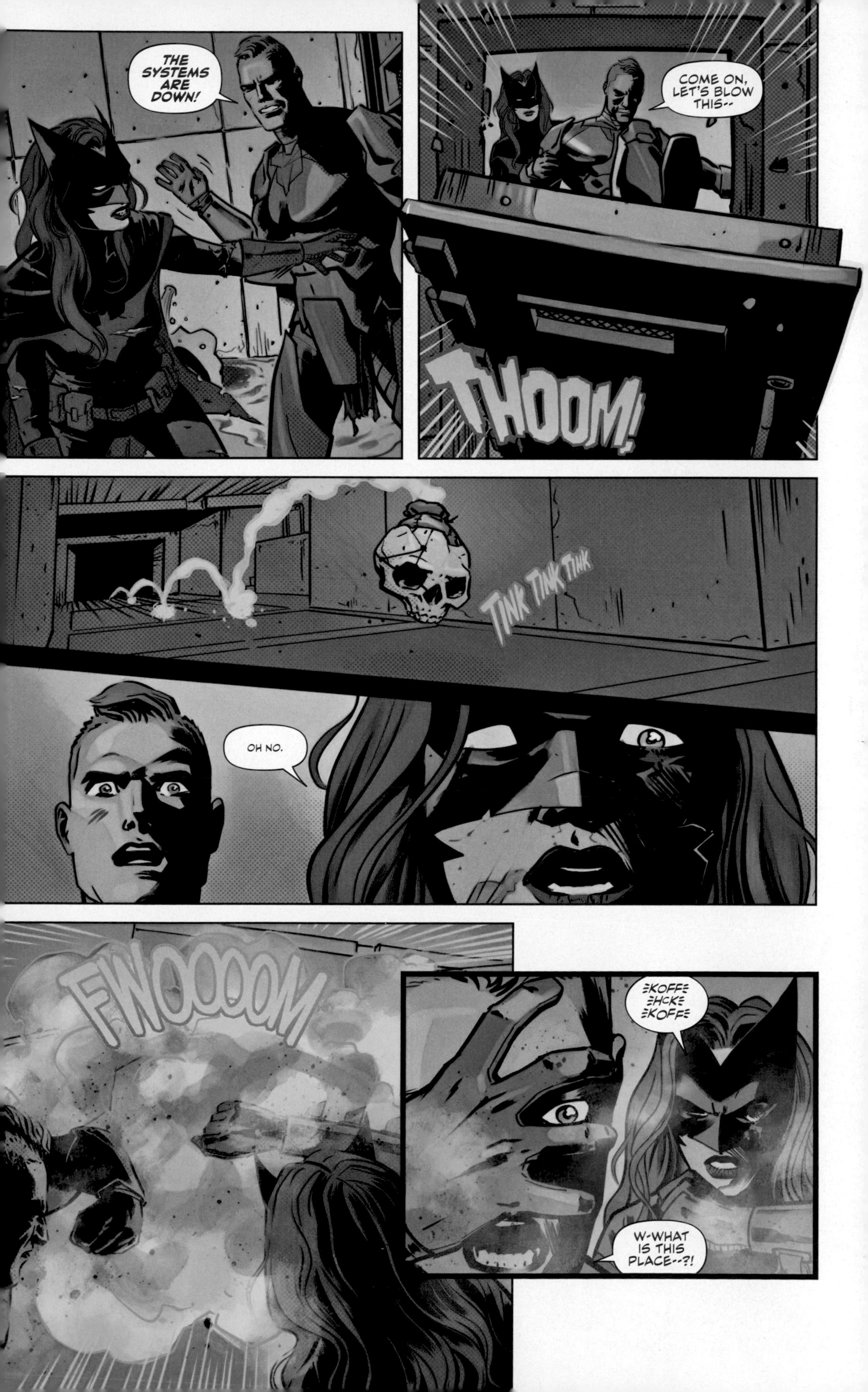
THE SYSTEMS ARE DOWN!
COME ON, LET'S BLOW THIS--
THOOM!
TINK TINK TINK
OH NO.
FWOOOOM
KOFF HCK KOFF
W-WHAT IS THIS PLACE--?!

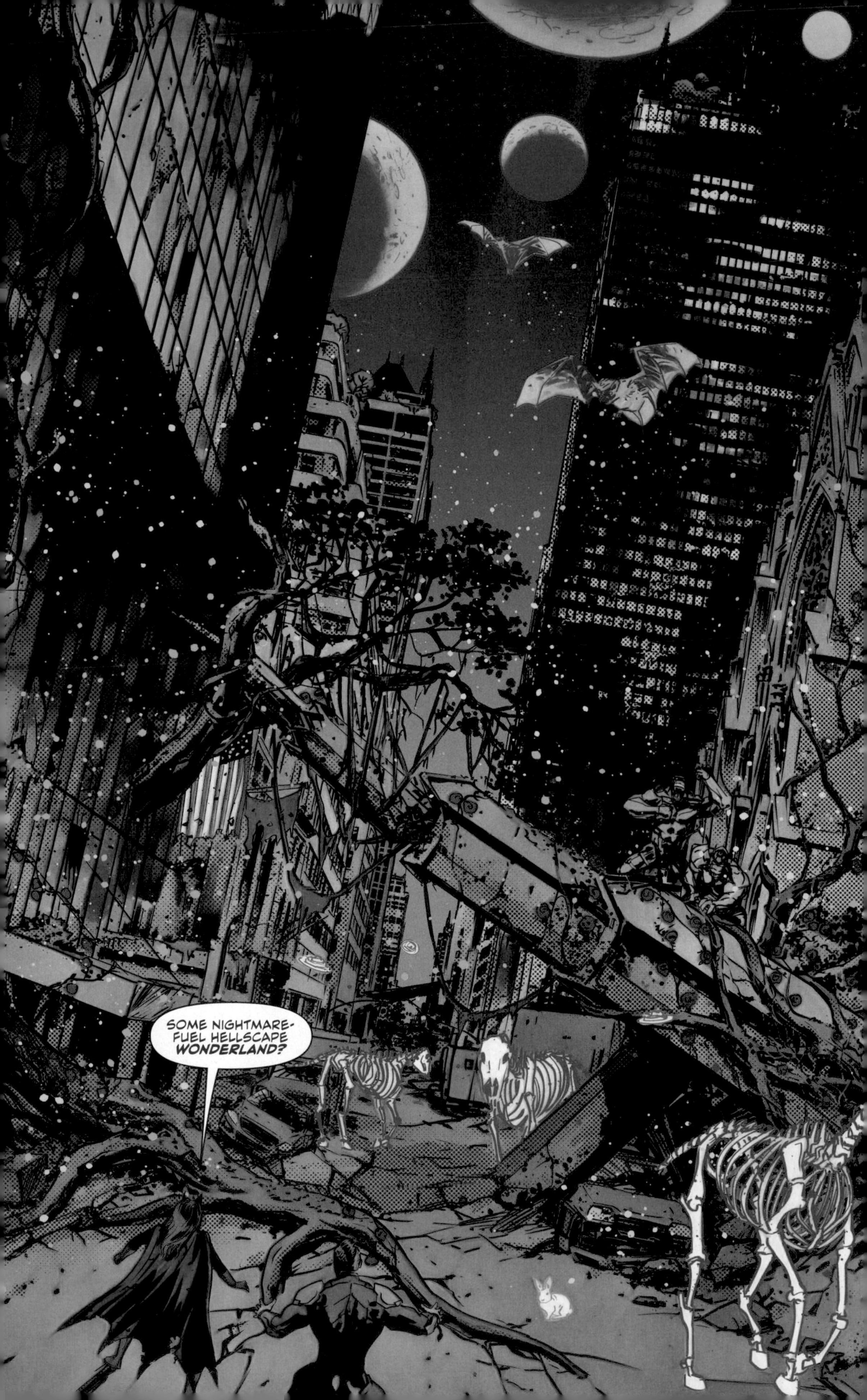
SOME NIGHTMARE-FUEL HELLSCAPE WONDERLAND?

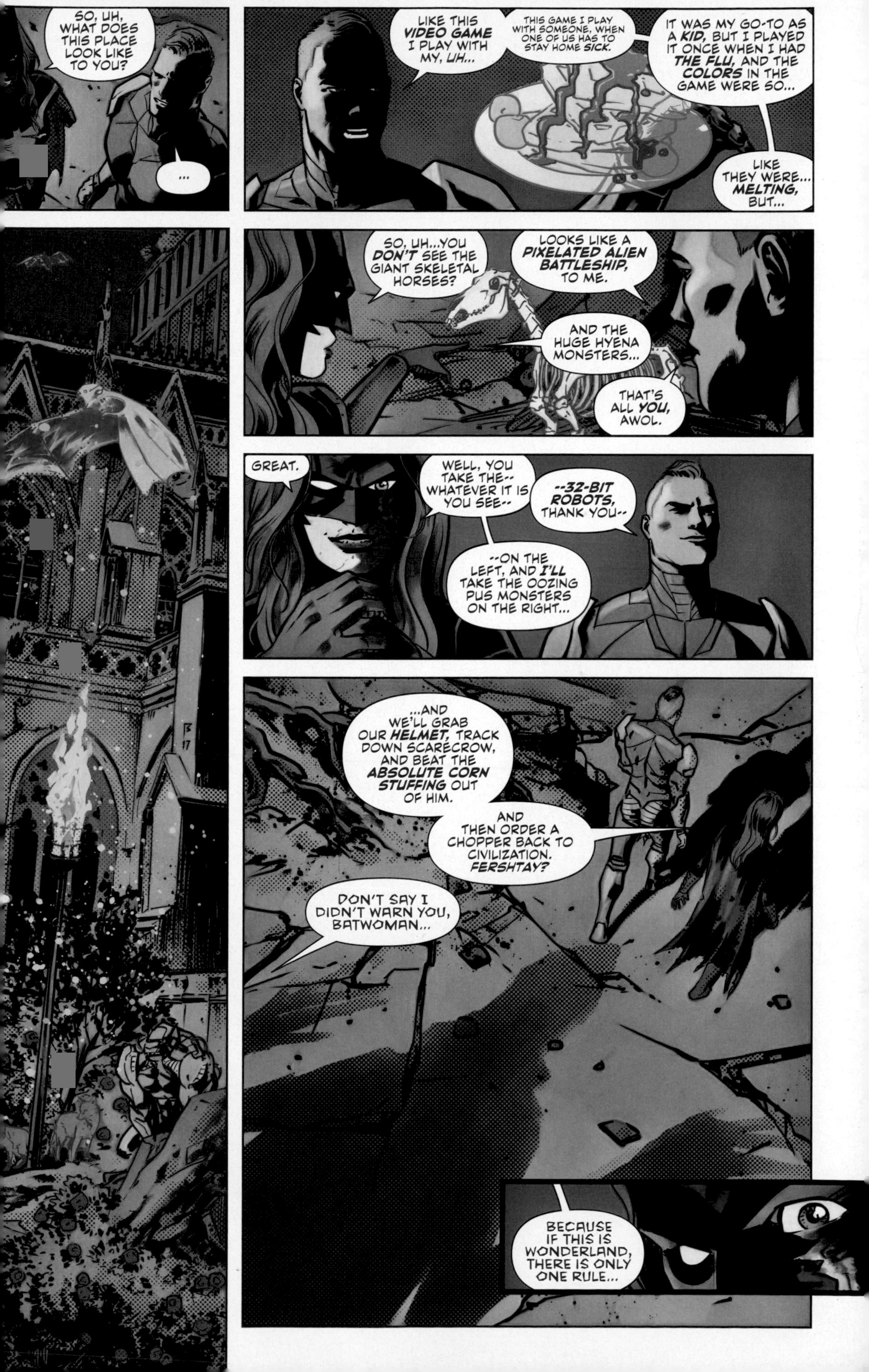

SO, UH, WHAT DOES THIS PLACE LOOK LIKE TO YOU?
...
LIKE THIS VIDEO GAME I PLAY WITH MY, UH...
THIS GAME I PLAY WITH SOMEONE, WHEN ONE OF US HAS TO STAY HOME SICK.
IT WAS MY GO-TO AS A KID, BUT I PLAYED IT ONCE WHEN I HAD THE FLU, AND THE COLORS IN THE GAME WERE SO...
LIKE THEY WERE... MELTING, BUT...
SO, UH...YOU DON'T SEE THE GIANT SKELETAL HORSES?
LOOKS LIKE A PIXELATED ALIEN BATTLESHIP, TO ME.
AND THE HUGE HYENA MONSTERS...
THAT'S ALL YOU, AWOL.
GREAT.
WELL, YOU TAKE THE-- WHATEVER IT IS YOU SEE--
--32-BIT ROBOTS, THANK YOU--
--ON THE LEFT, AND I'LL TAKE THE OOZING PUS MONSTERS ON THE RIGHT...
...AND WE'LL GRAB OUR HELMET, TRACK DOWN SCARECROW, AND BEAT THE ABSOLUTE CORN STUFFING OUT OF HIM.
AND THEN ORDER A CHOPPER BACK TO CIVILIZATION. FERSHTAY?
DON'T SAY I DIDN'T WARN YOU, BATWOMAN...
BECAUSE IF THIS IS WONDERLAND, THERE IS ONLY ONE RULE...

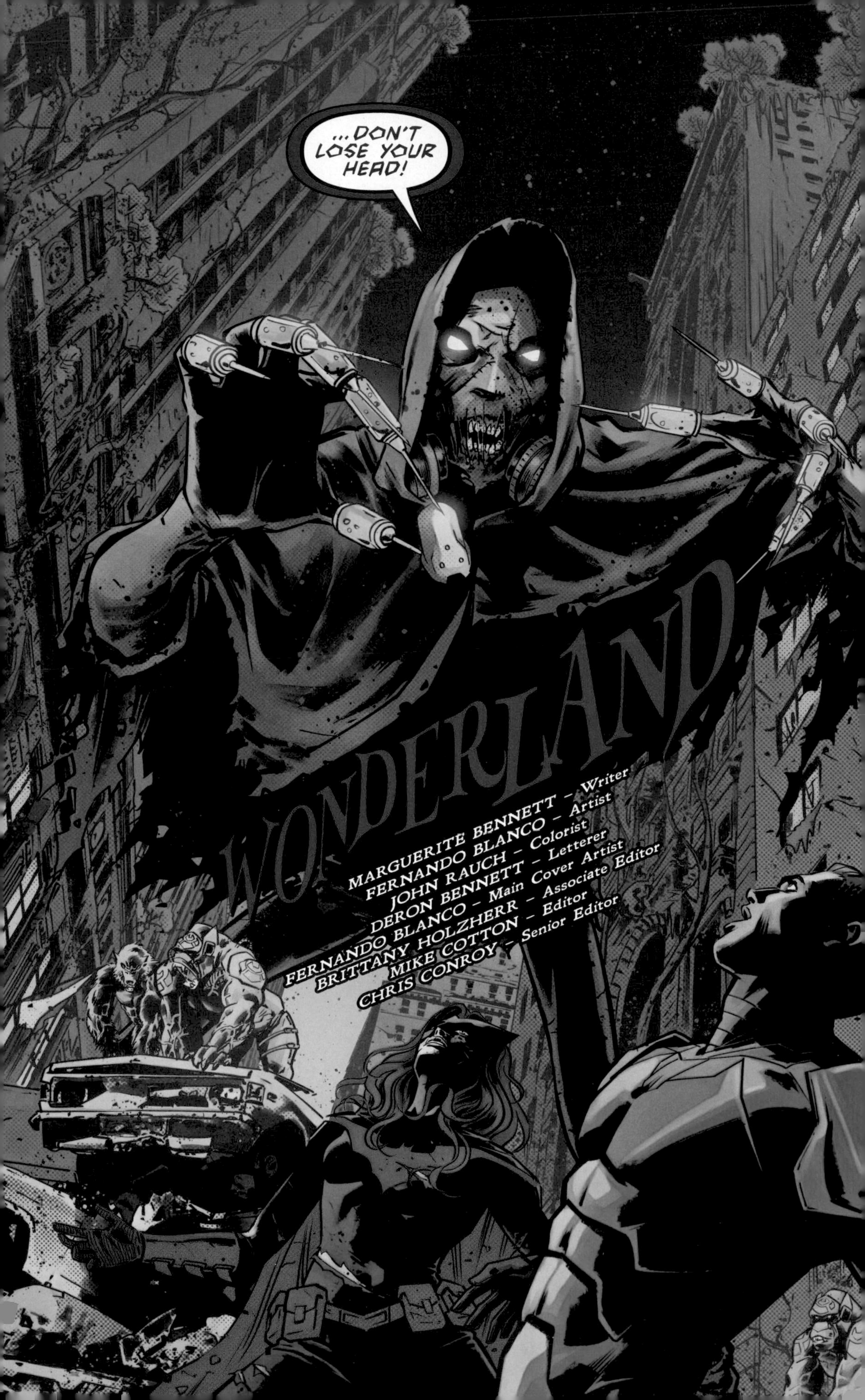
...DON'T LOSE YOUR HEAD!
WONDERLAND
MARGUERITE BENNETT - Writer
FERNANDO BLANCO - Artist
JOHN RAUCH - Colorist
DERON BENNETT - Letterer
FERNANDO BLANCO - Main Cover Artist
BRITTANY HOLZHERR - Associate Editor
MIKE COTTON - Editor
CHRIS CONROY - Senior Editor

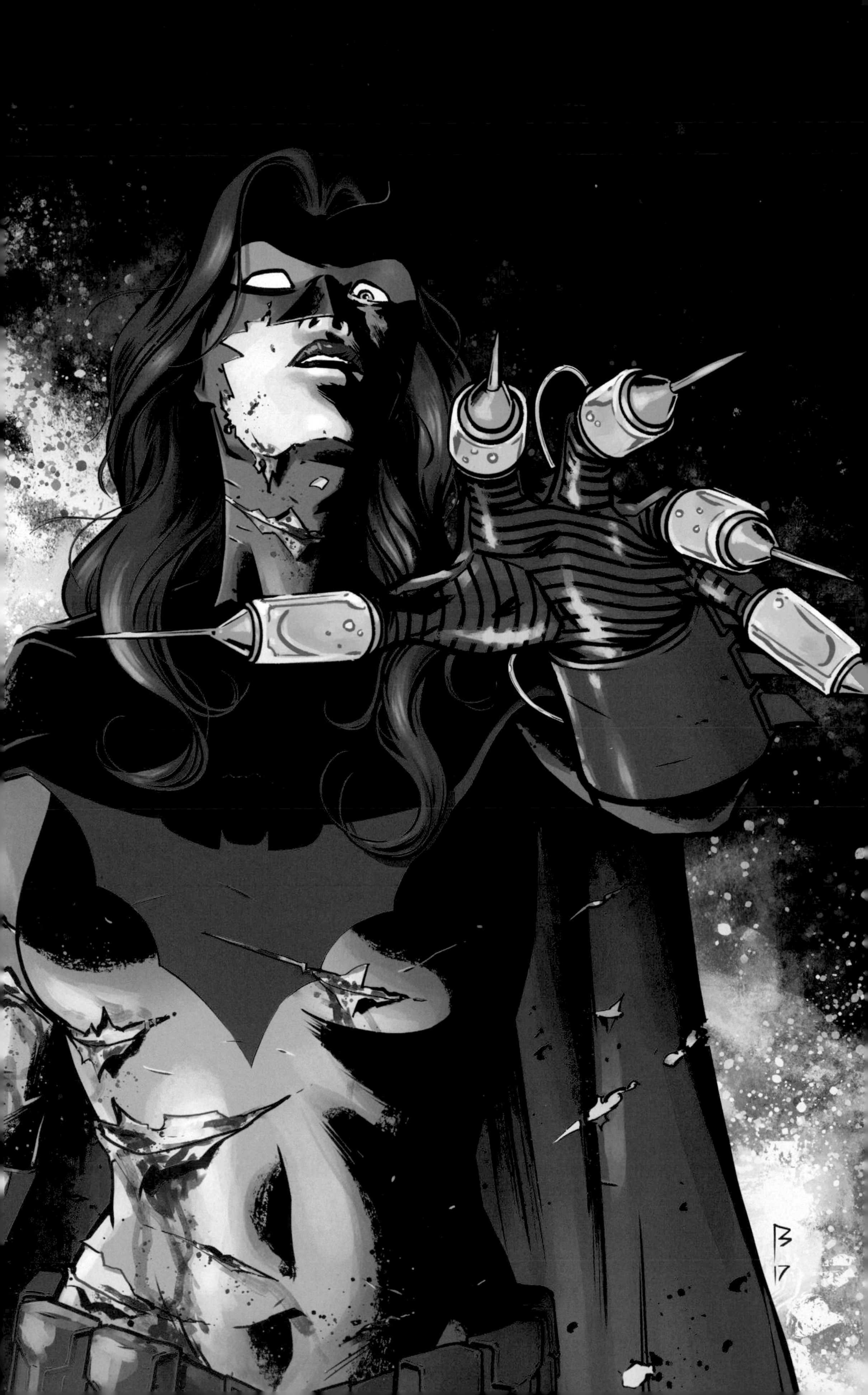

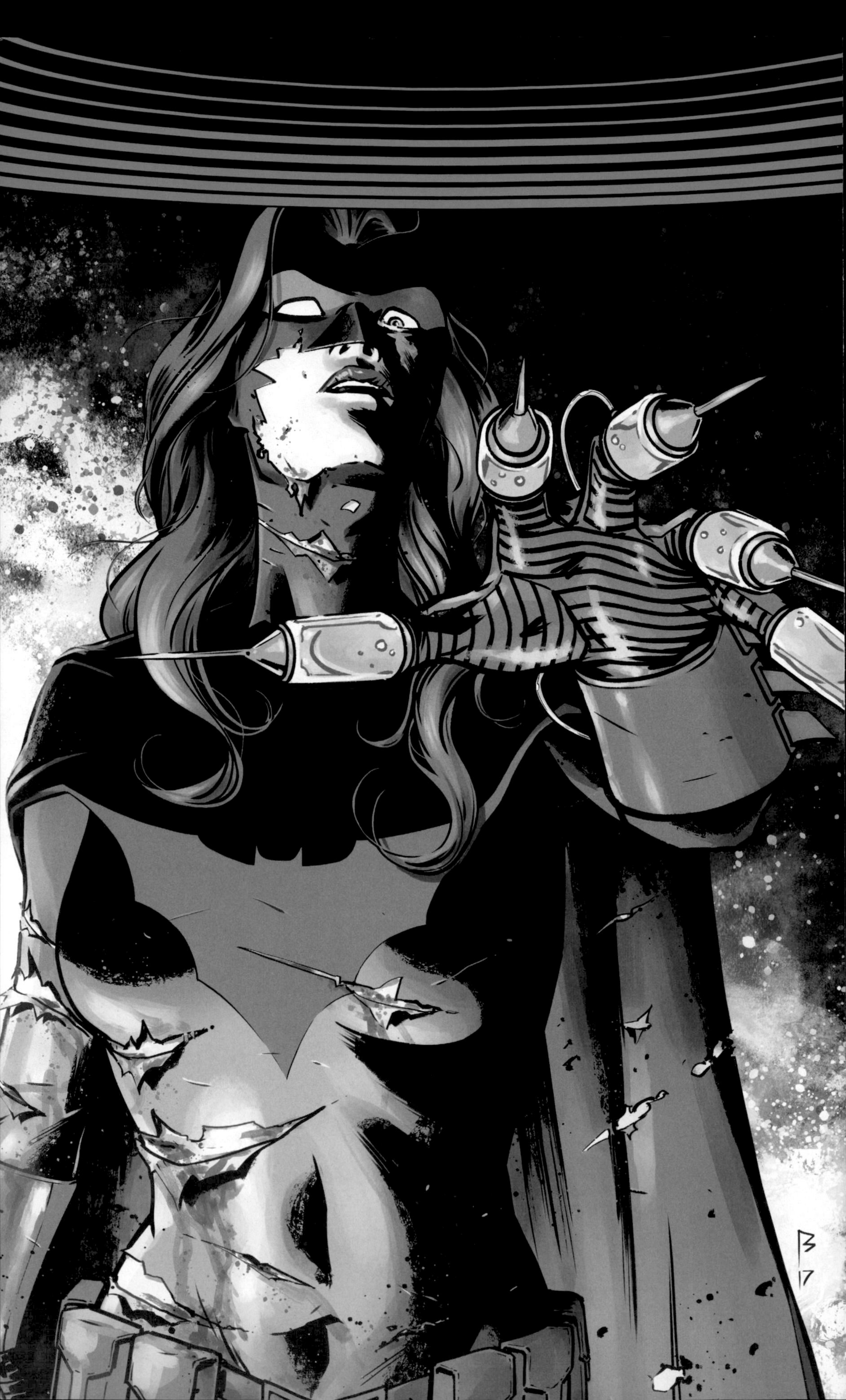

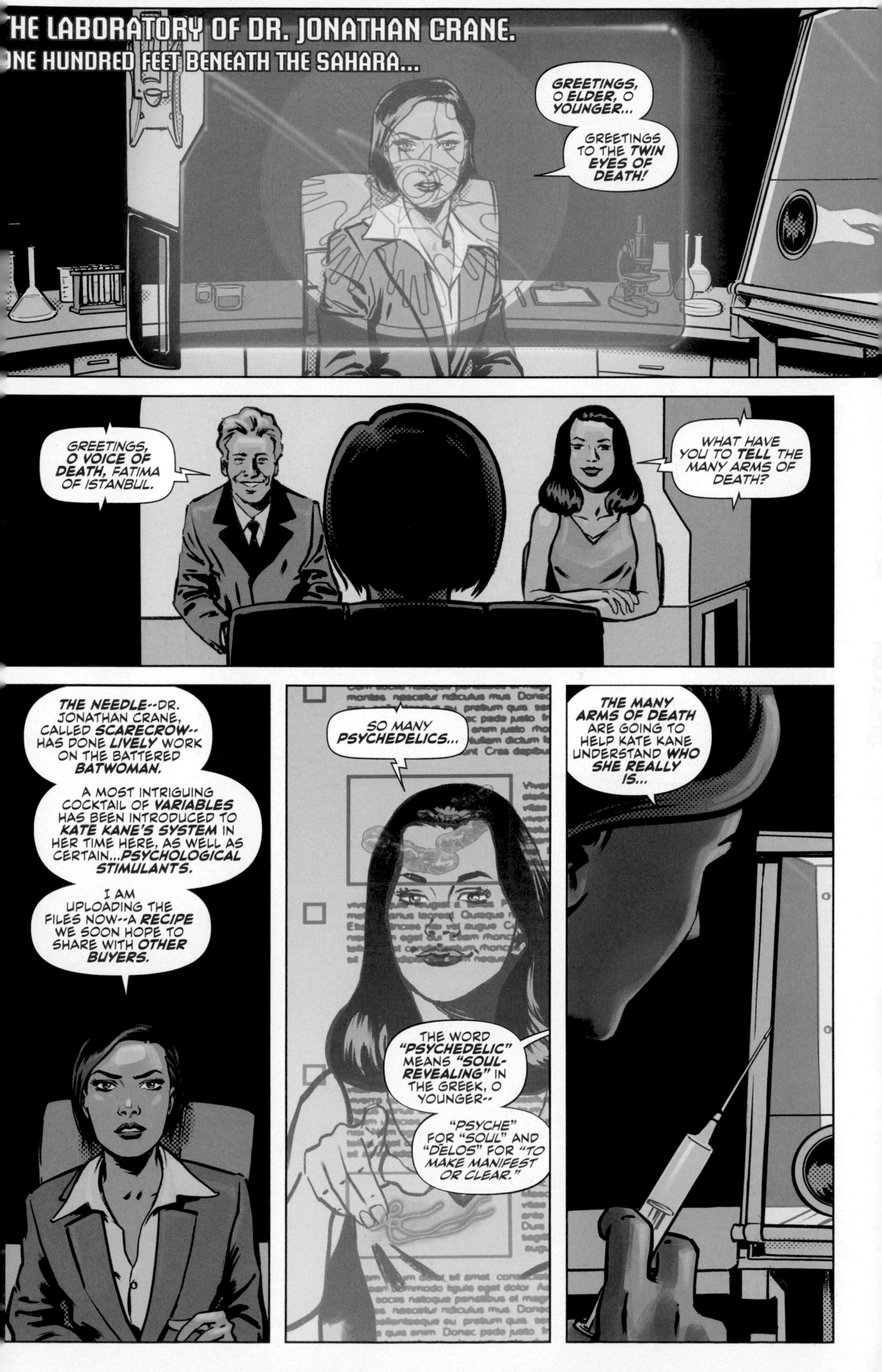
THE LABORATORY OF DR. JONATHAN CRANE.
ONE HUNDRED FEET BENEATH THE SAHARA...
GREETINGS, O ELDER, O YOUNGER...
GREETINGS TO THE TWIN EYES OF DEATH!
GREETINGS, O VOICE OF DEATH, FATIMA OF ISTANBUL.
WHAT HAVE YOU TO TELL THE MANY ARMS OF DEATH?
THE NEEDLE--DR. JONATHAN CRANE, CALLED SCARECROW--HAS DONE LIVELY WORK ON THE BATTERED BATWOMAN.
A MOST INTRIGUING COCKTAIL OF VARIABLES HAS BEEN INTRODUCED TO KATE KANE'S SYSTEM IN HER TIME HERE, AS WELL AS CERTAIN...PSYCHOLOGICAL STIMULANTS.
I AM UPLOADING THE FILES NOW--A RECIPE WE SOON HOPE TO SHARE WITH OTHER BUYERS.
SO MANY PSYCHEDELICS...
THE WORD "PSYCHEDELIC" MEANS "SOUL-REVEALING" IN THE GREEK, O YOUNGER--
"PSYCHE" FOR "SOUL" AND "DELOS" FOR "TO MAKE MANIFEST OR CLEAR."
THE MANY ARMS OF DEATH ARE GOING TO HELP KATE KANE UNDERSTAND WHO SHE REALLY IS...

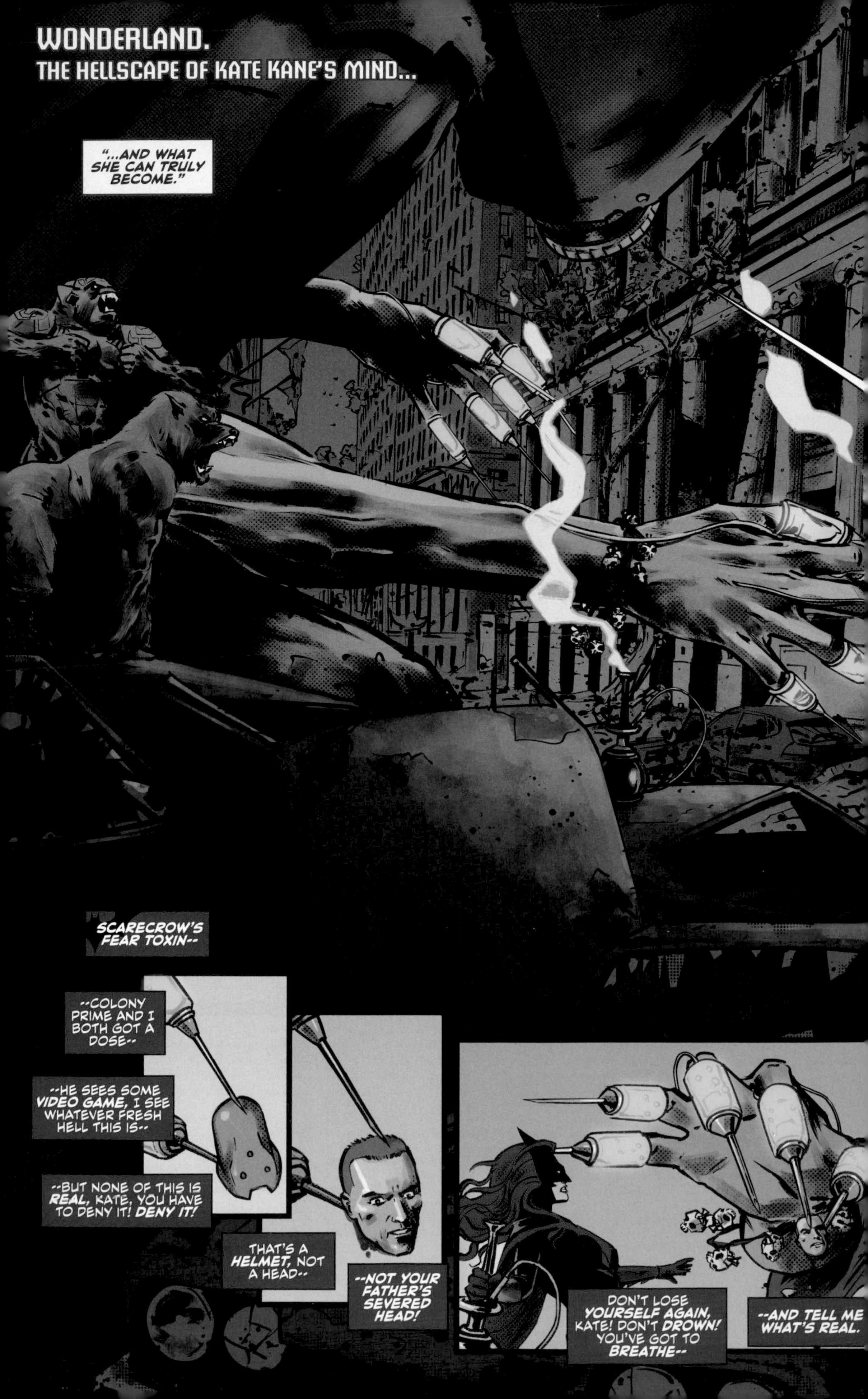
WONDERLAND.
THE HELLSCAPE OF KATE KANE'S MIND...
"...AND WHAT SHE CAN TRULY BECOME."
SCARECROW'S FEAR TOXIN--
--COLONY PRIME AND I BOTH GOT A DOSE--
--HE SEES SOME VIDEO GAME, I SEE WHATEVER FRESH HELL THIS IS--
--BUT NONE OF THIS IS REAL, KATE, YOU HAVE TO DENY IT! DENY IT!
THAT'S A HELMET, NOT A HEAD--
--NOT YOUR FATHER'S SEVERED HEAD!
DON'T LOSE YOURSELF AGAIN, KATE! DON'T DROWN! YOU'VE GOT TO BREATHE--
--AND TELL ME WHAT'S REAL.

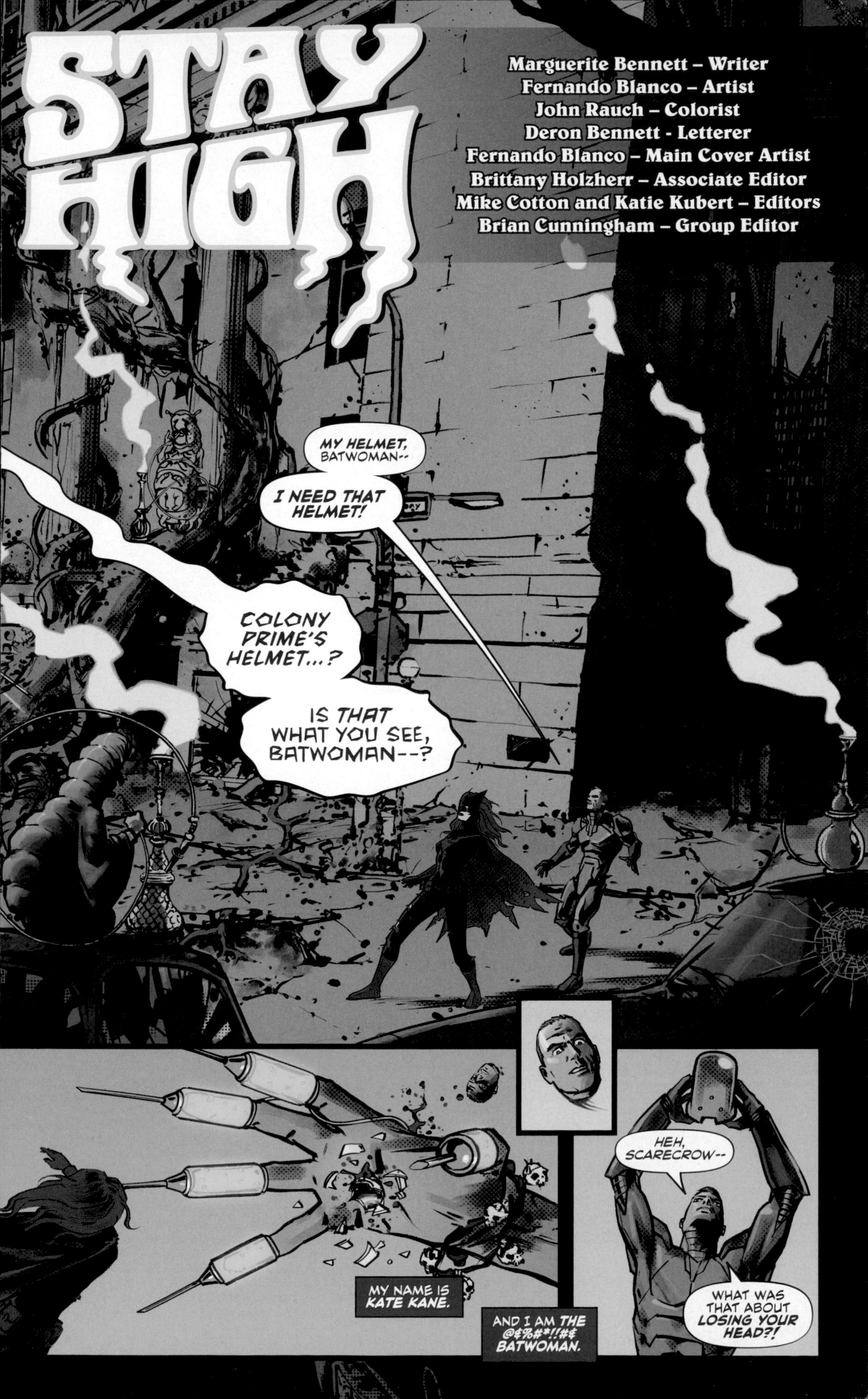
STAY HIGH
Marguerite Bennett – Writer
Fernando Blanco – Artist
John Rauch – Colorist
Deron Bennett - Letterer
Fernando Blanco – Main Cover Artist
Brittany Holzherr – Associate Editor
Mike Cotton and Katie Kubert – Editors
Brian Cunningham – Group Editor
MY HELMET, BATWOMAN--
I NEED THAT HELMET!
COLONY PRIME'S HELMET...?
IS THAT WHAT YOU SEE, BATWOMAN--?
MY NAME IS KATE KANE.
AND I AM THE @$%#*!!#$ BATWOMAN.
HEH, SCARECROW--
WHAT WAS THAT ABOUT LOSING YOUR HEAD?!

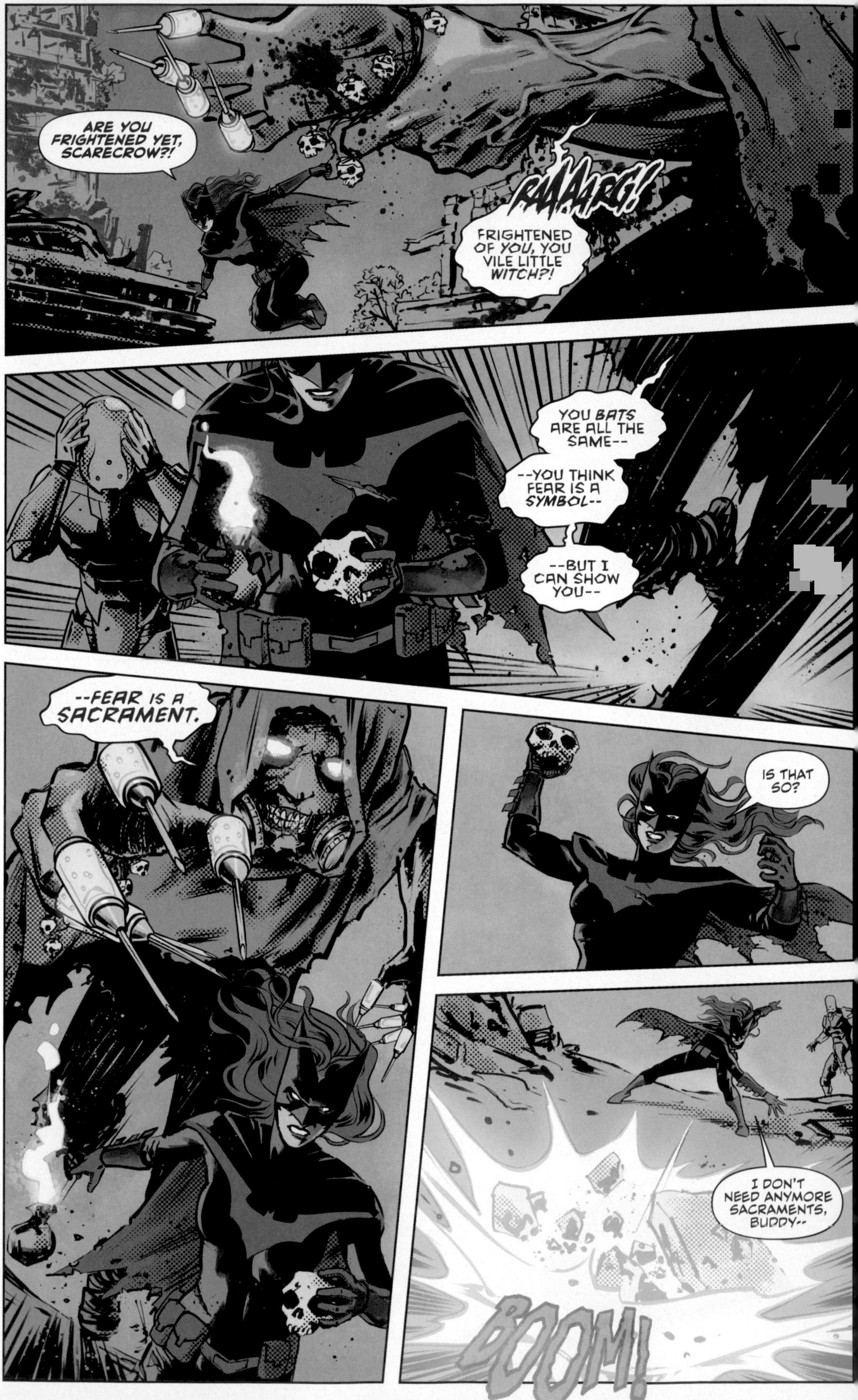
ARE YOU FRIGHTENED YET, SCARECROW?!
RAAAARG!
FRIGHTENED OF YOU, YOU VILE LITTLE WITCH?!
YOU BATS ARE ALL THE SAME--
--YOU THINK FEAR IS A SYMBOL--
--BUT I CAN SHOW YOU--
--FEAR IS A SACRAMENT.
IS THAT SO?
I DON'T NEED ANYMORE SACRAMENTS, BUDDY--
BOOM!

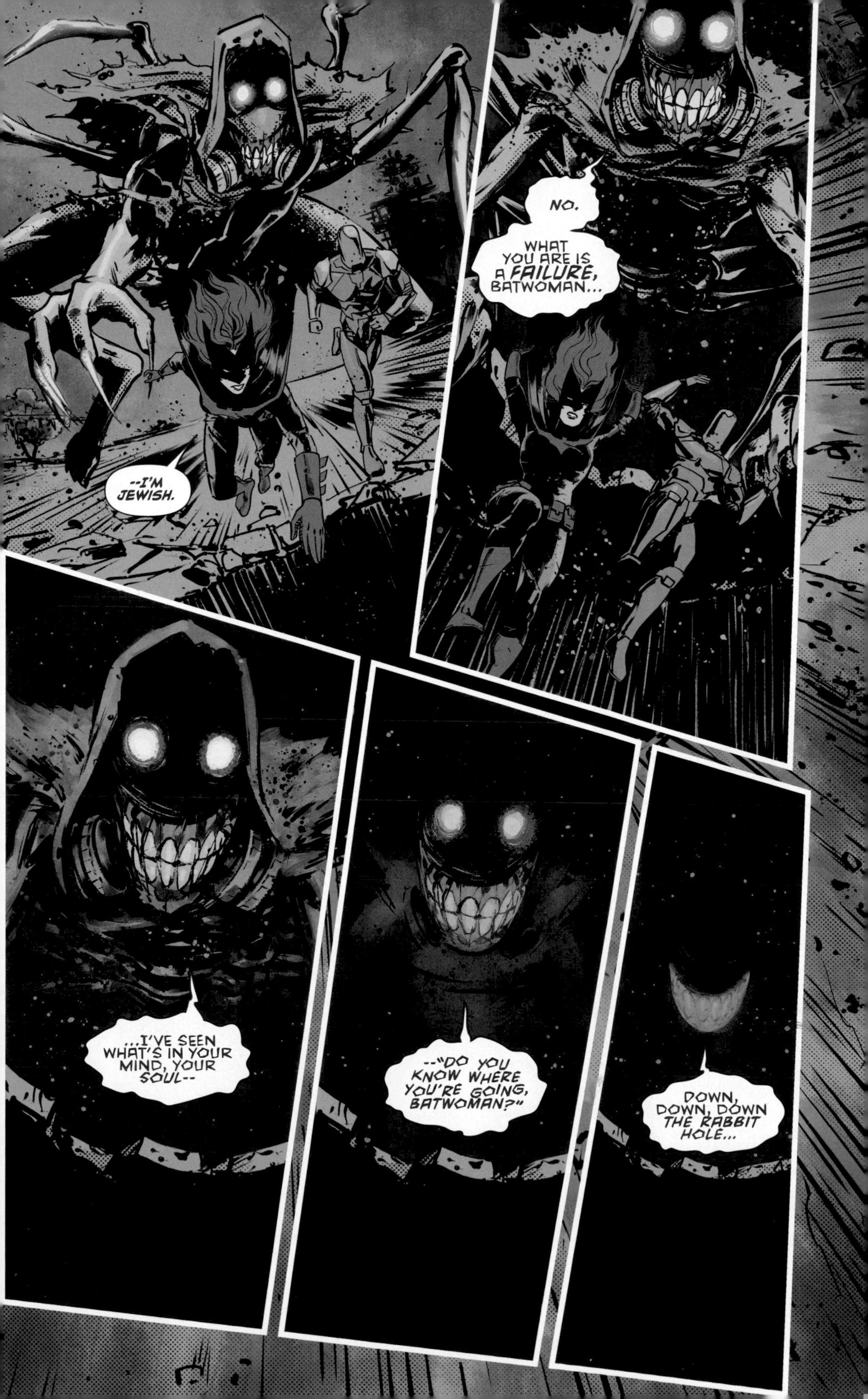
--I'M JEWISH.
NO.
WHAT YOU ARE IS A FAILURE, BATWOMAN...
...I'VE SEEN WHAT'S IN YOUR MIND, YOUR SOUL--
--"DO YOU KNOW WHERE YOU'RE GOING, BATWOMAN?"
DOWN, DOWN, DOWN THE RABBIT HOLE...

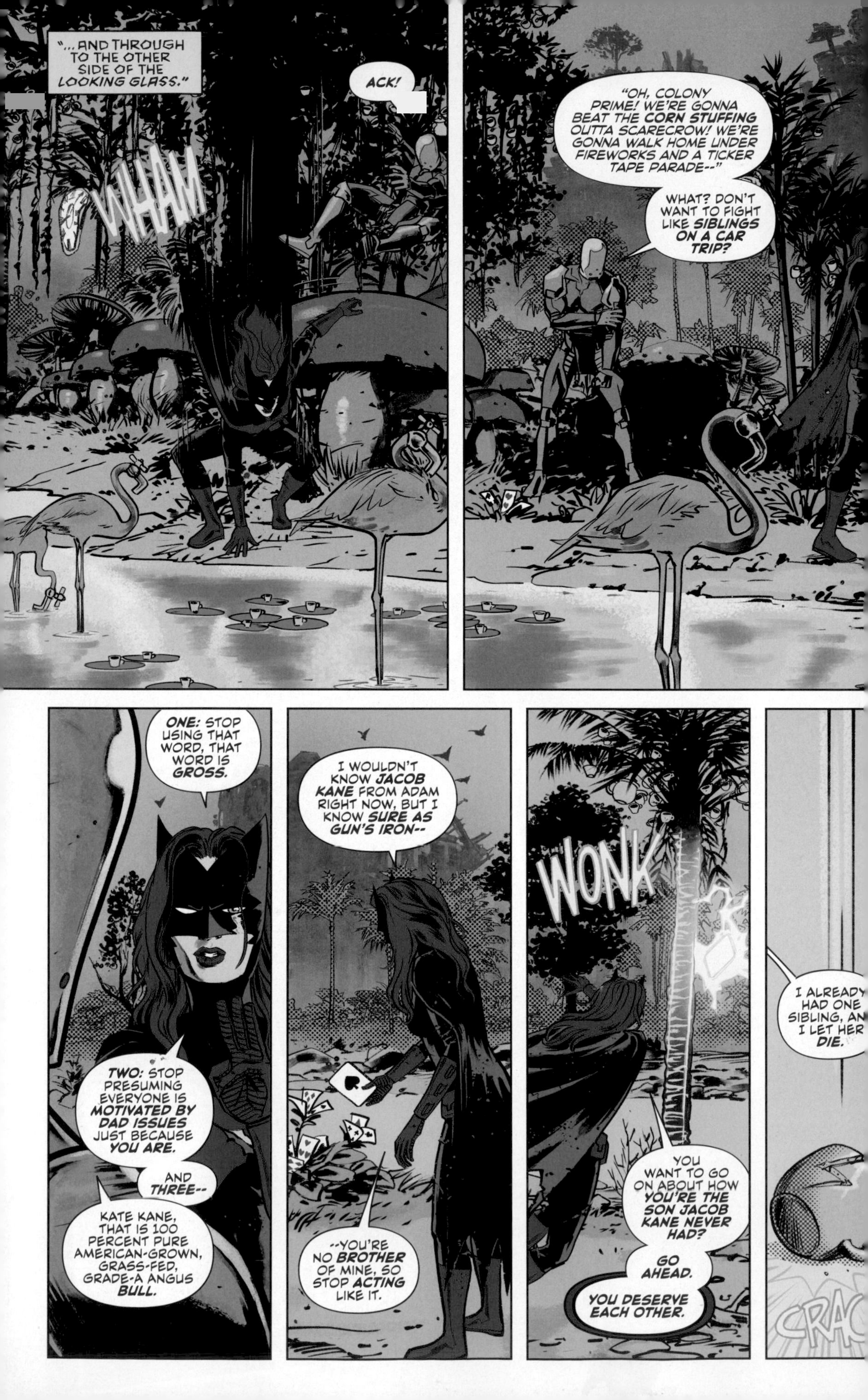
"...AND THROUGH TO THE OTHER SIDE OF THE LOOKING GLASS."
ACK!
WHAM
"OH, COLONY PRIME! WE'RE GONNA BEAT THE CORN STUFFING OUTTA SCARECROW! WE'RE GONNA WALK HOME UNDER FIREWORKS AND A TICKER TAPE PARADE--"
WHAT? DON'T WANT TO FIGHT LIKE SIBLINGS ON A CAR TRIP?
ONE: STOP USING THAT WORD, THAT WORD IS GROSS.
TWO: STOP PRESUMING EVERYONE IS MOTIVATED BY DAD ISSUES JUST BECAUSE YOU ARE.
AND THREE--
KATE KANE, THAT IS 100 PERCENT PURE AMERICAN-GROWN, GRASS-FED, GRADE-A ANGUS BULL.
I WOULDN'T KNOW JACOB KANE FROM ADAM RIGHT NOW, BUT I KNOW SURE AS GUN'S IRON--
--YOU'RE NO BROTHER OF MINE, SO STOP ACTING LIKE IT.
WONK
YOU WANT TO GO ON ABOUT HOW YOU'RE THE SON JACOB KANE NEVER HAD?
GO AHEAD.
YOU DESERVE EACH OTHER.
I ALREADY HAD ONE SIBLING, AN I LET HER DIE.

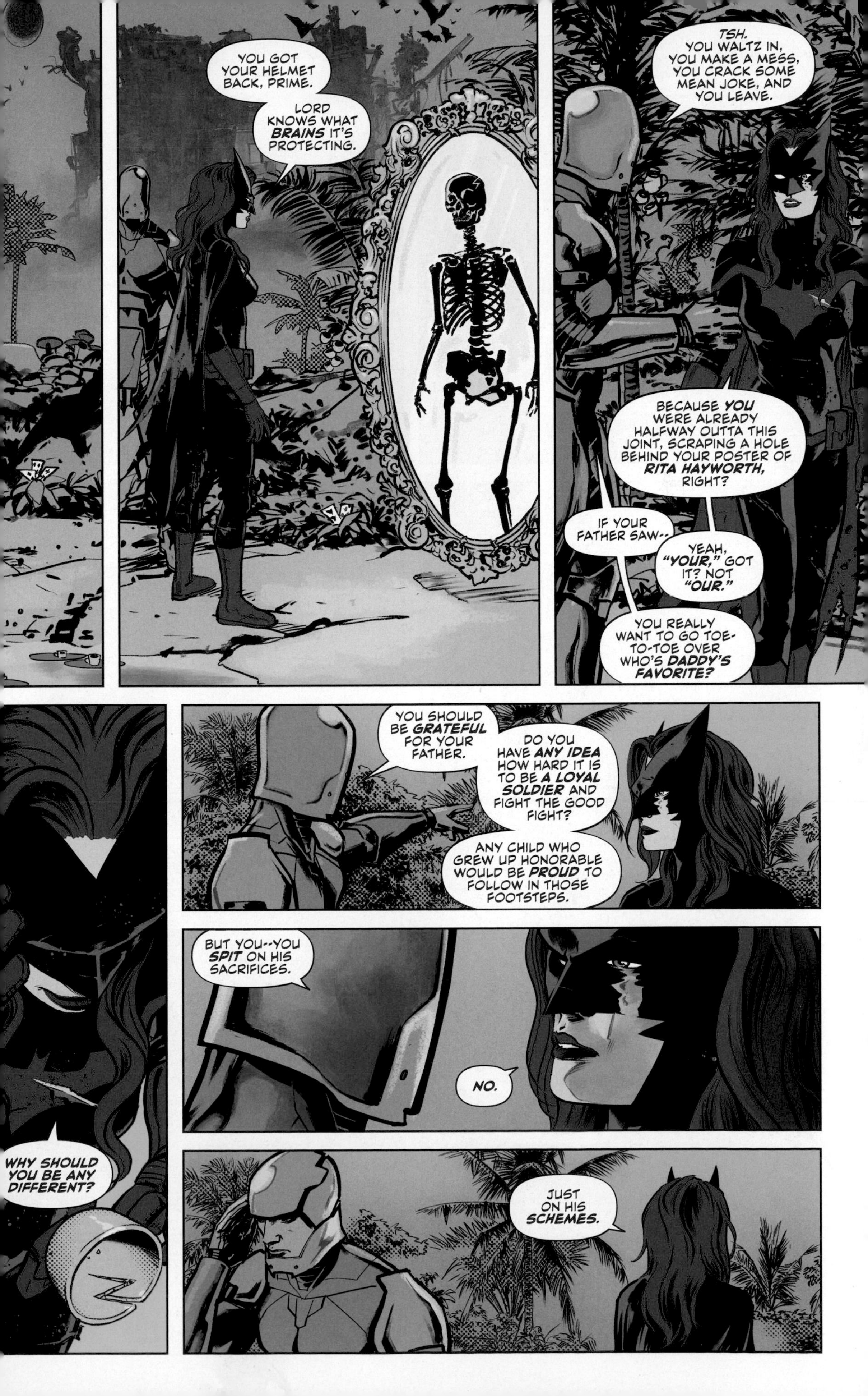
YOU GOT YOUR HELMET BACK, PRIME.
LORD KNOWS WHAT BRAINS IT'S PROTECTING.
TSH. YOU WALTZ IN, YOU MAKE A MESS, YOU CRACK SOME MEAN JOKE, AND YOU LEAVE.
BECAUSE YOU WERE ALREADY HALFWAY OUTTA THIS JOINT, SCRAPING A HOLE BEHIND YOUR POSTER OF RITA HAYWORTH, RIGHT?
IF YOUR FATHER SAW--
YEAH, "YOUR," GOT IT? NOT "OUR."
YOU REALLY WANT TO GO TOE-TO-TOE OVER WHO'S DADDY'S FAVORITE?
YOU SHOULD BE GRATEFUL FOR YOUR FATHER.
DO YOU HAVE ANY IDEA HOW HARD IT IS TO BE A LOYAL SOLDIER AND FIGHT THE GOOD FIGHT?
ANY CHILD WHO GREW UP HONORABLE WOULD BE PROUD TO FOLLOW IN THOSE FOOTSTEPS.
BUT YOU--YOU SPIT ON HIS SACRIFICES.
NO.
JUST ON HIS SCHEMES.
WHY SHOULD YOU BE ANY DIFFERENT?

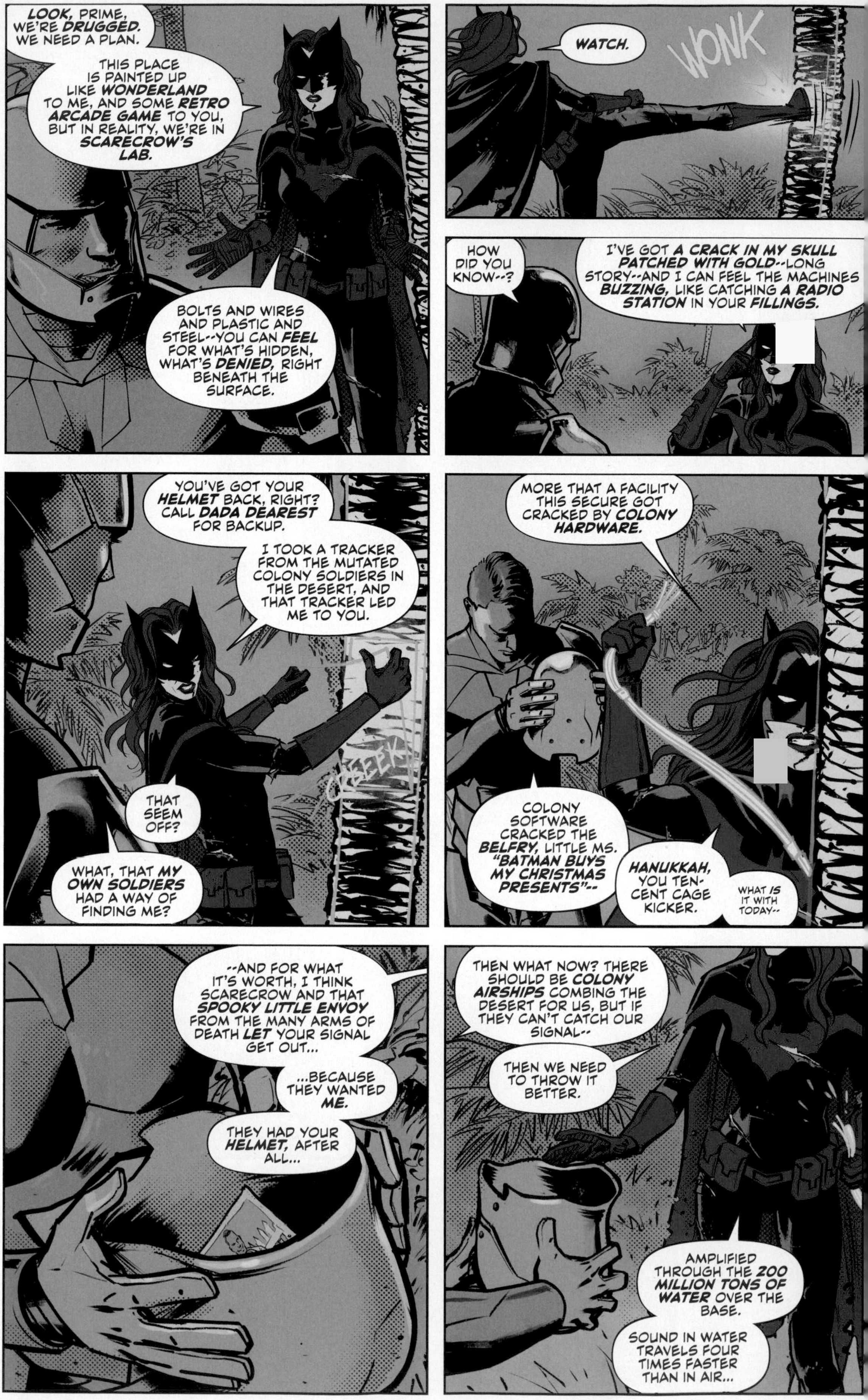

LOOK, PRIME, WE'RE DRUGGED. WE NEED A PLAN.
THIS PLACE IS PAINTED UP LIKE WONDERLAND TO ME, AND SOME RETRO ARCADE GAME TO YOU, BUT IN REALITY, WE'RE IN SCARECROW'S LAB.
BOLTS AND WIRES AND PLASTIC AND STEEL--YOU CAN FEEL FOR WHAT'S HIDDEN, WHAT'S DENIED, RIGHT BENEATH THE SURFACE.
WATCH.
WONK
HOW DID YOU KNOW--?
I'VE GOT A CRACK IN MY SKULL PATCHED WITH GOLD--LONG STORY--AND I CAN FEEL THE MACHINES BUZZING, LIKE CATCHING A RADIO STATION IN YOUR FILLINGS.
YOU'VE GOT YOUR HELMET BACK, RIGHT? CALL DADA DEAREST FOR BACKUP.
I TOOK A TRACKER FROM THE MUTATED COLONY SOLDIERS IN THE DESERT, AND THAT TRACKER LED ME TO YOU.
THAT SEEM OFF?
WHAT, THAT MY OWN SOLDIERS HAD A WAY OF FINDING ME?
MORE THAT A FACILITY THIS SECURE GOT CRACKED BY COLONY HARDWARE.
COLONY SOFTWARE CRACKED THE BELFRY, LITTLE MS. "BATMAN BUYS MY CHRISTMAS PRESENTS"--
HANUKKAH, YOU TEN-CENT CAGE KICKER.
WHAT IS IT WITH TODAY--
--AND FOR WHAT IT'S WORTH, I THINK SCARECROW AND THAT SPOOKY LITTLE ENVOY FROM THE MANY ARMS OF DEATH LET YOUR SIGNAL GET OUT...
...BECAUSE THEY WANTED ME.
THEY HAD YOUR HELMET, AFTER ALL...
THEN WHAT NOW? THERE SHOULD BE COLONY AIRSHIPS COMBING THE DESERT FOR US, BUT IF THEY CAN'T CATCH OUR SIGNAL--
THEN WE NEED TO THROW IT BETTER.
AMPLIFIED THROUGH THE 200 MILLION TONS OF WATER OVER THE BASE.
SOUND IN WATER TRAVELS FOUR TIMES FASTER THAN IN AIR...

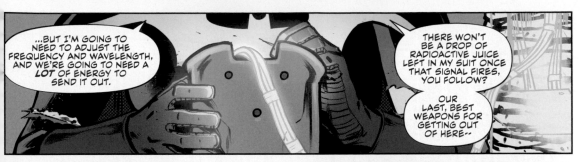

...BUT I'M GOING TO NEED TO ADJUST THE FREQUENCY AND WAVELENGTH, AND WE'RE GOING TO NEED A *LOT* OF ENERGY TO SEND IT OUT.

THERE WON'T BE A DROP OF RADIOACTIVE JUICE LEFT IN MY SUIT ONCE THAT SIGNAL FIRES, YOU FOLLOW?

OUR LAST, BEST WEAPONS FOR GETTING OUT OF HERE--

PLEASE DON'T SAY, *"WILL BE EACH OTHER."*

WELL, THEN *DON'T TIP YOUR HAND* LIKE THAT!

IF I KNOW IT ANNOYS YOU, I'M PRETTY MUCH *CONTRACTUALLY OBLIGATED* TO SAY IT NOW--

FINE.

"WILL BE EACH OTHER."

WHOOOM

I SEE YOU'VE BEEN LISTENING TO *JULIA PENNYWORTH,* AS FAR AS THE SCIENCE GOES, BATWOMAN.

I OWE JULIA...SO MANY ROUNDS OF *DOING THE DISHES.*

AND I BETTER NOT *BREAK A SINGLE--*

TSSSS

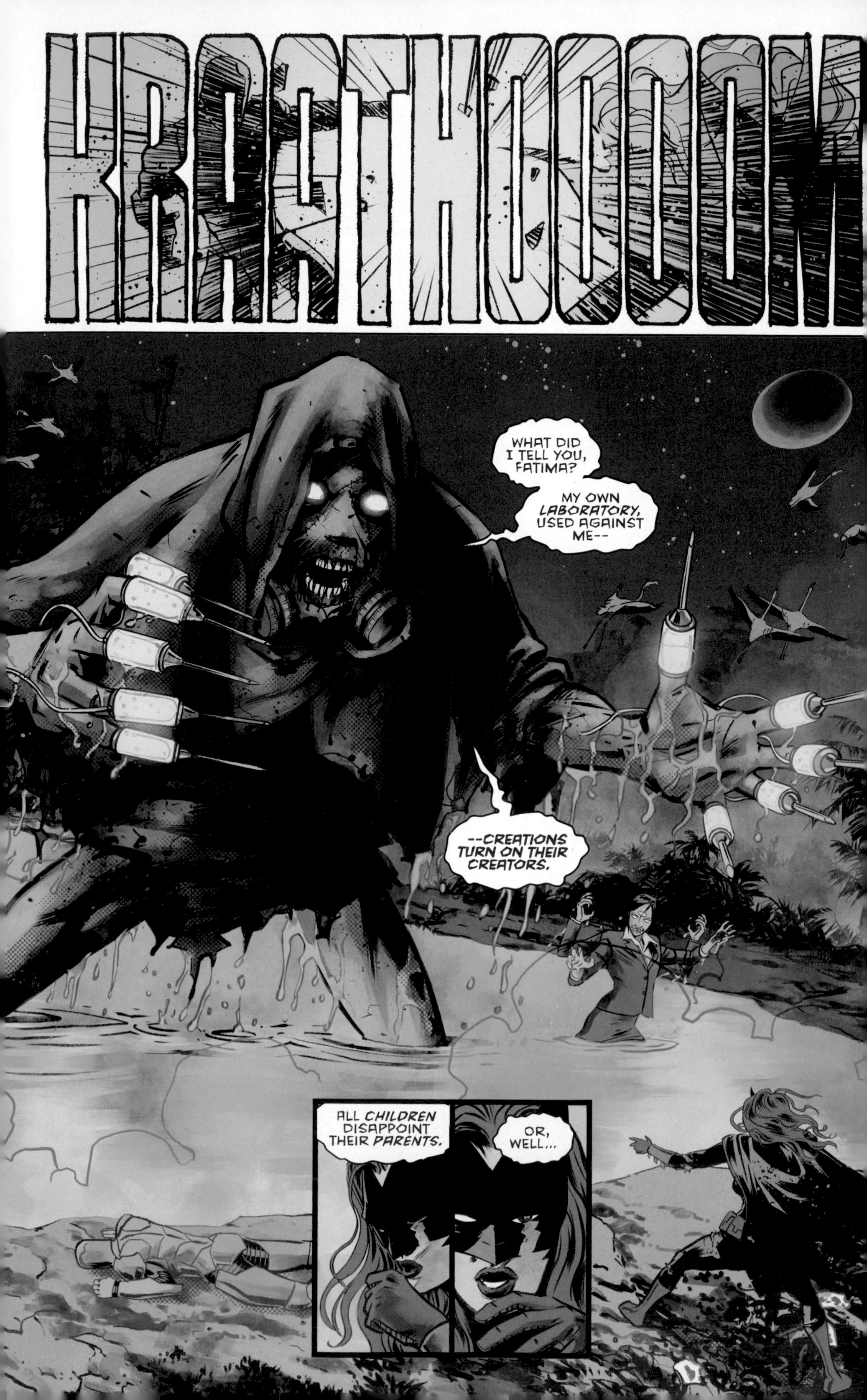
KRRATHOOOOOM
WHAT DID I TELL YOU, FATIMA?
MY OWN *LABORATORY*, USED AGAINST ME--
--CREATIONS TURN ON THEIR CREATORS.
ALL *CHILDREN* DISAPPOINT THEIR *PARENTS.*
OR, WELL...

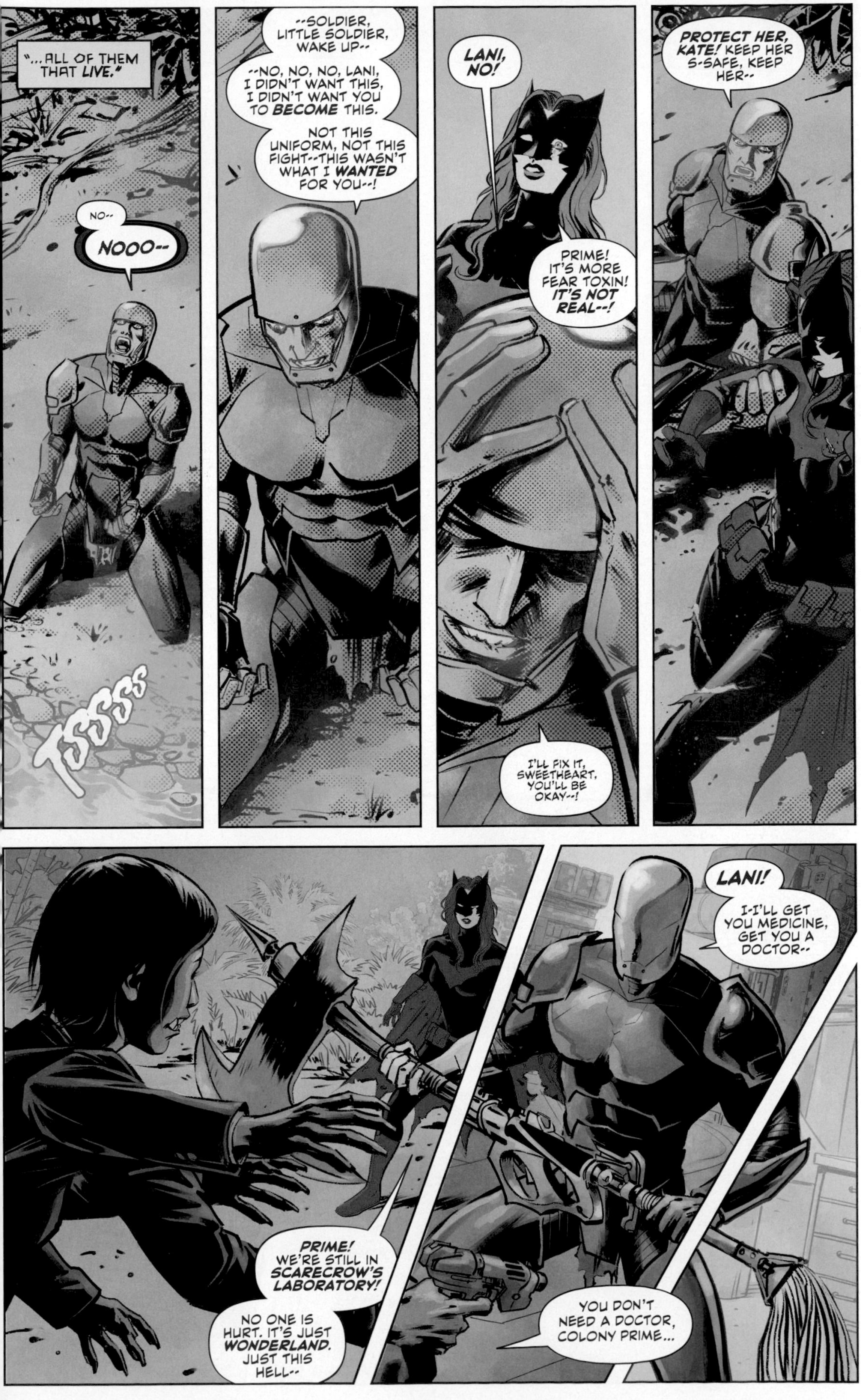
"...ALL OF THEM THAT LIVE."
NO--
NOOO--
TSSSSS
--SOLDIER, LITTLE SOLDIER, WAKE UP--
--NO, NO, NO, LANI, I DIDN'T WANT THIS, I DIDN'T WANT YOU TO BECOME THIS.
NOT THIS UNIFORM, NOT THIS FIGHT--THIS WASN'T WHAT I WANTED FOR YOU--!
LANI, NO!
PRIME! IT'S MORE FEAR TOXIN! IT'S NOT REAL--!
I'LL FIX IT, SWEETHEART, YOU'LL BE OKAY--!
PROTECT HER, KATE! KEEP HER S-SAFE, KEEP HER--
PRIME! WE'RE STILL IN SCARECROW'S LABORATORY!
NO ONE IS HURT. IT'S JUST WONDERLAND. JUST THIS HELL--
LANI!
I-I'LL GET YOU MEDICINE, GET YOU A DOCTOR--
YOU DON'T NEED A DOCTOR, COLONY PRIME...

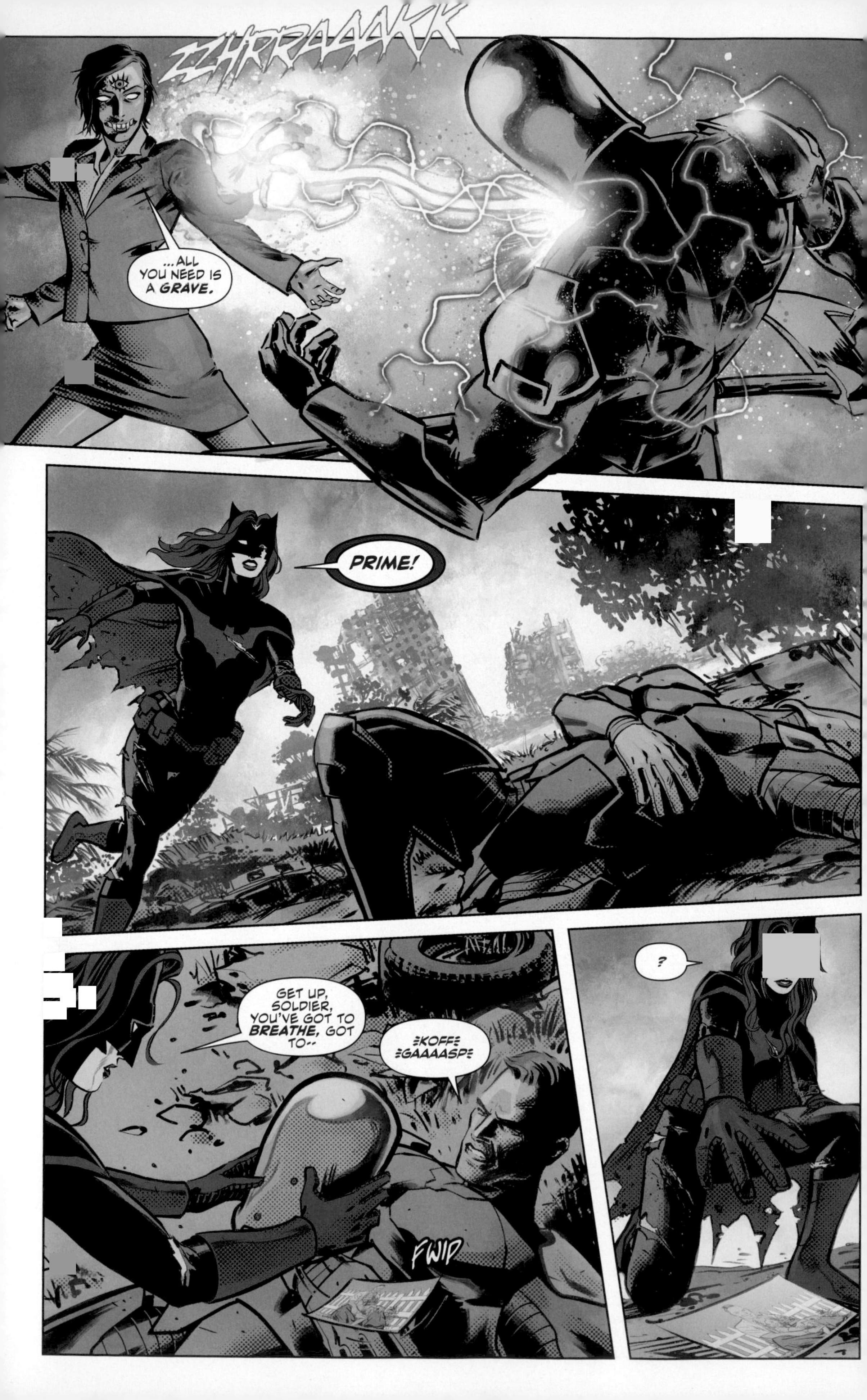
ZZHRRAAAKK
...ALL YOU NEED IS A GRAVE.
PRIME!
GET UP, SOLDIER, YOU'VE GOT TO BREATHE, GOT TO--
KOFF GAAAASP
FWIP
?

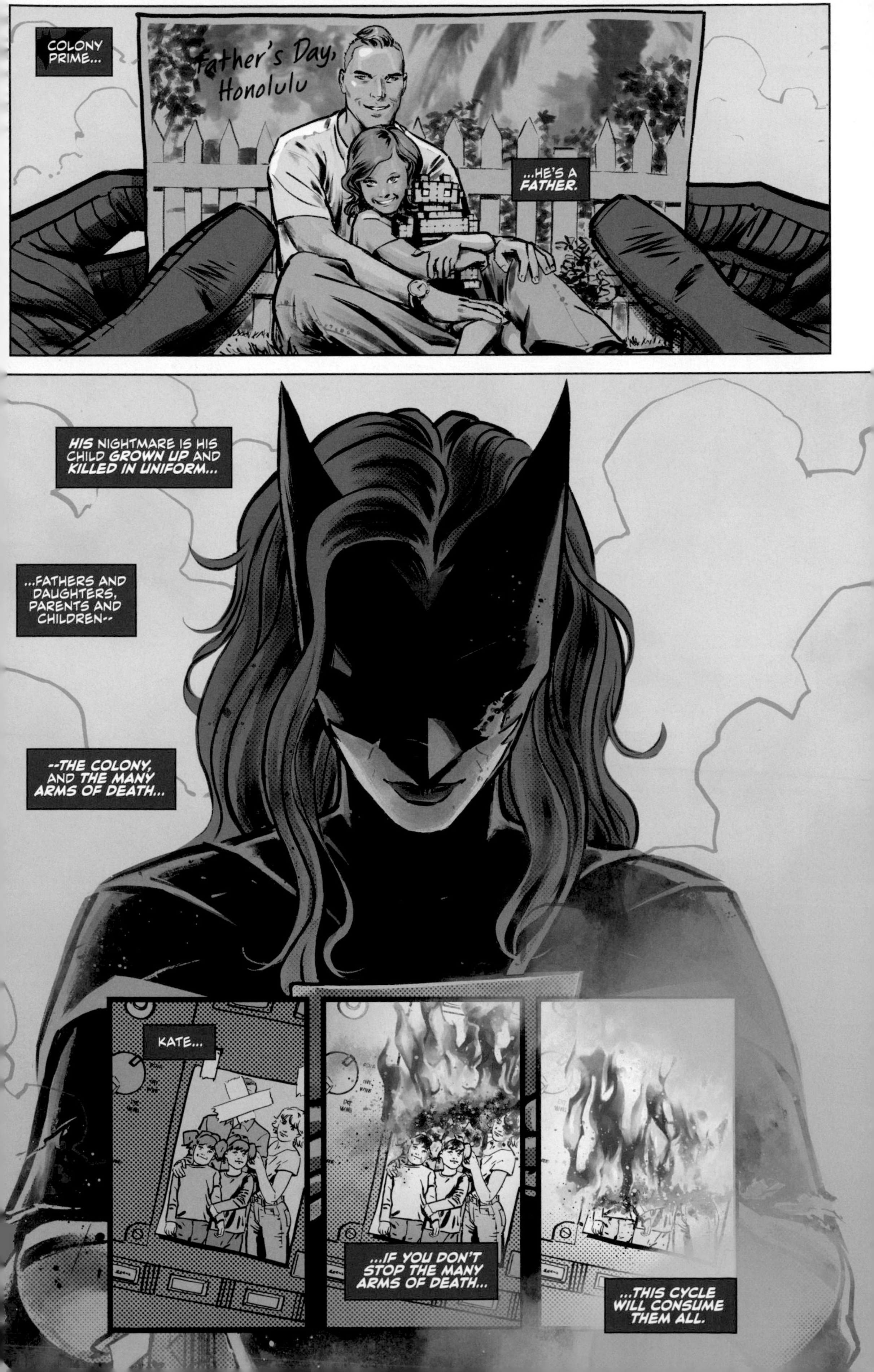

COLONY PRIME...
Father's Day, Honolulu
...HE'S A FATHER.
HIS NIGHTMARE IS HIS CHILD GROWN UP AND KILLED IN UNIFORM...
...FATHERS AND DAUGHTERS, PARENTS AND CHILDREN--
--THE COLONY, AND THE MANY ARMS OF DEATH...
KATE...
...IF YOU DON'T STOP THE MANY ARMS OF DEATH...
...THIS CYCLE WILL CONSUME THEM ALL.

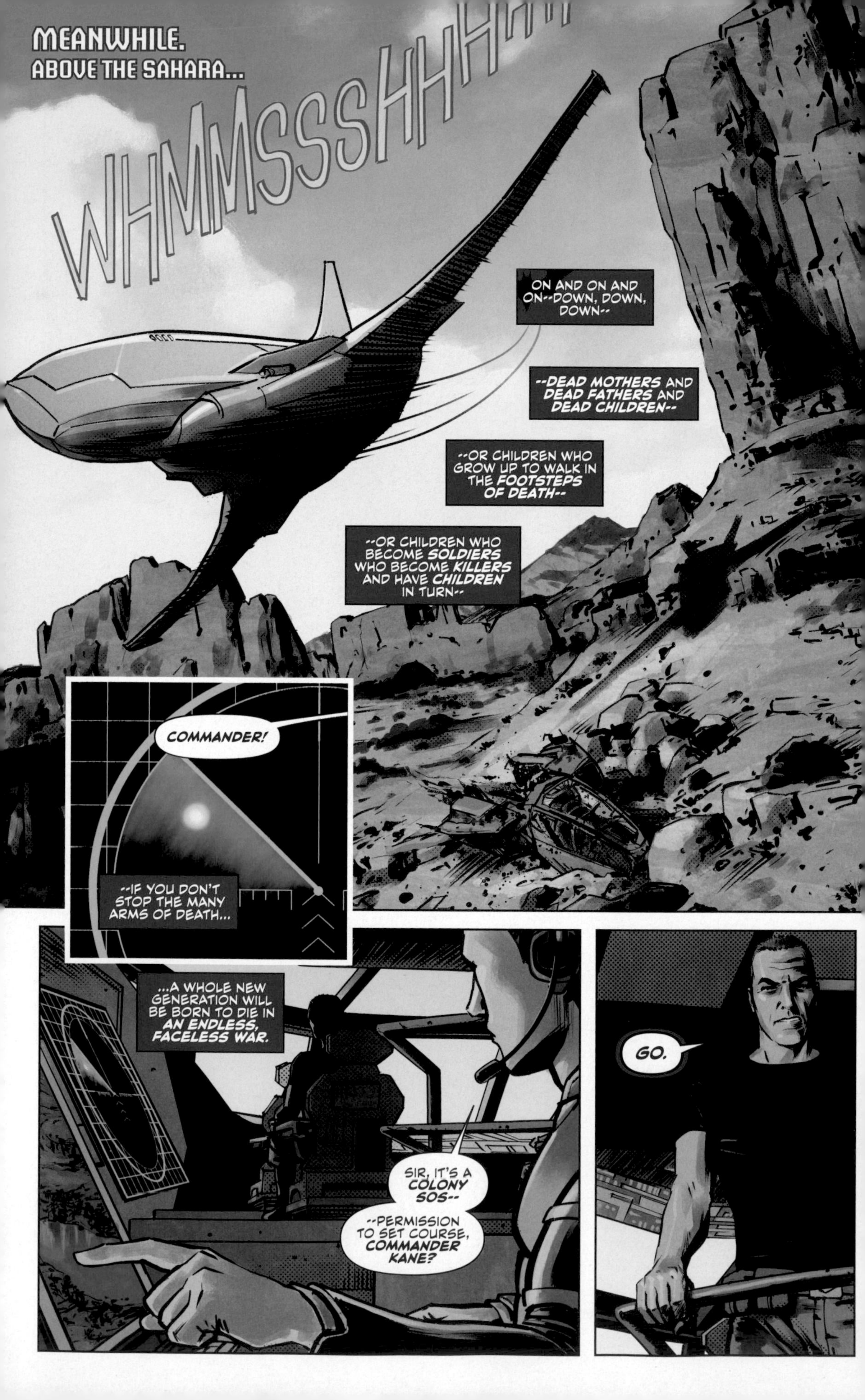
MEANWHILE. ABOVE THE SAHARA...
WHMMSSSSHHHH
ON AND ON AND ON--DOWN, DOWN, DOWN--
--DEAD MOTHERS AND DEAD FATHERS AND DEAD CHILDREN--
--OR CHILDREN WHO GROW UP TO WALK IN THE FOOTSTEPS OF DEATH--
--OR CHILDREN WHO BECOME SOLDIERS WHO BECOME KILLERS AND HAVE CHILDREN IN TURN--
COMMANDER!
--IF YOU DON'T STOP THE MANY ARMS OF DEATH...
...A WHOLE NEW GENERATION WILL BE BORN TO DIE IN AN ENDLESS, FACELESS WAR.
SIR, IT'S A COLONY SOS--
--PERMISSION TO SET COURSE, COMMANDER KANE?
GO.

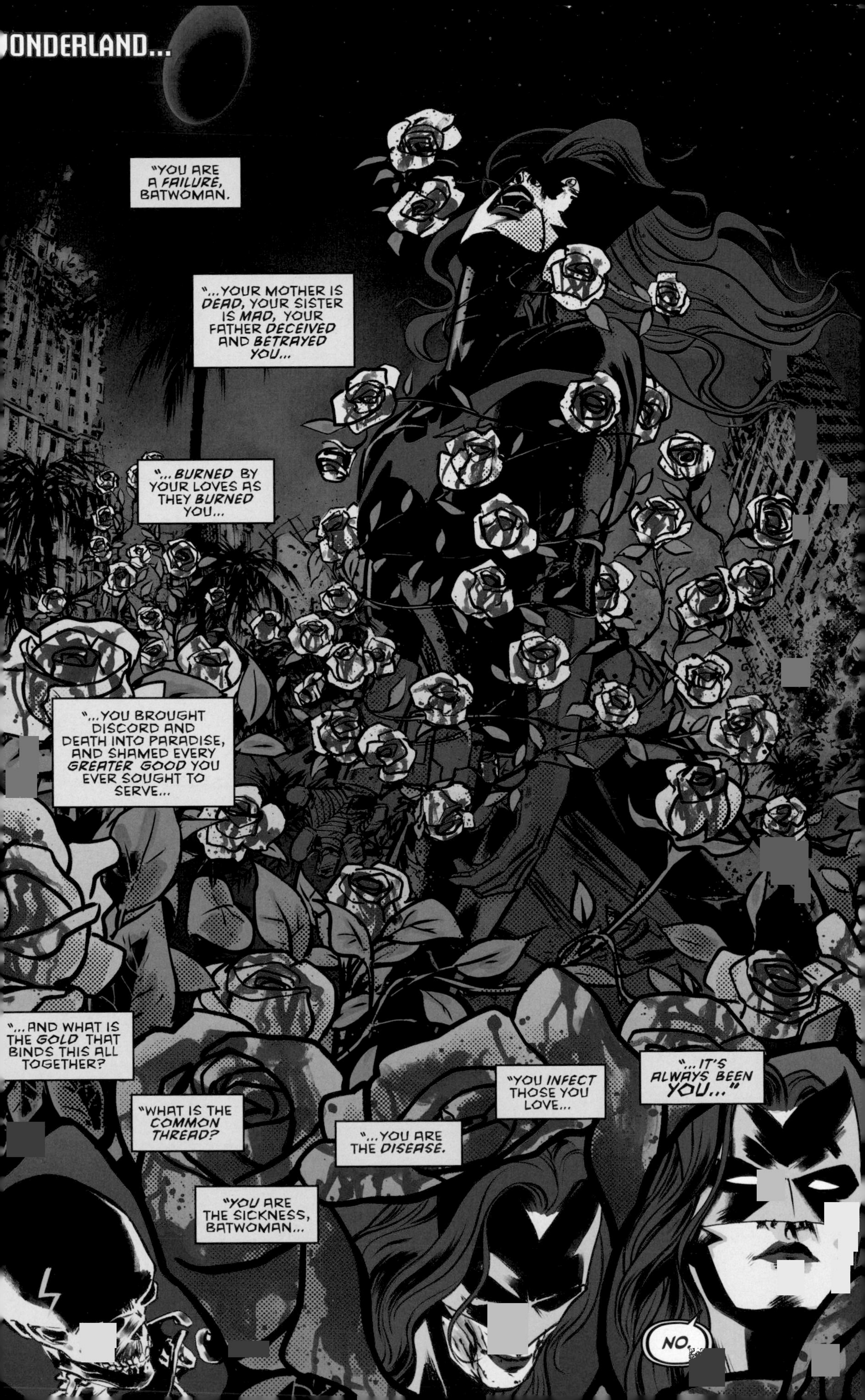

WONDERLAND...
"YOU ARE A FAILURE, BATWOMAN.
"...YOUR MOTHER IS DEAD, YOUR SISTER IS MAD, YOUR FATHER DECEIVED AND BETRAYED YOU...
"...BURNED BY YOUR LOVES AS THEY BURNED YOU...
"...YOU BROUGHT DISCORD AND DEATH INTO PARADISE, AND SHAMED EVERY GREATER GOOD YOU EVER SOUGHT TO SERVE...
"...AND WHAT IS THE GOLD THAT BINDS THIS ALL TOGETHER?
"WHAT IS THE COMMON THREAD?
"YOU ARE THE SICKNESS, BATWOMAN...
"...YOU ARE THE DISEASE.
"YOU INFECT THOSE YOU LOVE...
"...IT'S ALWAYS BEEN YOU..."
NO.

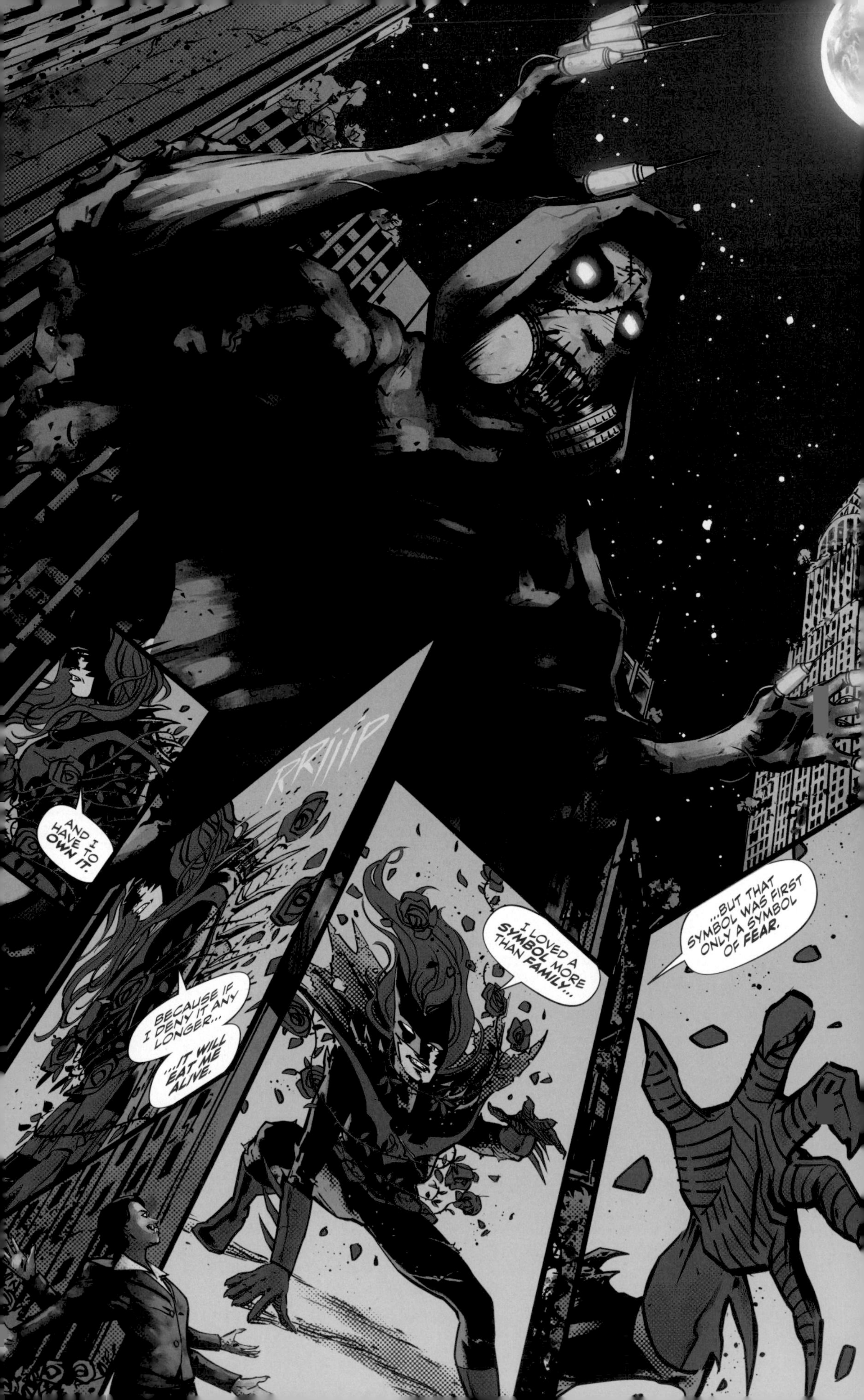
AND I HAVE TO OWN IT.
RRiiiip
BECAUSE IF I DENY IT ANY LONGER...
...IT WILL EAT ME ALIVE.
I LOVED A SYMBOL MORE THAN FAMILY...
...BUT THAT SYMBOL WAS FIRST ONLY A SYMBOL OF FEAR.

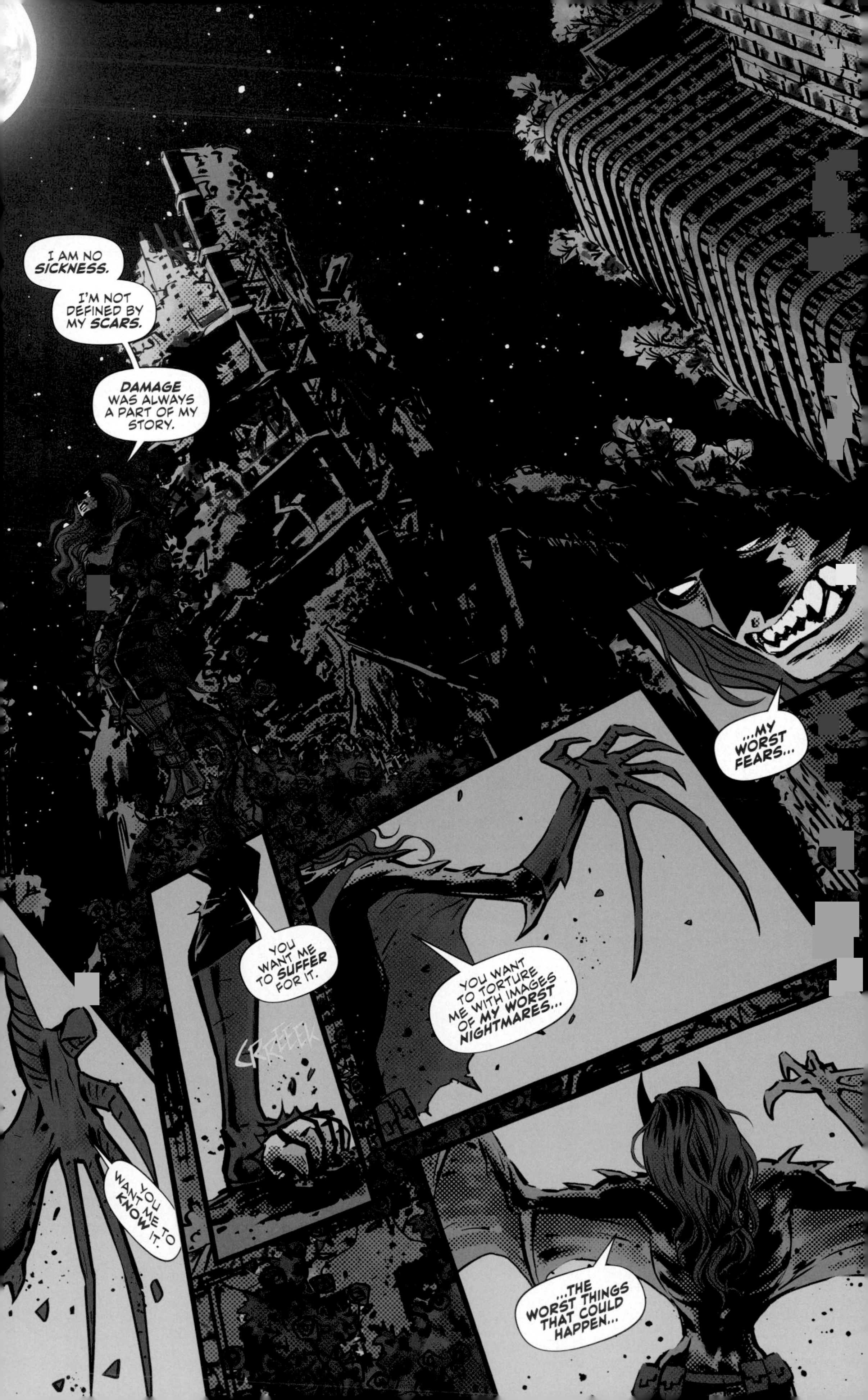
I AM NO SICKNESS.
I'M NOT DEFINED BY MY SCARS.
DAMAGE WAS ALWAYS A PART OF MY STORY.
...MY WORST FEARS...
YOU WANT TO TORTURE ME WITH IMAGES OF MY WORST NIGHTMARES...
YOU WANT ME TO SUFFER FOR IT.
CRREEEK
YOU WANT ME TO KNOW IT.
...THE WORST THINGS THAT COULD HAPPEN...

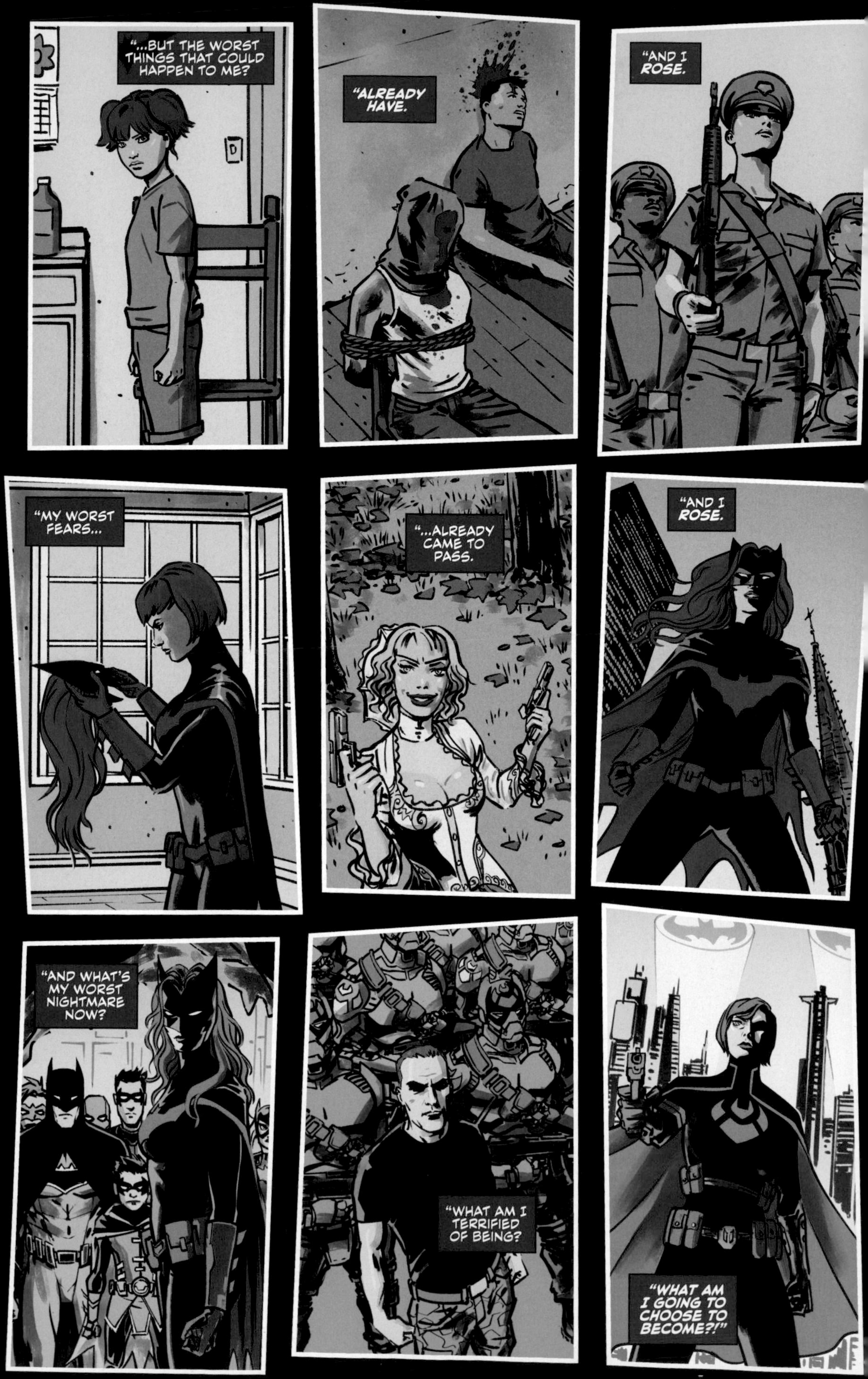
"...BUT THE WORST THINGS THAT COULD HAPPEN TO ME?
"ALREADY HAVE.
"AND I ROSE.
"MY WORST FEARS...
"...ALREADY CAME TO PASS.
"AND I ROSE.
"AND WHAT'S MY WORST NIGHTMARE NOW?
"WHAT AM I TERRIFIED OF BEING?
"WHAT AM I GOING TO CHOOSE TO BECOME?!"

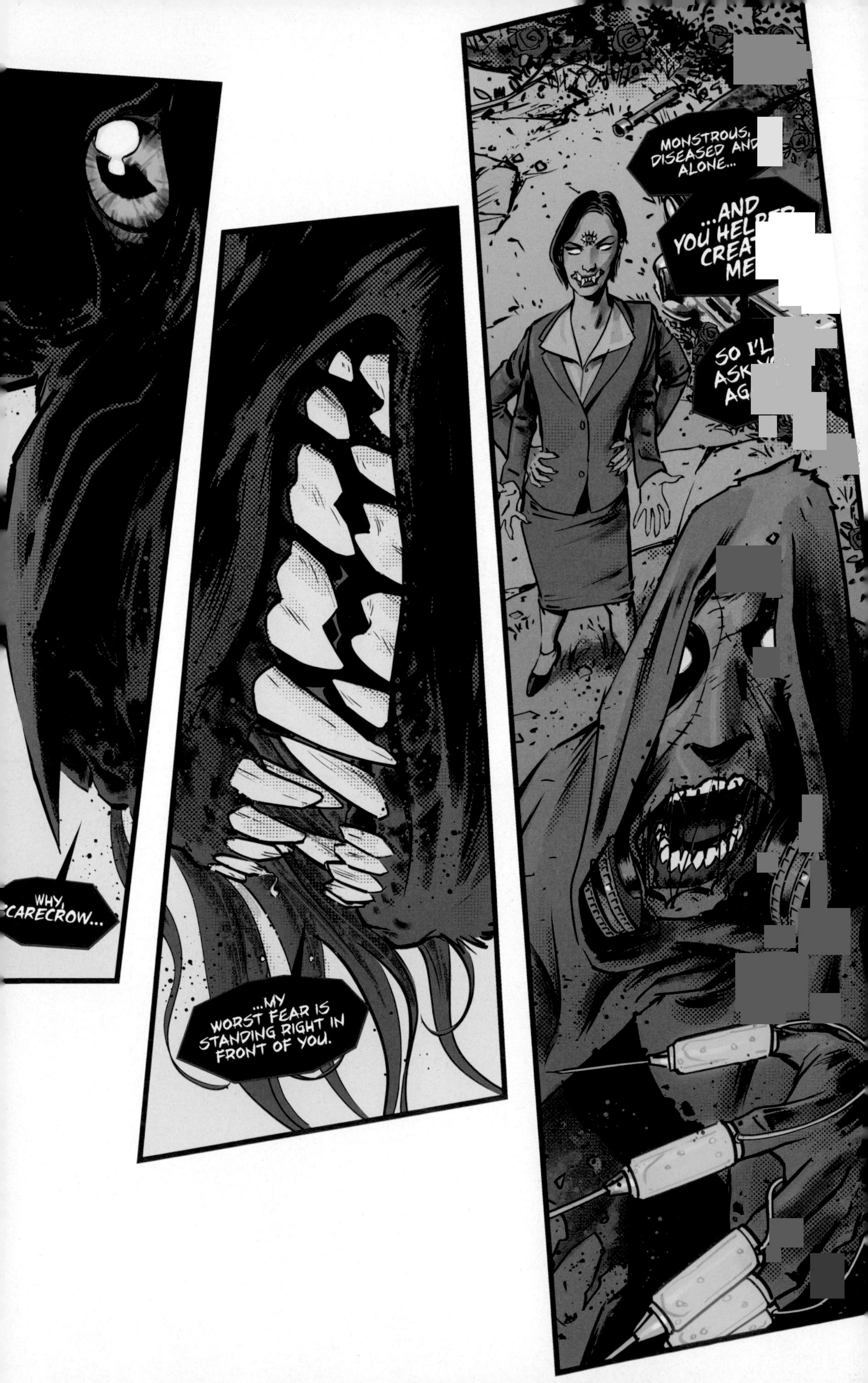
WHY, CARECROW...
...MY WORST FEAR IS STANDING RIGHT IN FRONT OF YOU.
MONSTROUS, DISEASED AND ALONE...
...AND YOU HELP CREAT ME
SO I'L ASK AG

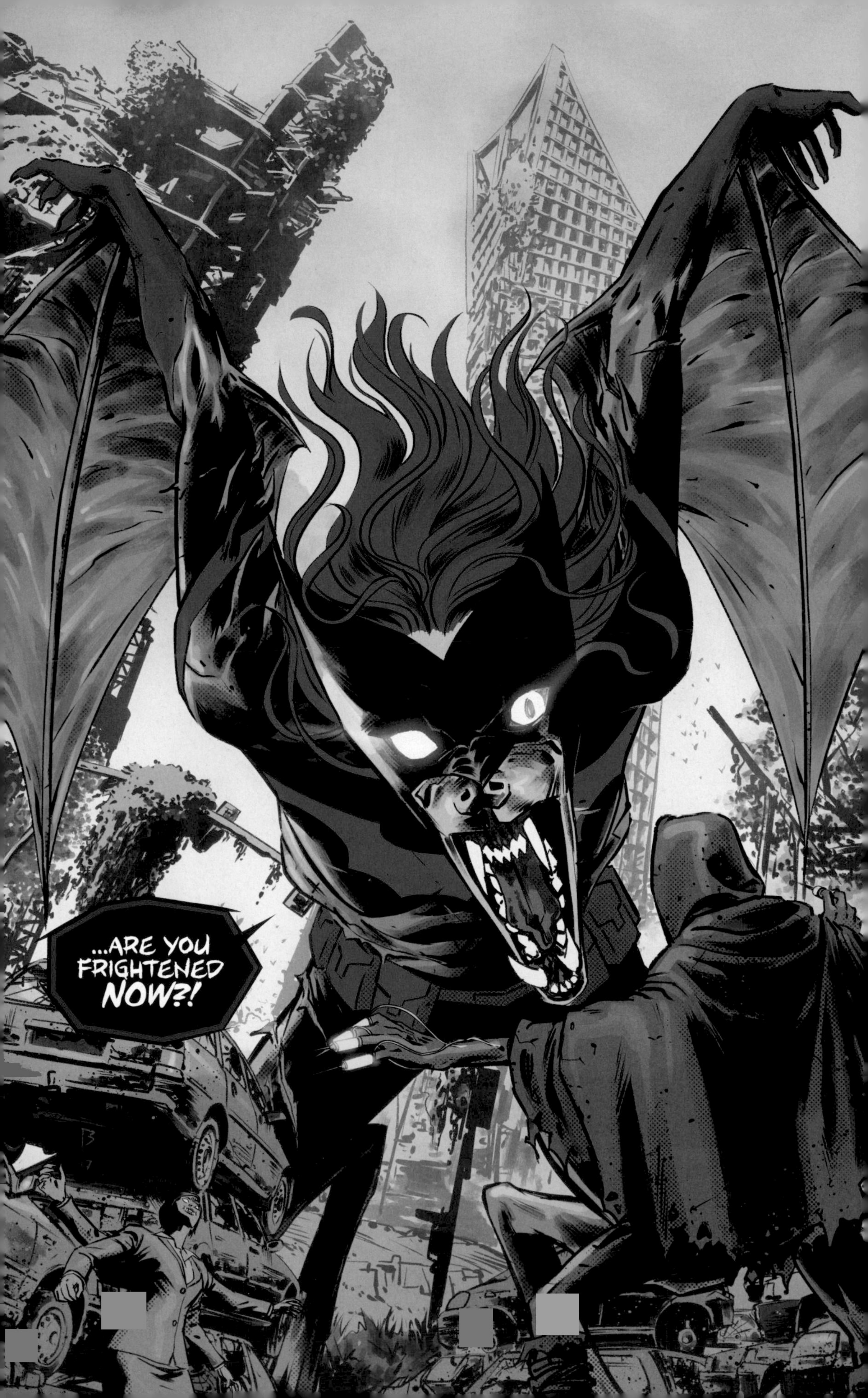
...ARE YOU FRIGHTENED NOW?!

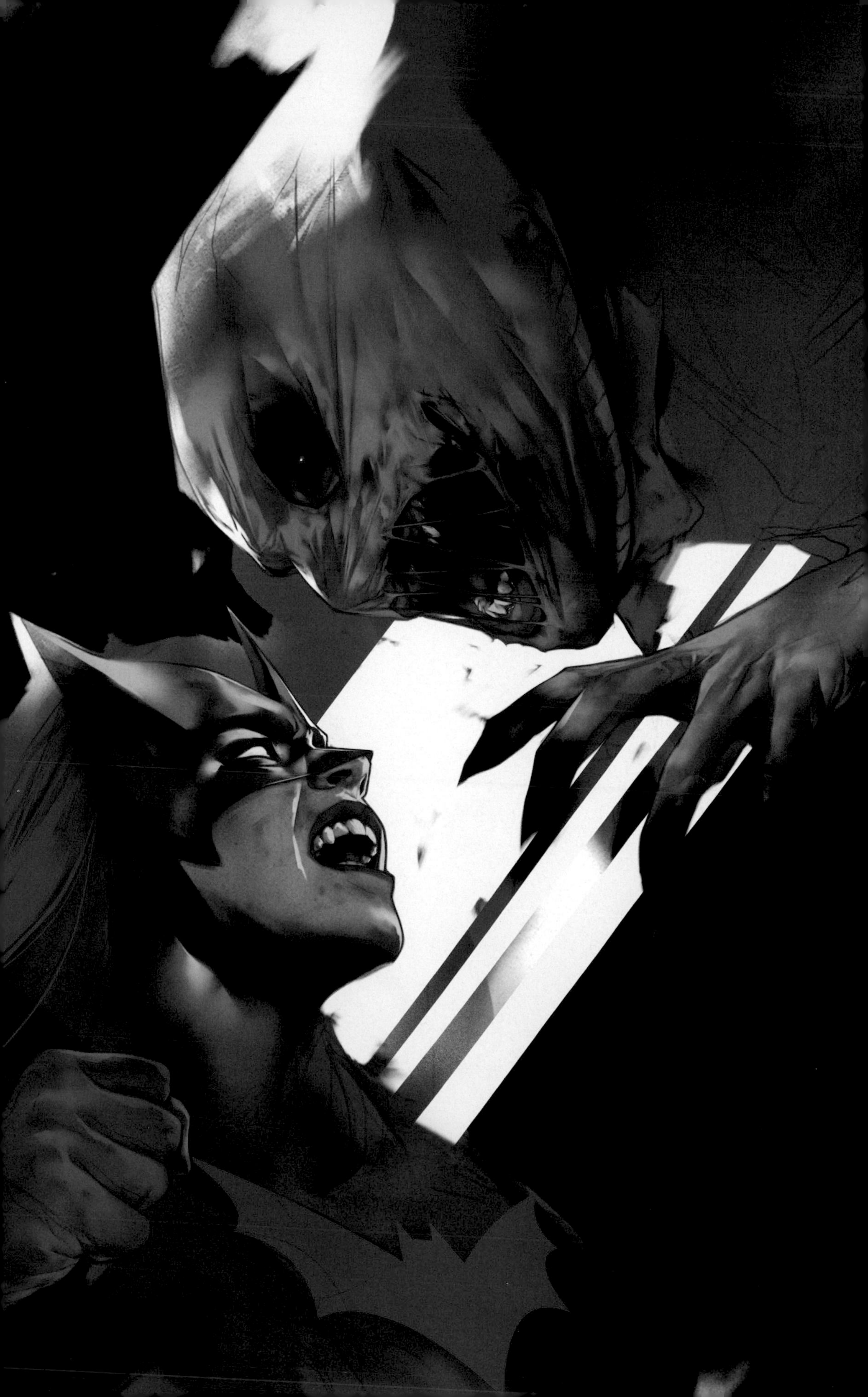

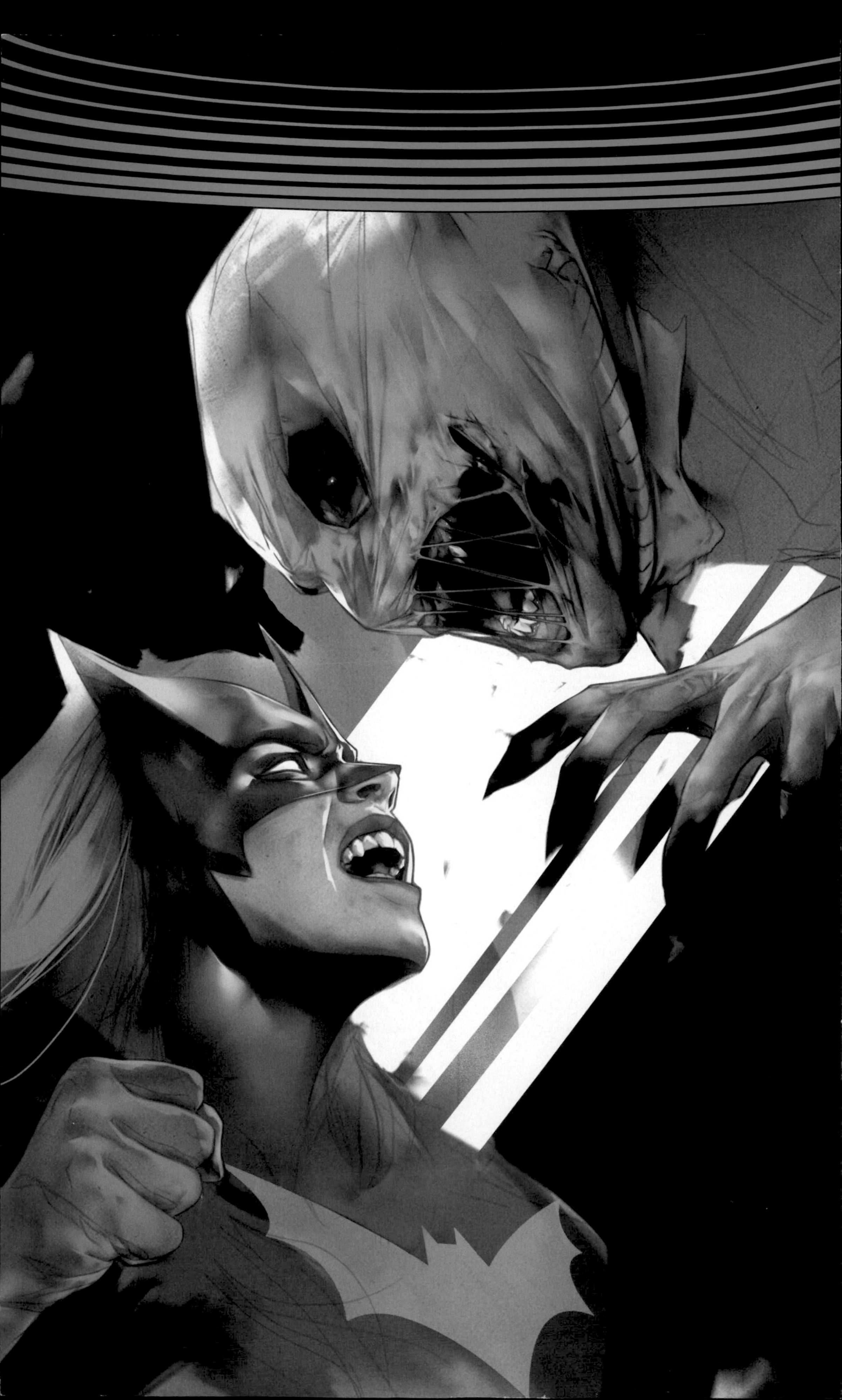

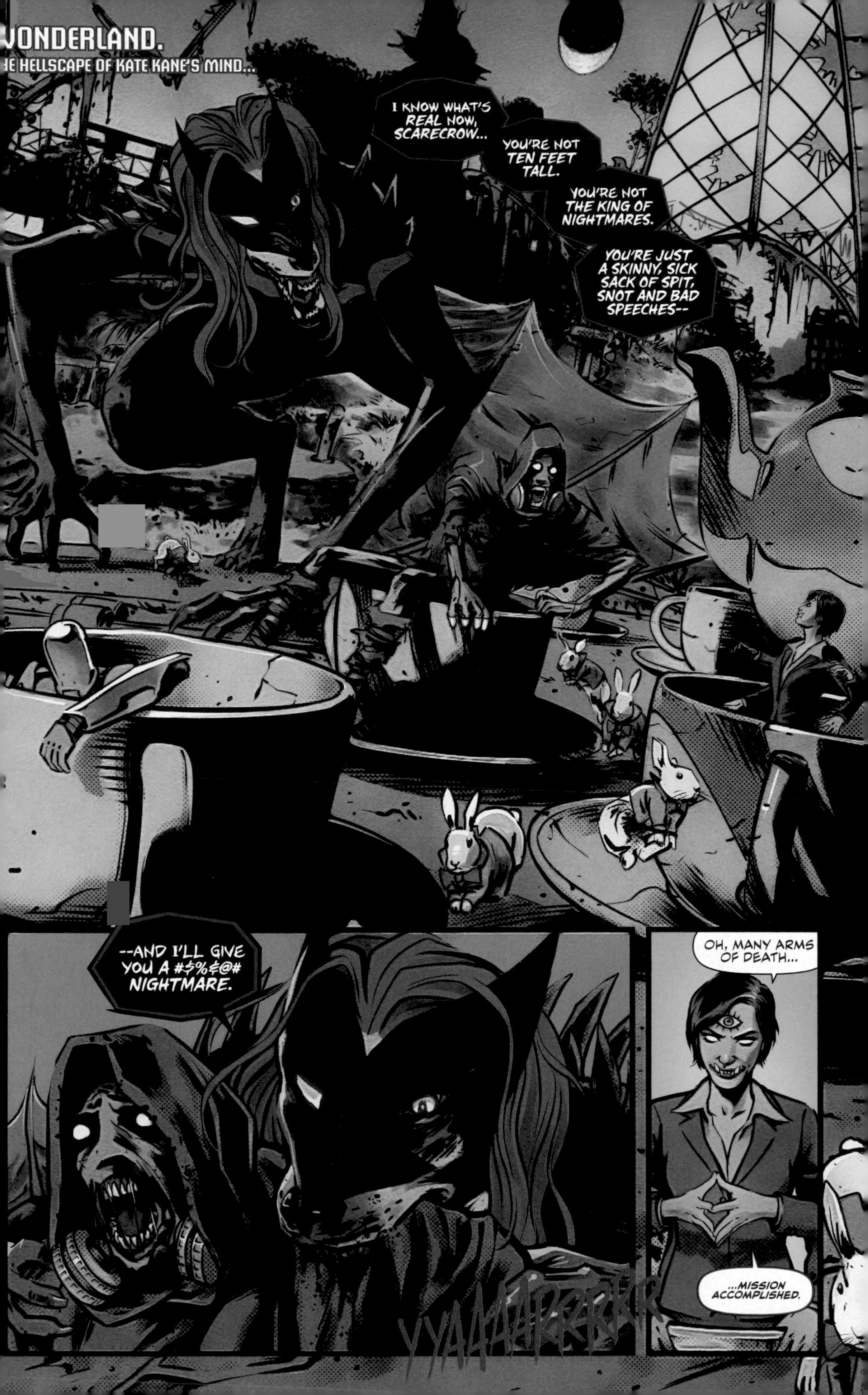
VONDERLAND.
IE HELLSCAPE OF KATE KANE'S MIND...
I KNOW WHAT'S REAL NOW, SCARECROW...
YOU'RE NOT TEN FEET TALL.
YOU'RE NOT THE KING OF NIGHTMARES.
YOU'RE JUST A SKINNY, SICK SACK OF SPIT, SNOT AND BAD SPEECHES--
--AND I'LL GIVE YOU A #$%&@# NIGHTMARE.
YYAAAARRRRRR
OH, MANY ARMS OF DEATH...
...MISSION ACCOMPLISHED.

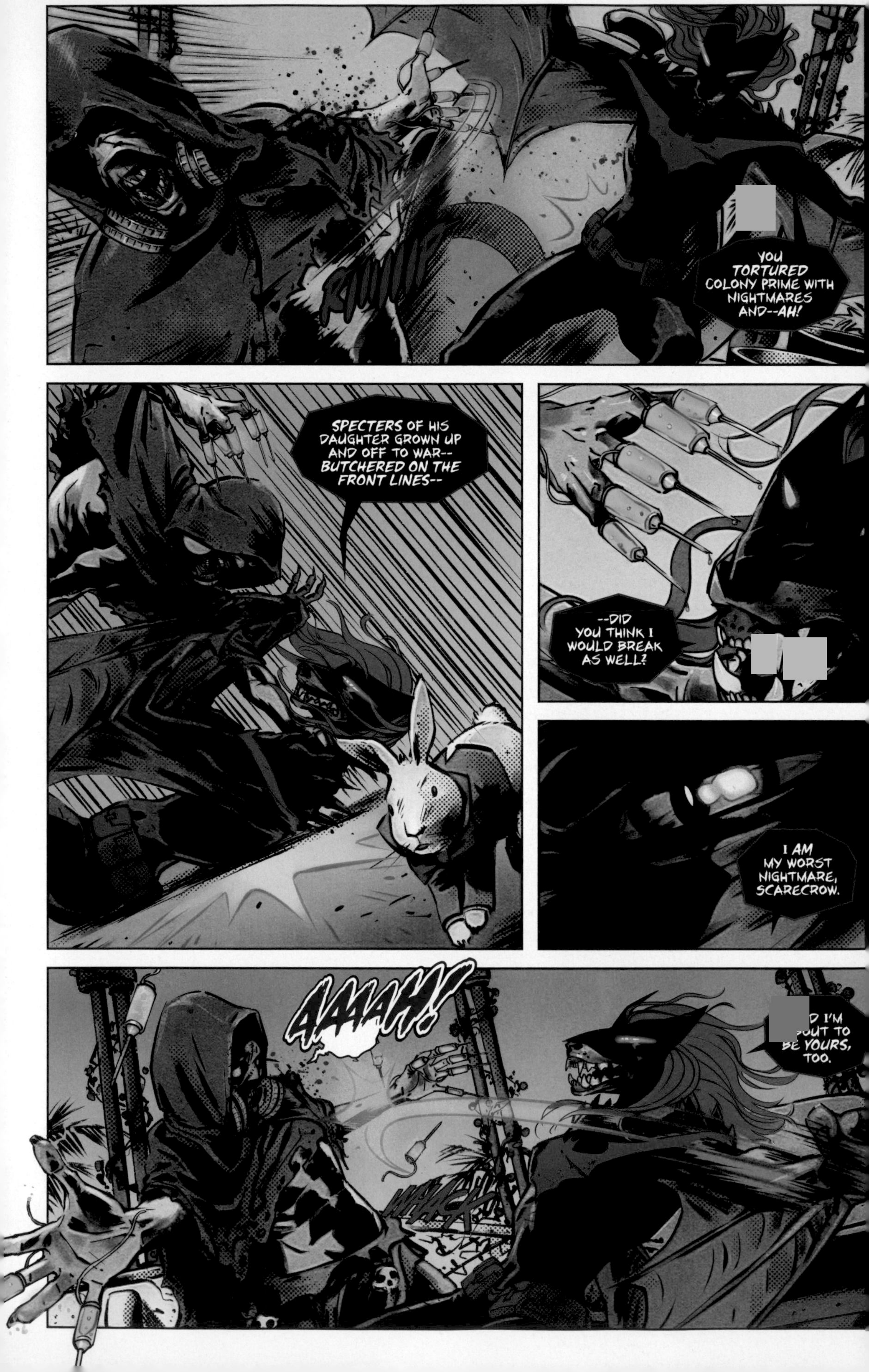
YOU TORTURED COLONY PRIME WITH NIGHTMARES AND--AH!
SPECTERS OF HIS DAUGHTER GROWN UP AND OFF TO WAR-- BUTCHERED ON THE FRONT LINES--
--DID YOU THINK I WOULD BREAK AS WELL?
I AM MY WORST NIGHTMARE, SCARECROW.
AAAAH!
D I'M
OUT TO
BE YOURS,
TOO.
WHACK

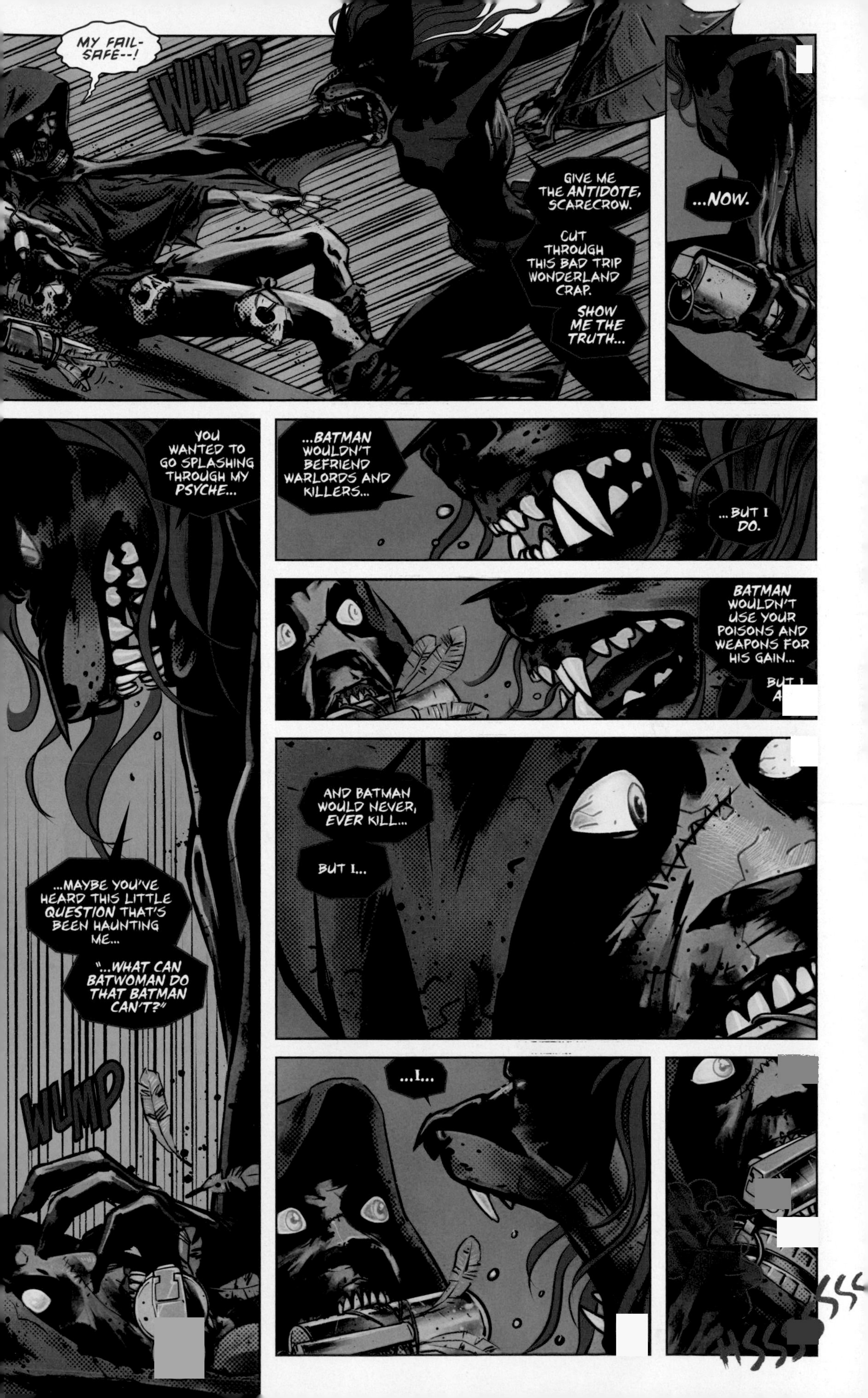
MY FAIL-SAFE--!
WUMP
GIVE ME THE ANTIDOTE, SCARECROW.
CUT THROUGH THIS BAD TRIP WONDERLAND CRAP.
SHOW ME THE TRUTH...
...NOW.
YOU WANTED TO GO SPLASHING THROUGH MY PSYCHE...
...BATMAN WOULDN'T BEFRIEND WARLORDS AND KILLERS...
...BUT I DO.
BATMAN WOULDN'T USE YOUR POISONS AND WEAPONS FOR HIS GAIN...
BUT I A
AND BATMAN WOULD NEVER, EVER KILL...
BUT I...
...MAYBE YOU'VE HEARD THIS LITTLE QUESTION THAT'S BEEN HAUNTING ME...
"...WHAT CAN BATWOMAN DO THAT BATMAN CAN'T?"
WUMP
...I...
HSSSSSS

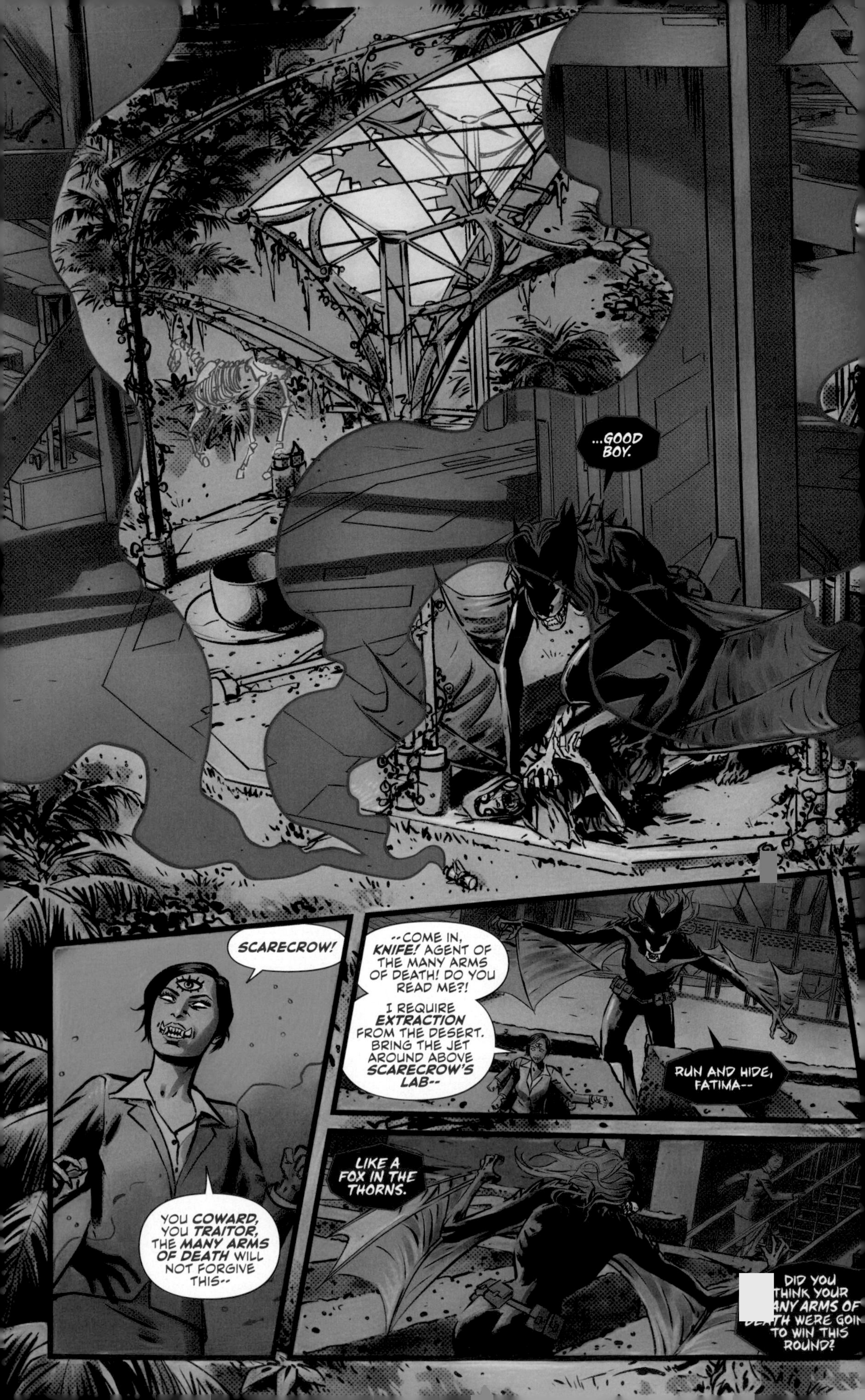
...GOOD BOY.
SCARECROW!
--COME IN, KNIFE! AGENT OF THE MANY ARMS OF DEATH! DO YOU READ ME?!
I REQUIRE EXTRACTION FROM THE DESERT. BRING THE JET AROUND ABOVE SCARECROW'S LAB--
RUN AND HIDE, FATIMA--
YOU COWARD, YOU TRAITOR, THE MANY ARMS OF DEATH WILL NOT FORGIVE THIS--
LIKE A FOX IN THE THORNS.
DID YOU THINK YOUR ANY ARMS OF TH WERE GOIN TO WIN THIS ROUND?

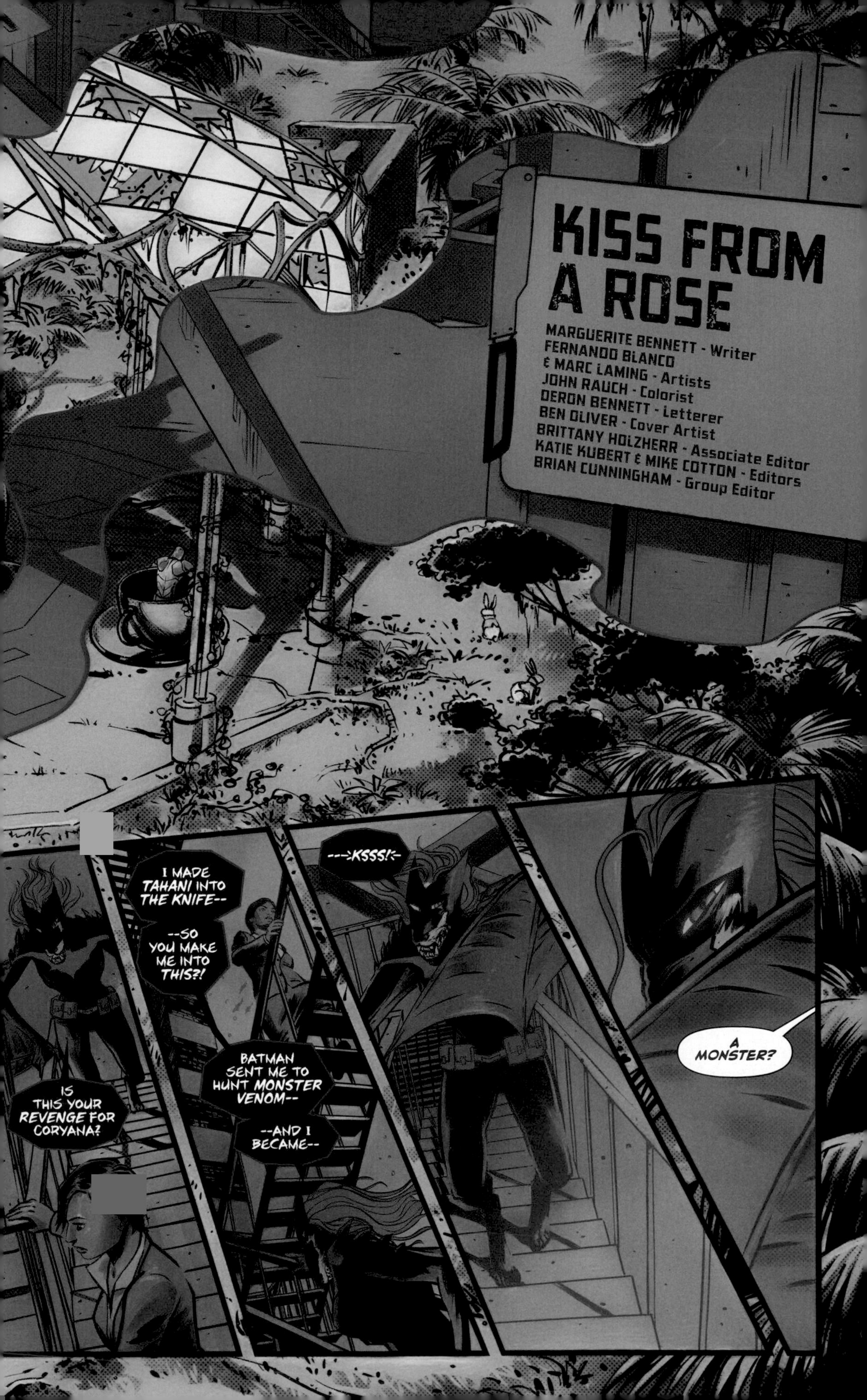
KISS FROM A ROSE
MARGUERITE BENNETT - Writer
FERNANDO BLANCO & MARC LAMING - Artists
JOHN RAUCH - Colorist
DERON BENNETT - Letterer
BEN OLIVER - Cover Artist
BRITTANY HOLZHERR - Associate Editor
KATIE KUBERT & MIKE COTTON - Editors
BRIAN CUNNINGHAM - Group Editor
IS THIS YOUR REVENGE FOR CORYANA?
I MADE TAHANI INTO THE KNIFE--
--SO YOU MAKE ME INTO THIS?!
BATMAN SENT ME TO HUNT MONSTER VENOM--
--AND I BECAME--
--KSSS!--
A MONSTER?

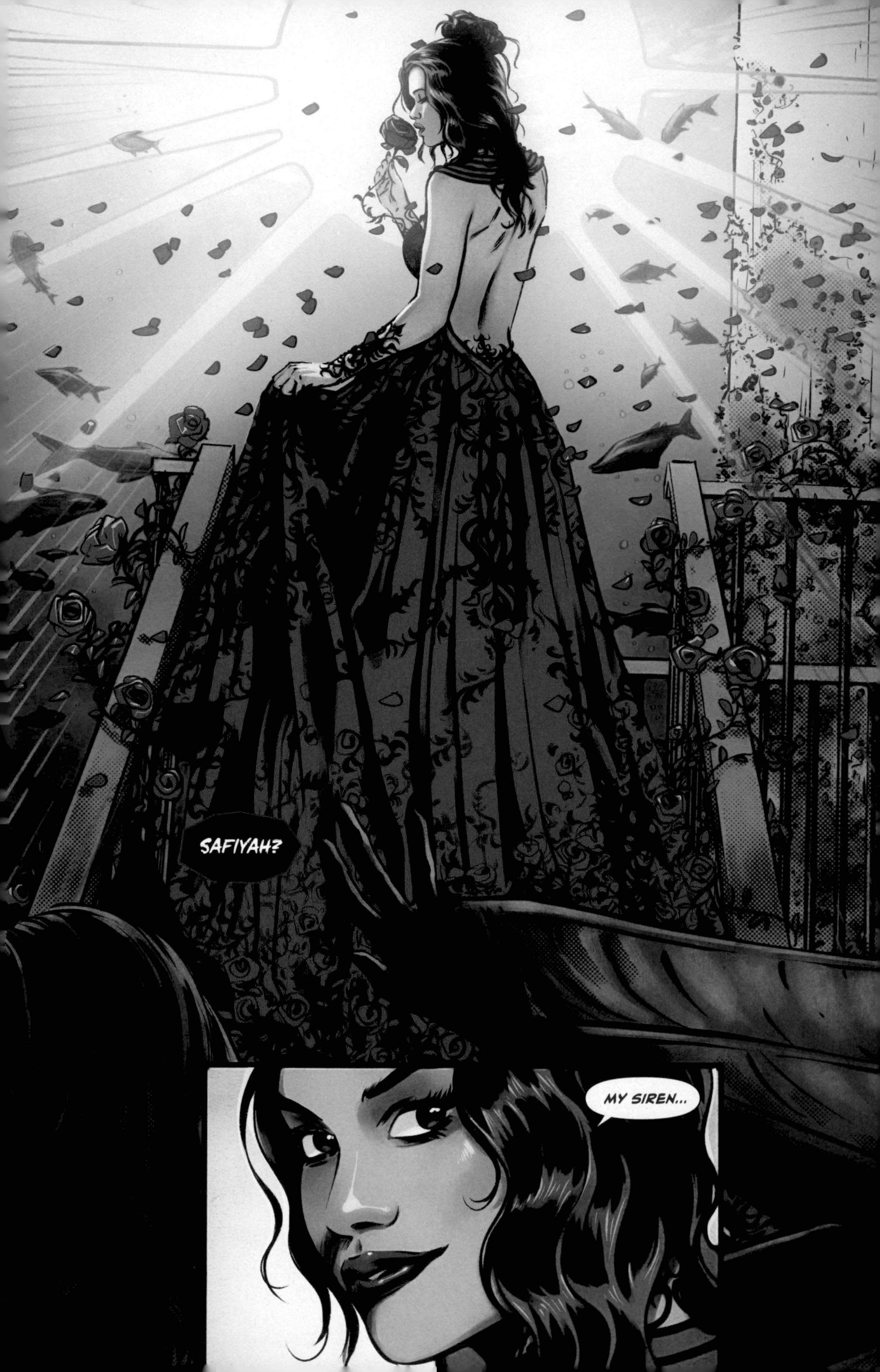
SAFIYAH?
MY SIREN...

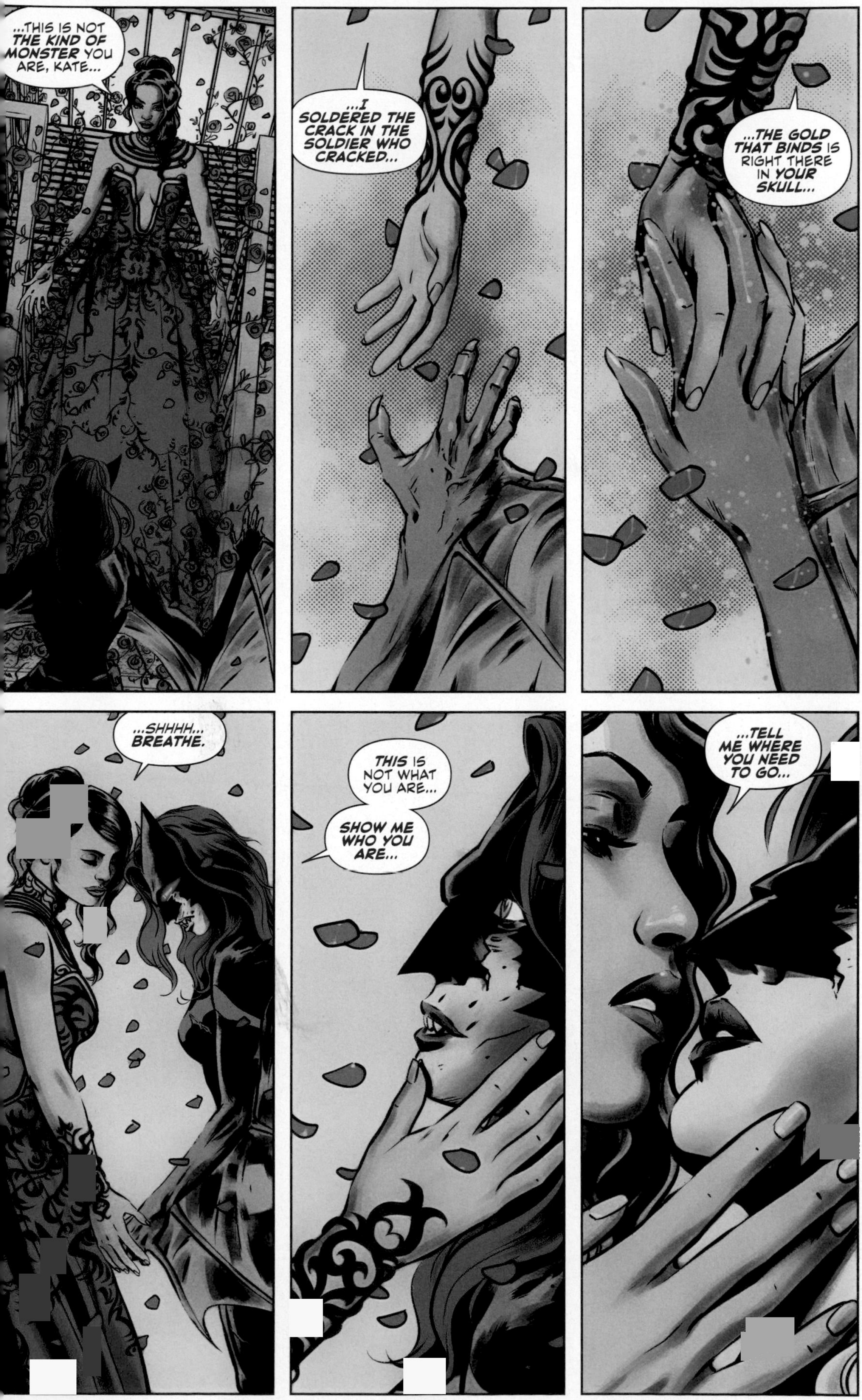
...THIS IS NOT THE KIND OF MONSTER YOU ARE, KATE...
...I SOLDERED THE CRACK IN THE SOLDIER WHO CRACKED...
...THE GOLD THAT BINDS IS RIGHT THERE IN YOUR SKULL...
...SHHHH... BREATHE.
THIS IS NOT WHAT YOU ARE...
SHOW ME WHO YOU ARE...
...TELL ME WHERE YOU NEED TO GO...

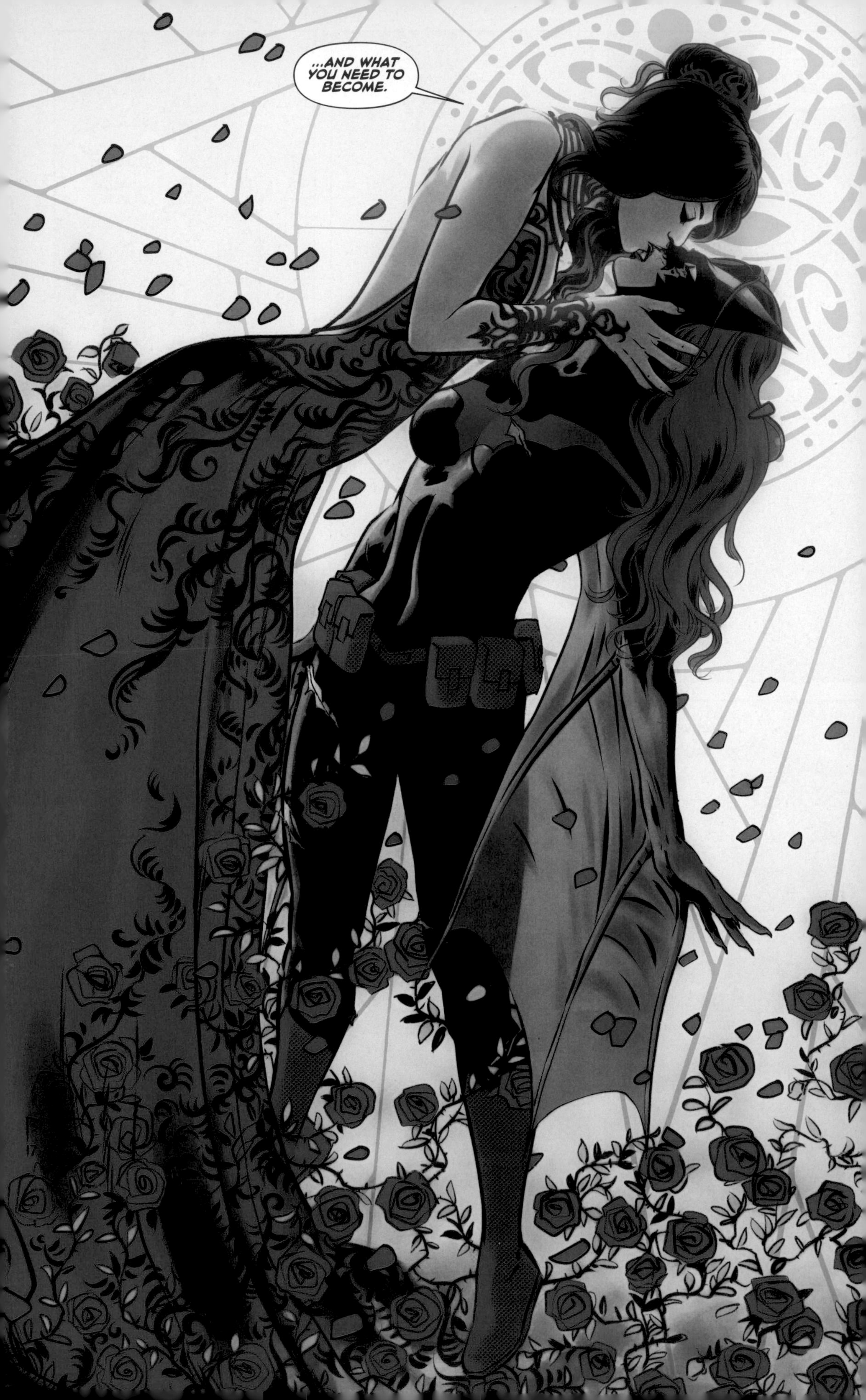
...AND WHAT YOU NEED TO BECOME.

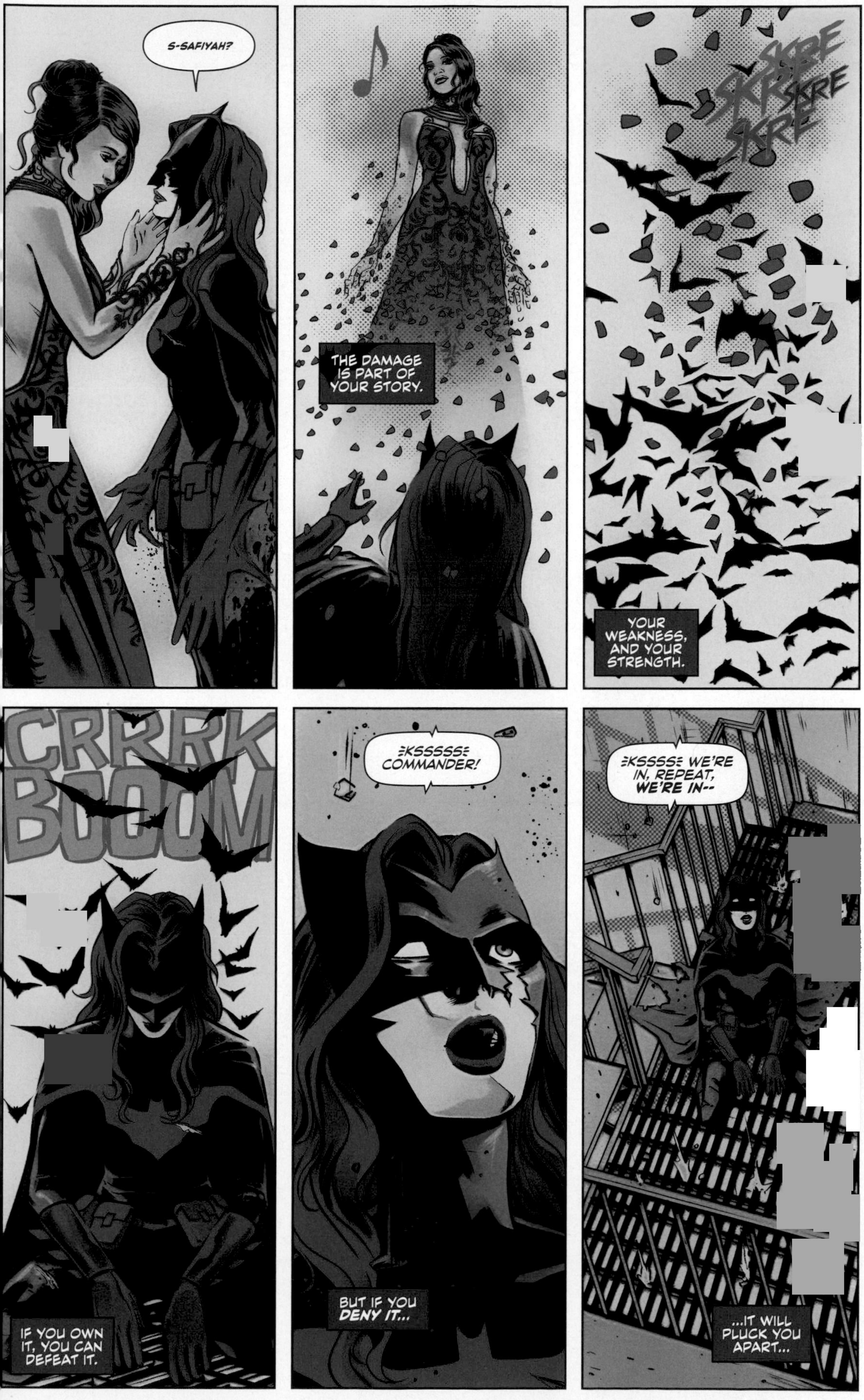
S-SAFIYAH?
THE DAMAGE IS PART OF YOUR STORY.
SKRE SKRE SKRE SKRE
YOUR WEAKNESS, AND YOUR STRENGTH.
CRRRK BOOOM
IF YOU OWN IT, YOU CAN DEFEAT IT.
=KSSSSS= COMMANDER!
BUT IF YOU DENY IT...
=KSSSS= WE'RE IN, REPEAT, WE'RE IN--
...IT WILL PLUCK YOU APART...

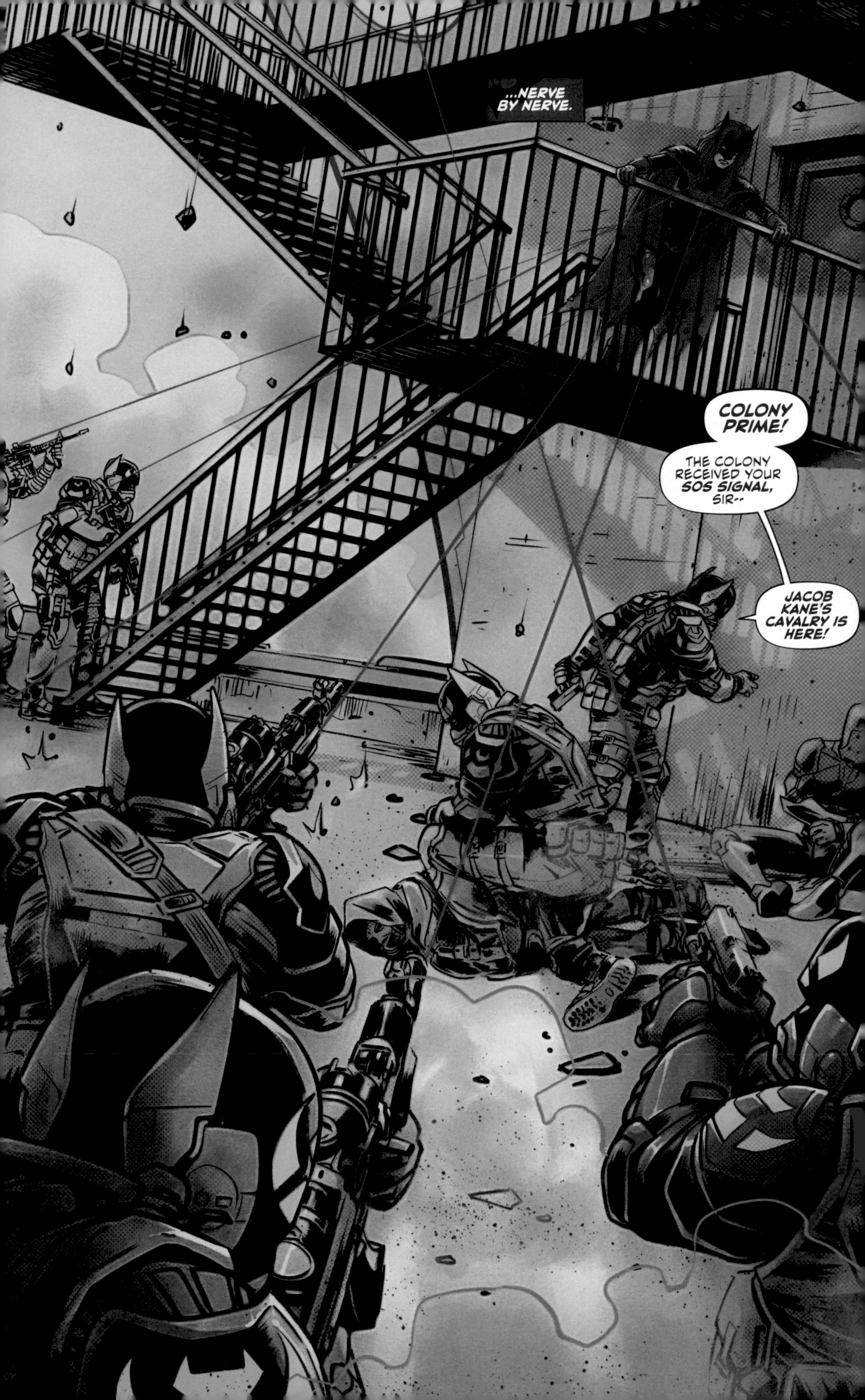
...NERVE BY NERVE.
COLONY PRIME!
THE COLONY RECEIVED YOUR SOS SIGNAL, SIR--
JACOB KANE'S CAVALRY IS HERE!

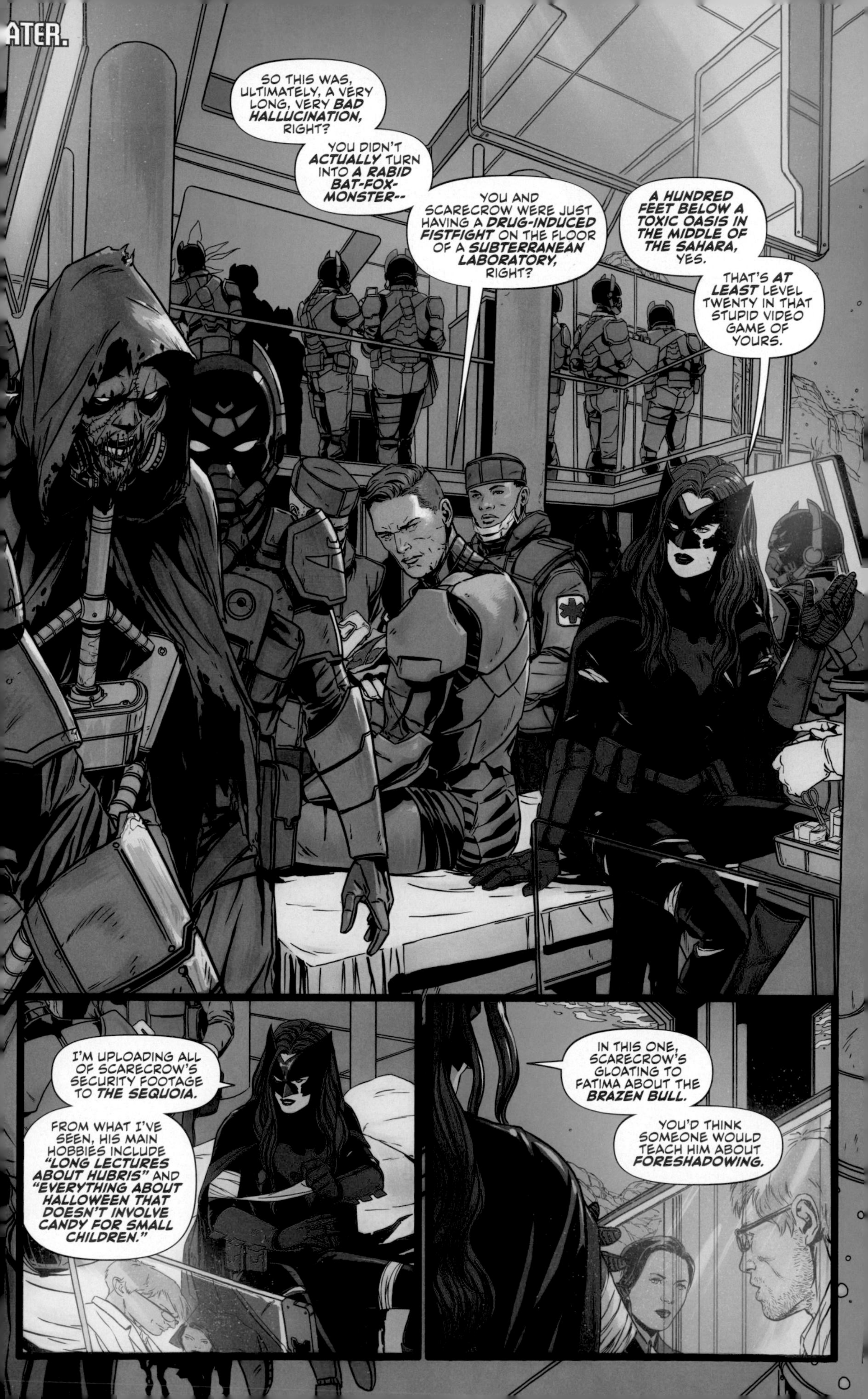

ATER.
SO THIS WAS, ULTIMATELY, A VERY LONG, VERY BAD HALLUCINATION, RIGHT?
YOU DIDN'T ACTUALLY TURN INTO A RABID BAT-FOX-MONSTER--
YOU AND SCARECROW WERE JUST HAVING A DRUG-INDUCED FISTFIGHT ON THE FLOOR OF A SUBTERRANEAN LABORATORY, RIGHT?
A HUNDRED FEET BELOW A TOXIC OASIS IN THE MIDDLE OF THE SAHARA, YES.
THAT'S AT LEAST LEVEL TWENTY IN THAT STUPID VIDEO GAME OF YOURS.
I'M UPLOADING ALL OF SCARECROW'S SECURITY FOOTAGE TO THE SEQUOIA.
FROM WHAT I'VE SEEN, HIS MAIN HOBBIES INCLUDE "LONG LECTURES ABOUT HUBRIS" AND "EVERYTHING ABOUT HALLOWEEN THAT DOESN'T INVOLVE CANDY FOR SMALL CHILDREN."
IN THIS ONE, SCARECROW'S GLOATING TO FATIMA ABOUT THE BRAZEN BULL.
YOU'D THINK SOMEONE WOULD TEACH HIM ABOUT FORESHADOWING.

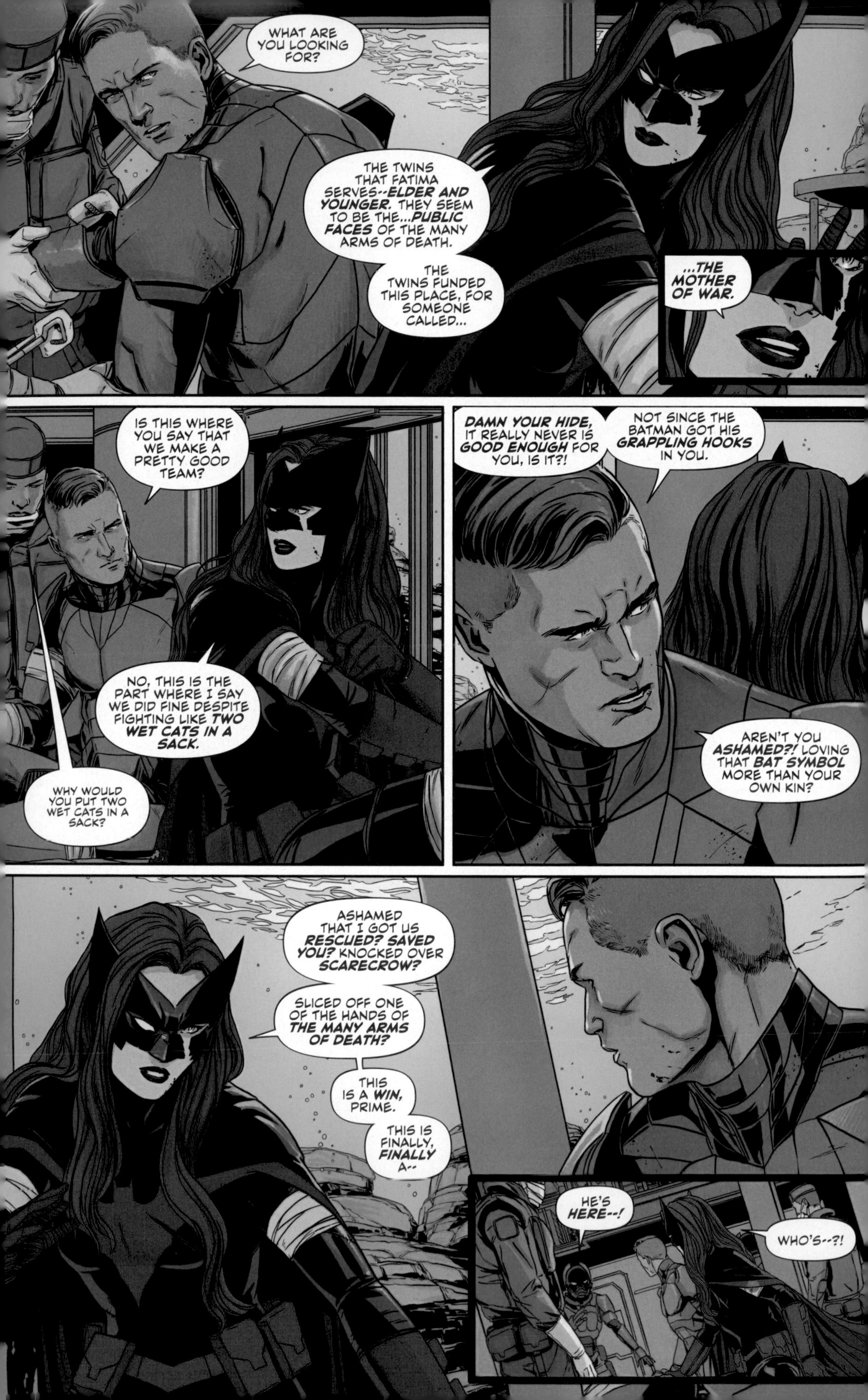

WHAT ARE YOU LOOKING FOR?
THE TWINS THAT FATIMA SERVES--ELDER AND YOUNGER. THEY SEEM TO BE THE...PUBLIC FACES OF THE MANY ARMS OF DEATH.
THE TWINS FUNDED THIS PLACE, FOR SOMEONE CALLED...
...THE MOTHER OF WAR.
IS THIS WHERE YOU SAY THAT WE MAKE A PRETTY GOOD TEAM?
NO, THIS IS THE PART WHERE I SAY WE DID FINE DESPITE FIGHTING LIKE TWO WET CATS IN A SACK.
WHY WOULD YOU PUT TWO WET CATS IN A SACK?
DAMN YOUR HIDE, IT REALLY NEVER IS GOOD ENOUGH FOR YOU, IS IT?!
NOT SINCE THE BATMAN GOT HIS GRAPPLING HOOKS IN YOU.
AREN'T YOU ASHAMED?! LOVING THAT BAT SYMBOL MORE THAN YOUR OWN KIN?
ASHAMED THAT I GOT US RESCUED? SAVED YOU? KNOCKED OVER SCARECROW?
SLICED OFF ONE OF THE HANDS OF THE MANY ARMS OF DEATH?
THIS IS A WIN, PRIME.
THIS IS FINALLY, FINALLY A--
HE'S HERE--!
WHO'S--?!

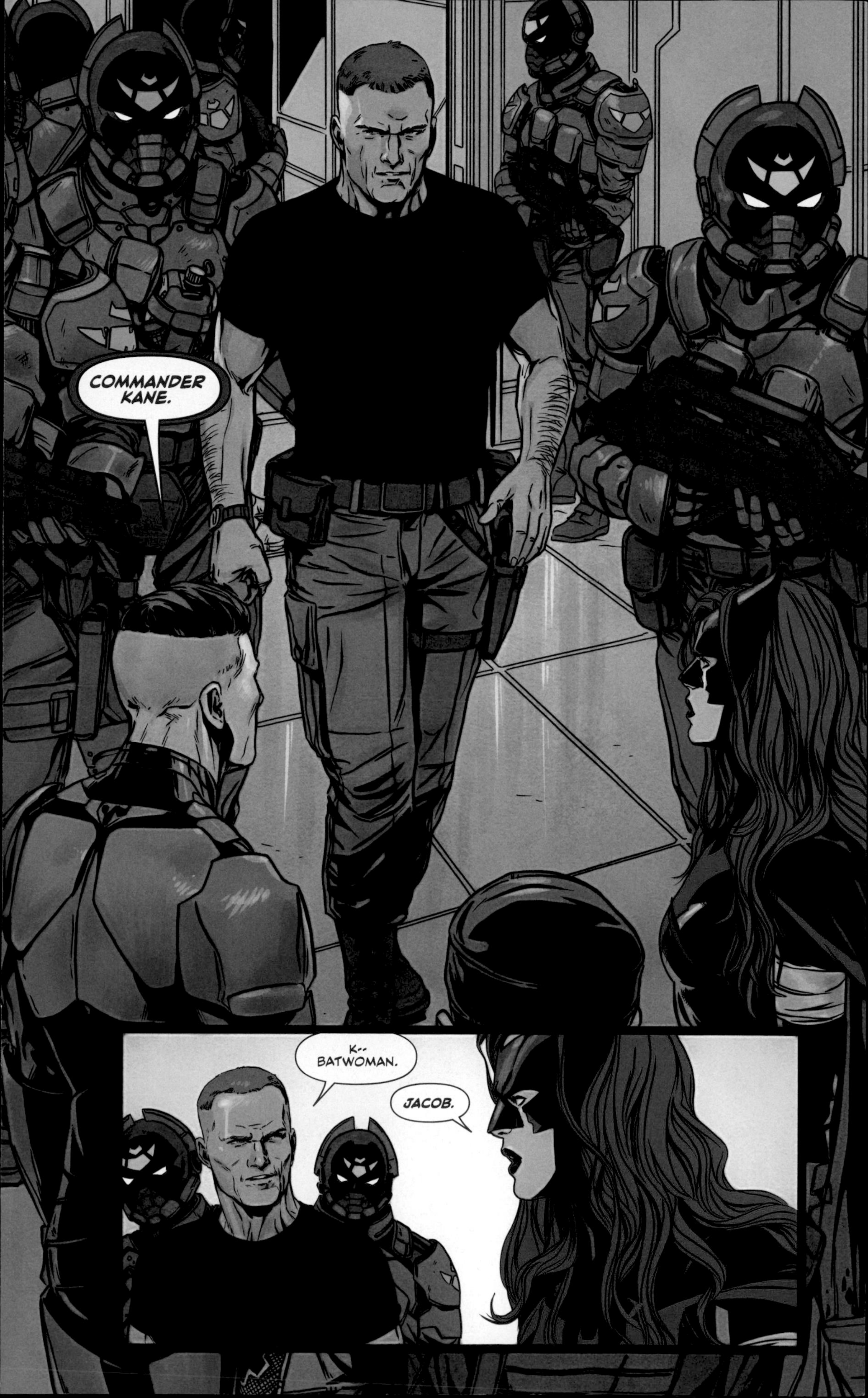
COMMANDER KANE.
K-- BATWOMAN.
JACOB.

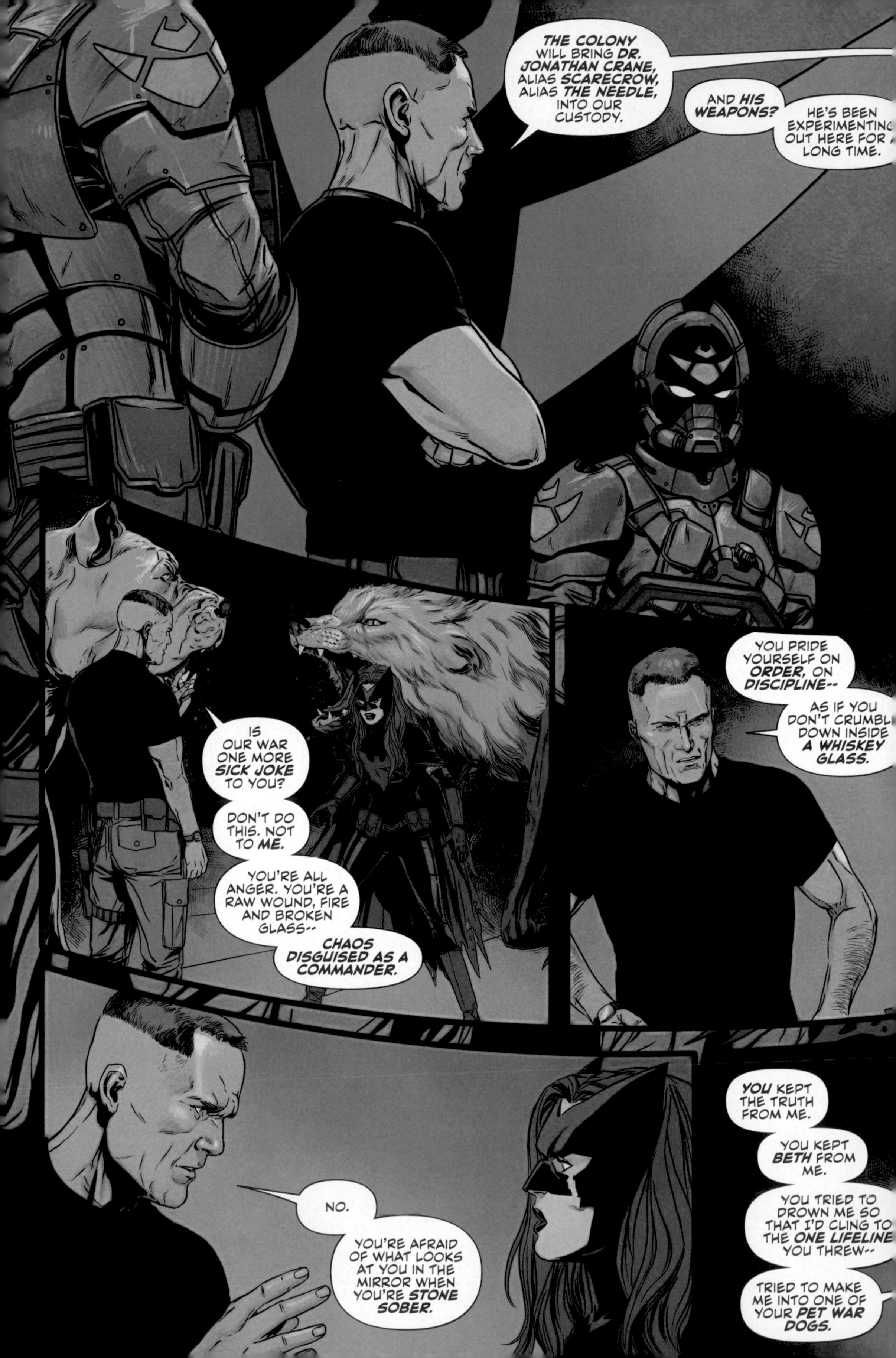
THE COLONY WILL BRING DR. JONATHAN CRANE, ALIAS SCARECROW, ALIAS THE NEEDLE, INTO OUR CUSTODY.
AND HIS WEAPONS?
HE'S BEEN EXPERIMENTING OUT HERE FOR A LONG TIME.
IS OUR WAR ONE MORE SICK JOKE TO YOU?
DON'T DO THIS. NOT TO ME.
YOU'RE ALL ANGER. YOU'RE A RAW WOUND, FIRE AND BROKEN GLASS--
CHAOS DISGUISED AS A COMMANDER.
YOU PRIDE YOURSELF ON ORDER, ON DISCIPLINE--
AS IF YOU DON'T CRUMBLE DOWN INSIDE A WHISKEY GLASS.
NO.
YOU'RE AFRAID OF WHAT LOOKS AT YOU IN THE MIRROR WHEN YOU'RE STONE SOBER.
YOU KEPT THE TRUTH FROM ME.
YOU KEPT BETH FROM ME.
YOU TRIED TO DROWN ME SO THAT I'D CLING TO THE ONE LIFELINE YOU THREW--
TRIED TO MAKE ME INTO ONE OF YOUR PET WAR DOGS.

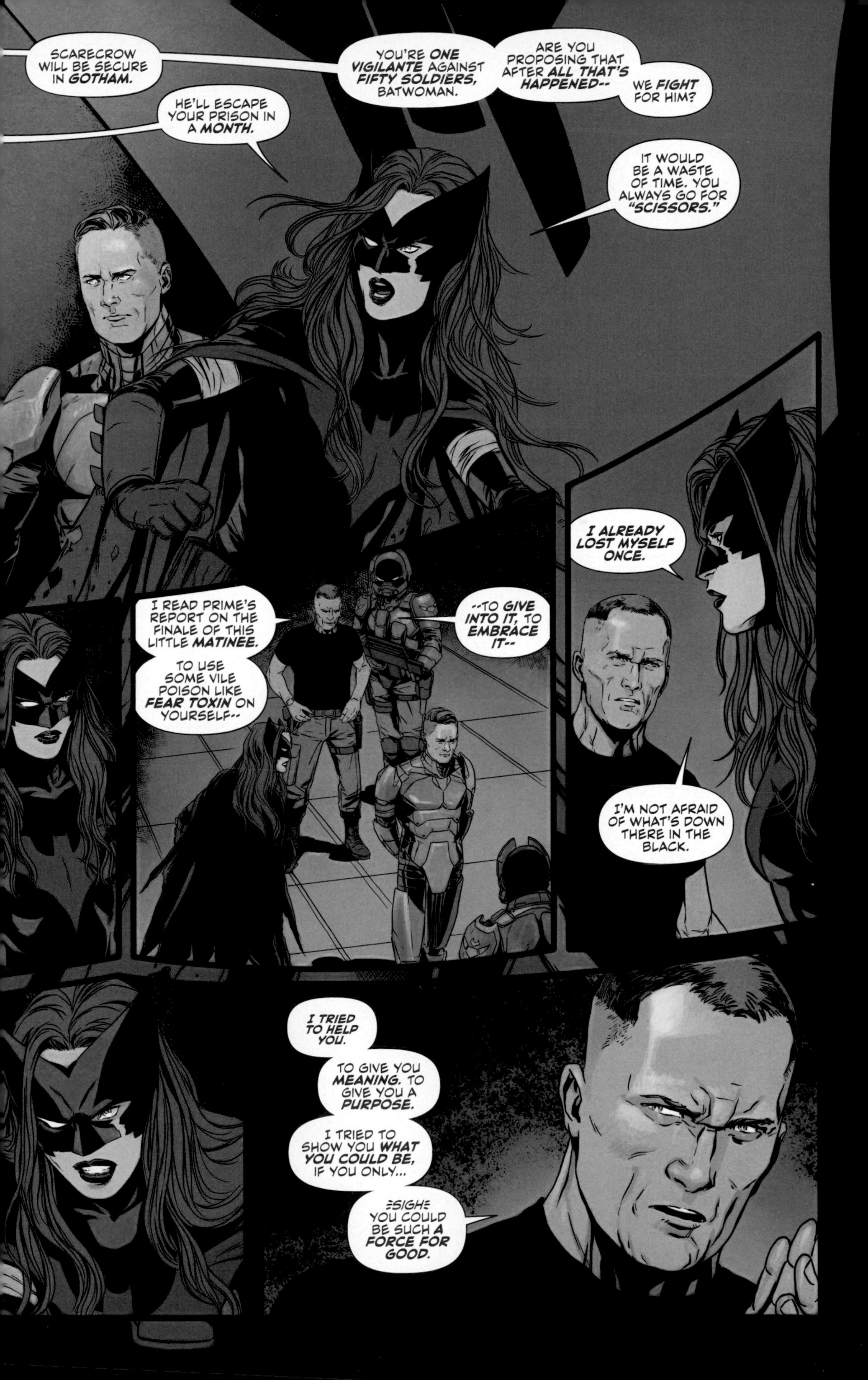
SCARECROW WILL BE SECURE IN GOTHAM.
YOU'RE ONE VIGILANTE AGAINST FIFTY SOLDIERS, BATWOMAN.
ARE YOU PROPOSING THAT AFTER ALL THAT'S HAPPENED--
WE FIGHT FOR HIM?
HE'LL ESCAPE YOUR PRISON IN A MONTH.
IT WOULD BE A WASTE OF TIME. YOU ALWAYS GO FOR "SCISSORS."
I READ PRIME'S REPORT ON THE FINALE OF THIS LITTLE MATINEE.
TO USE SOME VILE POISON LIKE FEAR TOXIN ON YOURSELF--
--TO GIVE INTO IT, TO EMBRACE IT--
I ALREADY LOST MYSELF ONCE.
I'M NOT AFRAID OF WHAT'S DOWN THERE IN THE BLACK.
I TRIED TO HELP YOU.
TO GIVE YOU MEANING. TO GIVE YOU A PURPOSE.
I TRIED TO SHOW YOU WHAT YOU COULD BE, IF YOU ONLY...
=SIGH= YOU COULD BE SUCH A FORCE FOR GOOD.

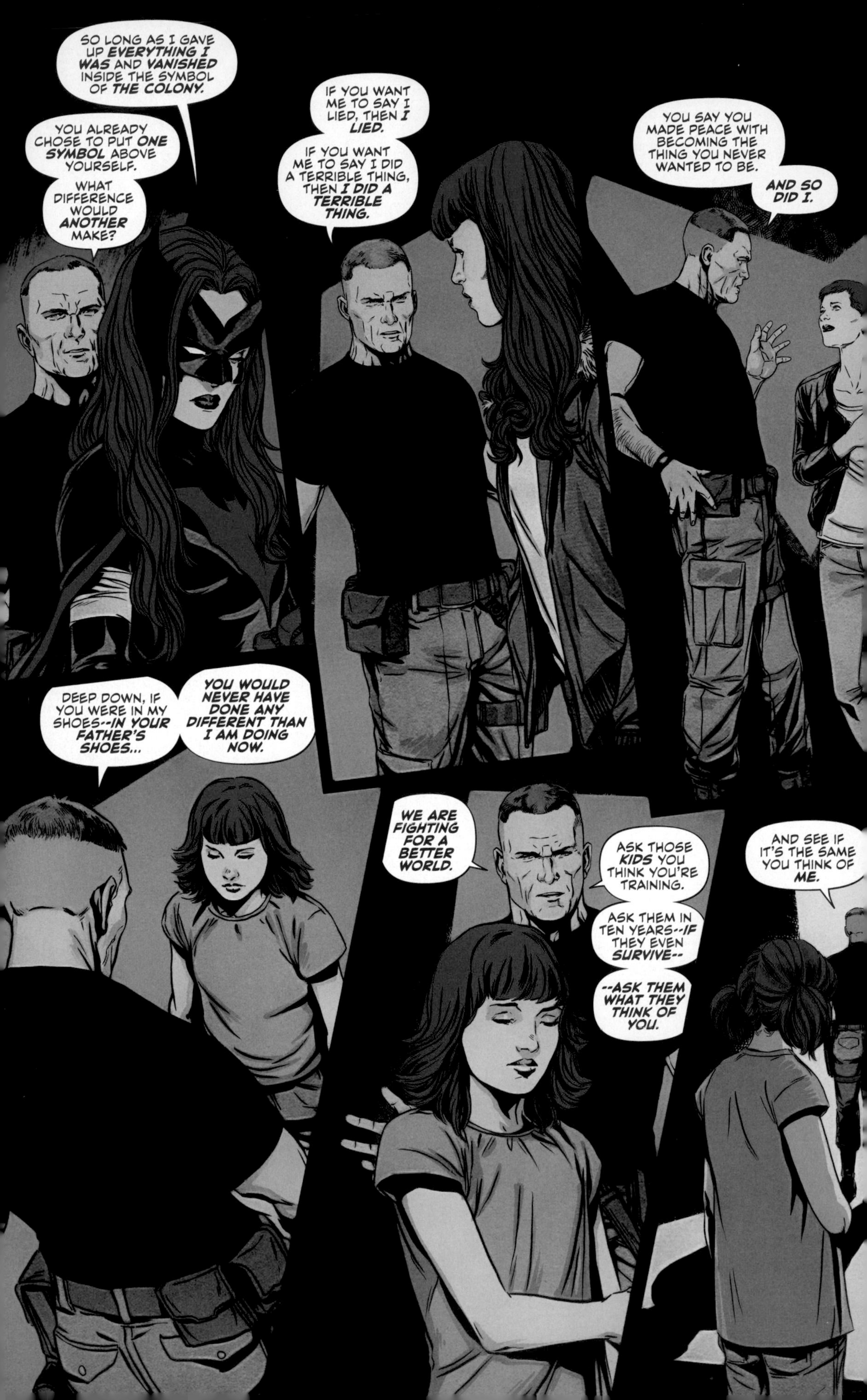
SO LONG AS I GAVE UP EVERYTHING I WAS AND VANISHED INSIDE THE SYMBOL OF THE COLONY.
YOU ALREADY CHOSE TO PUT ONE SYMBOL ABOVE YOURSELF.
WHAT DIFFERENCE WOULD ANOTHER MAKE?
IF YOU WANT ME TO SAY I LIED, THEN I LIED.
IF YOU WANT ME TO SAY I DID A TERRIBLE THING, THEN I DID A TERRIBLE THING.
YOU SAY YOU MADE PEACE WITH BECOMING THE THING YOU NEVER WANTED TO BE.
AND SO DID I.
DEEP DOWN, IF YOU WERE IN MY SHOES--IN YOUR FATHER'S SHOES...
YOU WOULD NEVER HAVE DONE ANY DIFFERENT THAN I AM DOING NOW.
WE ARE FIGHTING FOR A BETTER WORLD.
ASK THOSE KIDS YOU THINK YOU'RE TRAINING.
ASK THEM IN TEN YEARS--IF THEY EVEN SURVIVE--
--ASK THEM WHAT THEY THINK OF YOU.
AND SEE IF IT'S THE SAME YOU THINK OF ME.

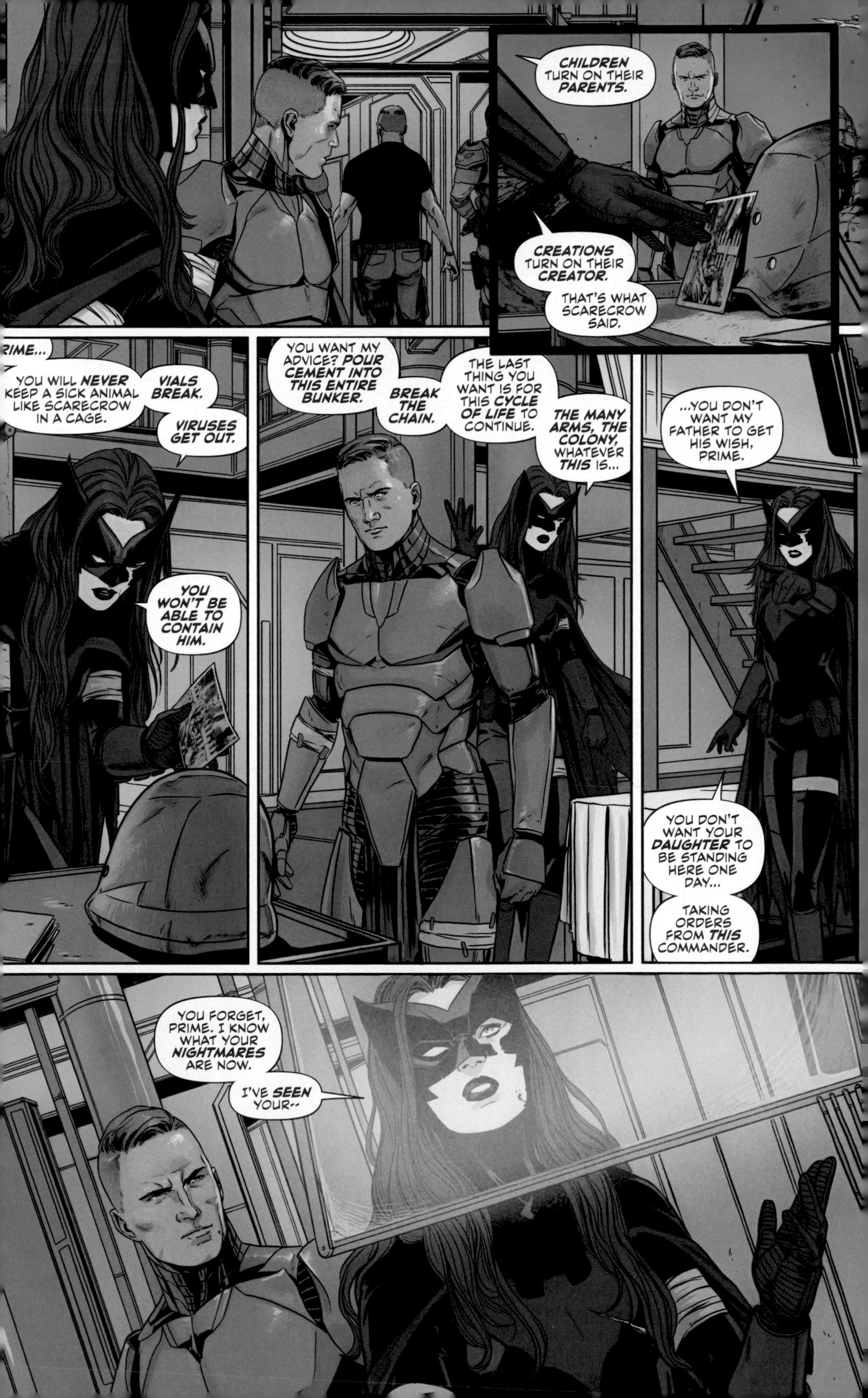

CHILDREN TURN ON THEIR PARENTS.
CREATIONS TURN ON THEIR CREATOR.
THAT'S WHAT SCARECROW SAID.
...PRIME...
YOU WILL NEVER KEEP A SICK ANIMAL LIKE SCARECROW IN A CAGE.
VIALS BREAK.
VIRUSES GET OUT.
YOU WON'T BE ABLE TO CONTAIN HIM.
YOU WANT MY ADVICE? POUR CEMENT INTO THIS ENTIRE BUNKER.
BREAK THE CHAIN.
THE LAST THING YOU WANT IS FOR THIS CYCLE OF LIFE TO CONTINUE.
THE MANY ARMS, THE COLONY, WHATEVER THIS IS...
...YOU DON'T WANT MY FATHER TO GET HIS WISH, PRIME.
YOU DON'T WANT YOUR DAUGHTER TO BE STANDING HERE ONE DAY...
TAKING ORDERS FROM THIS COMMANDER.
YOU FORGET, PRIME. I KNOW WHAT YOUR NIGHTMARES ARE NOW.
I'VE SEEN YOUR--

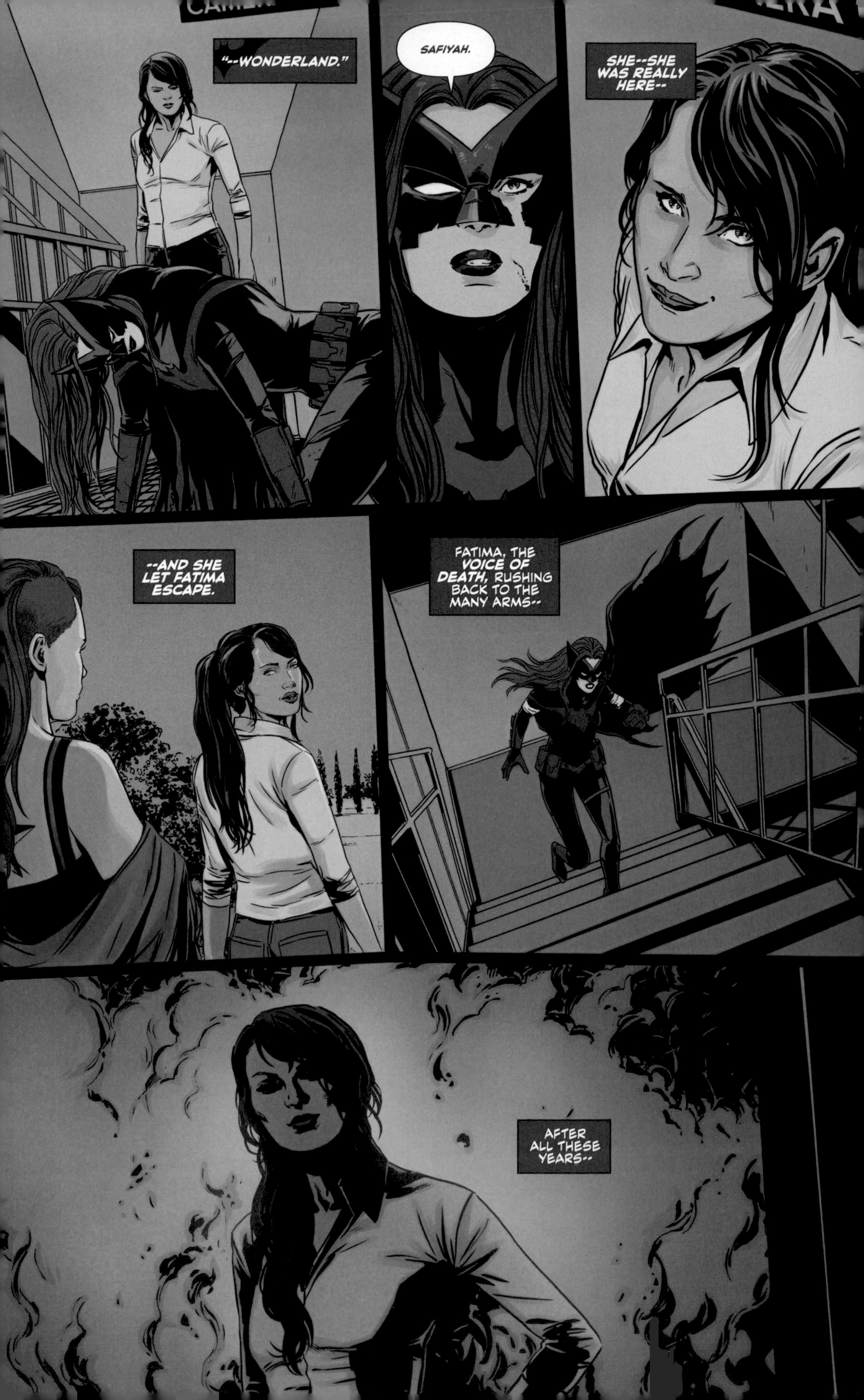
"--WONDERLAND."
SAFIYAH.
SHE--SHE WAS REALLY HERE--
--AND SHE LET FATIMA ESCAPE.
FATIMA, THE VOICE OF DEATH, RUSHING BACK TO THE MANY ARMS--
AFTER ALL THESE YEARS--

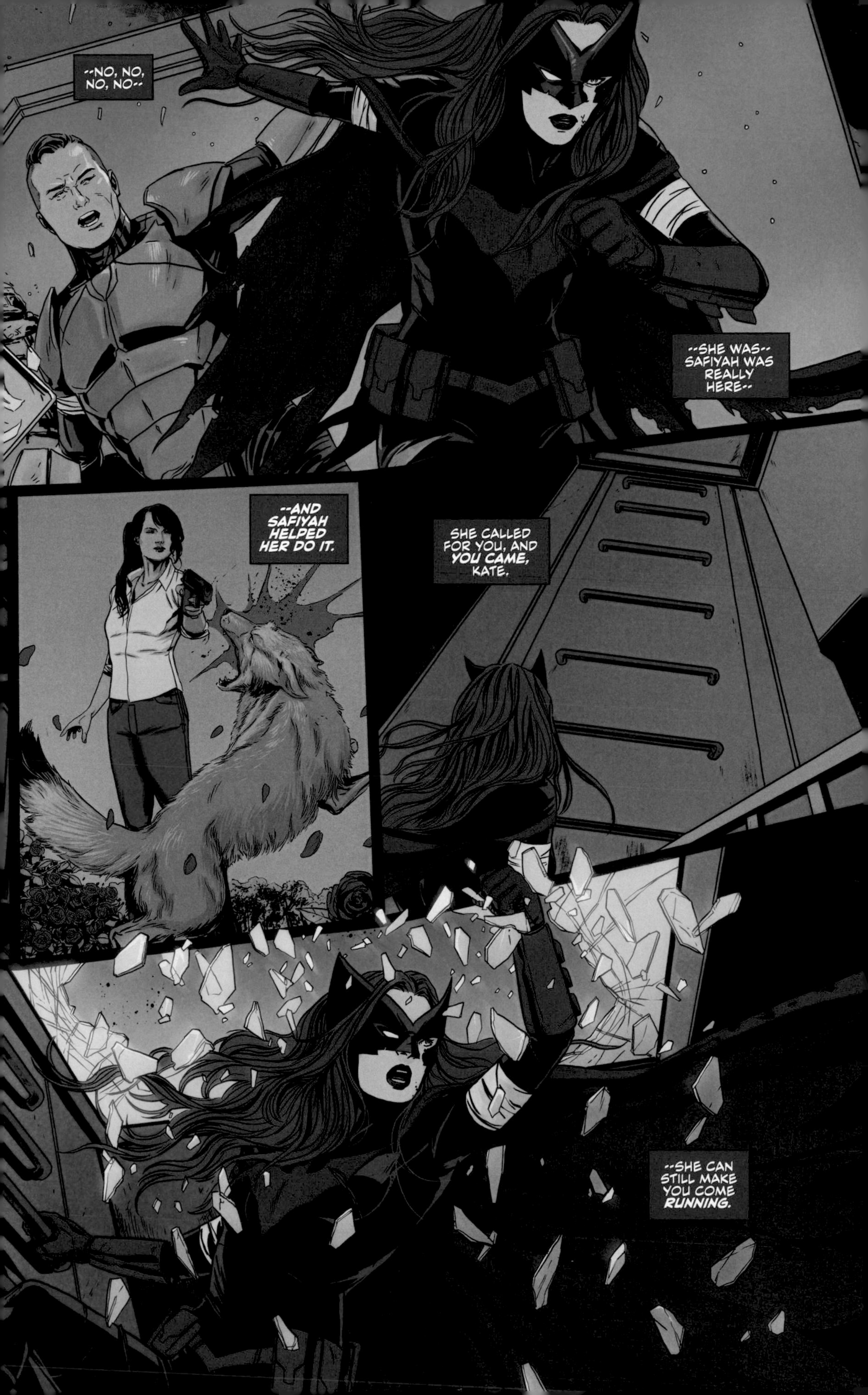
--NO, NO, NO, NO--
--SHE WAS-- SAFIYAH WAS REALLY HERE--
--AND SAFIYAH HELPED HER DO IT.
SHE CALLED FOR YOU, AND YOU CAME, KATE.
--SHE CAN STILL MAKE YOU COME RUNNING.

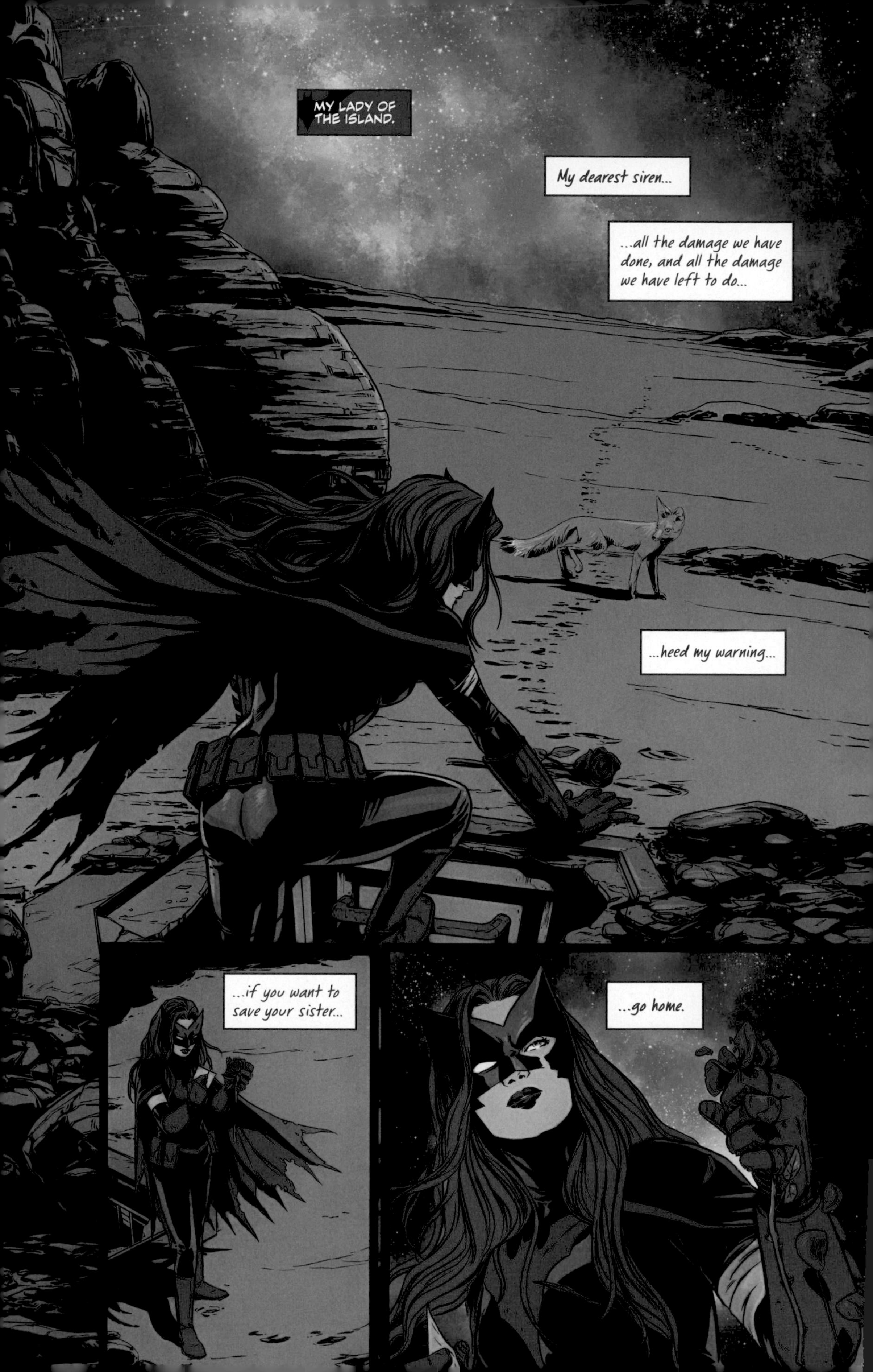
MY LADY OF THE ISLAND.
My dearest siren...
...all the damage we have done, and all the damage we have left to do...
...heed my warning...
...if you want to save your sister...
...go home.

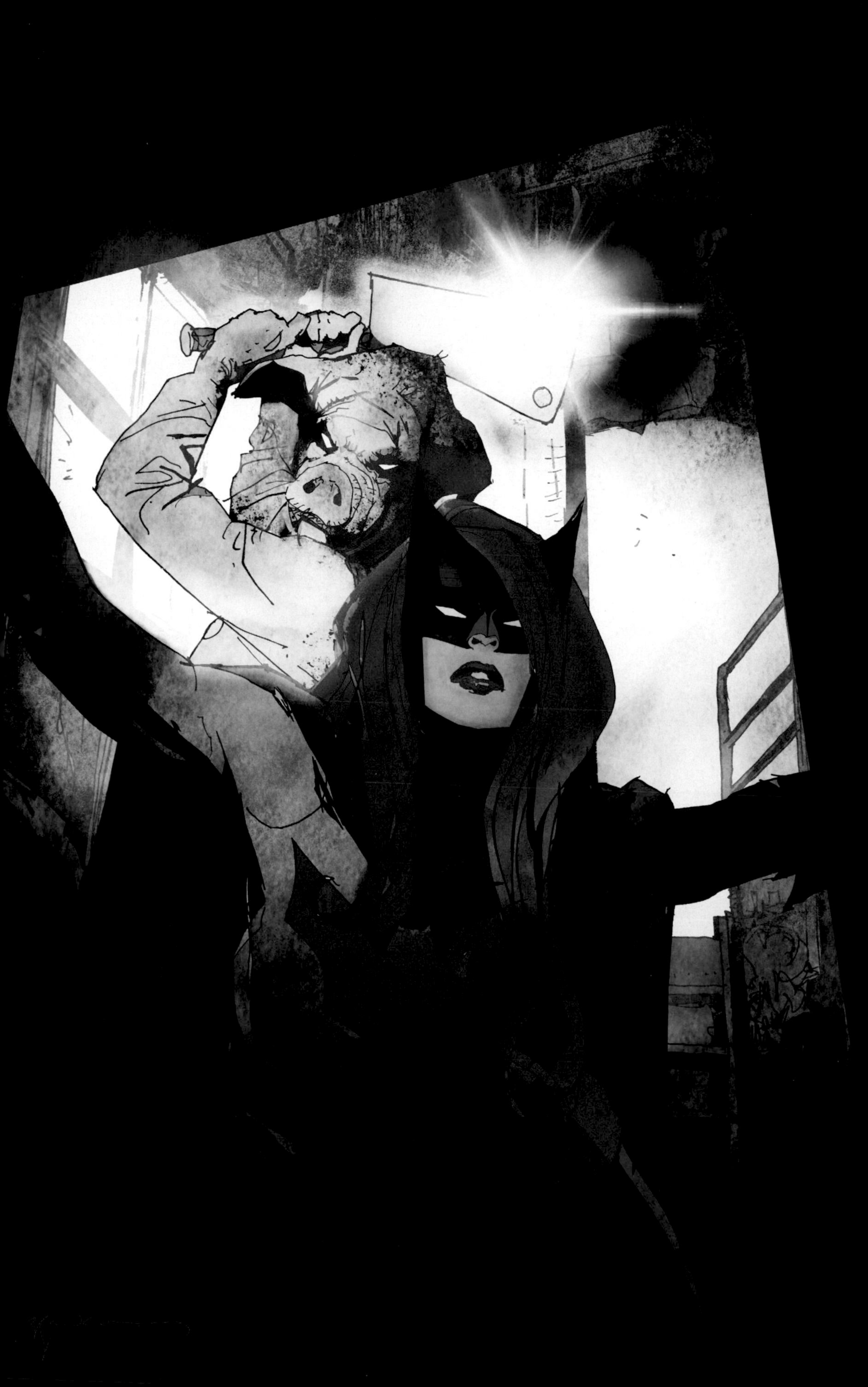

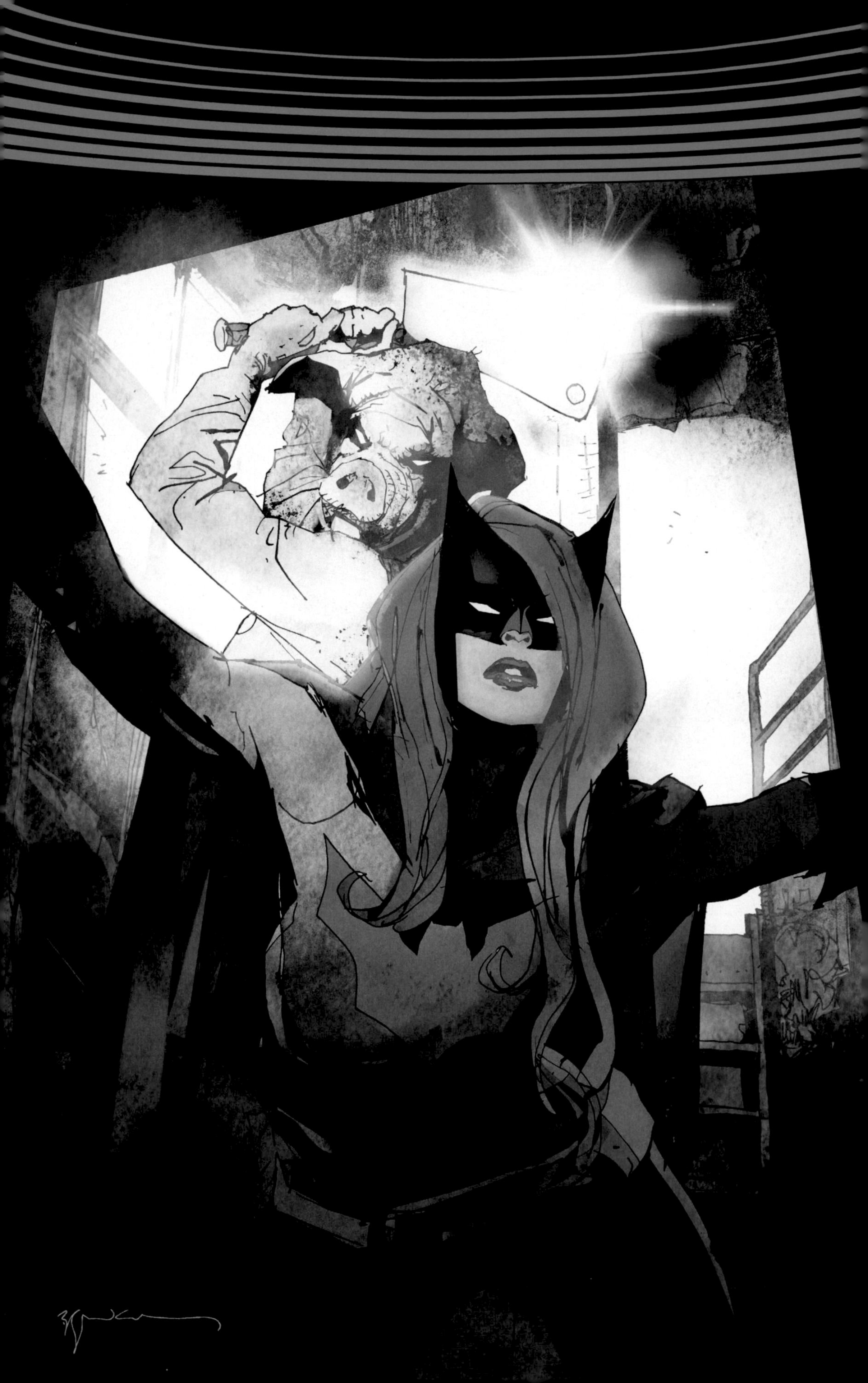

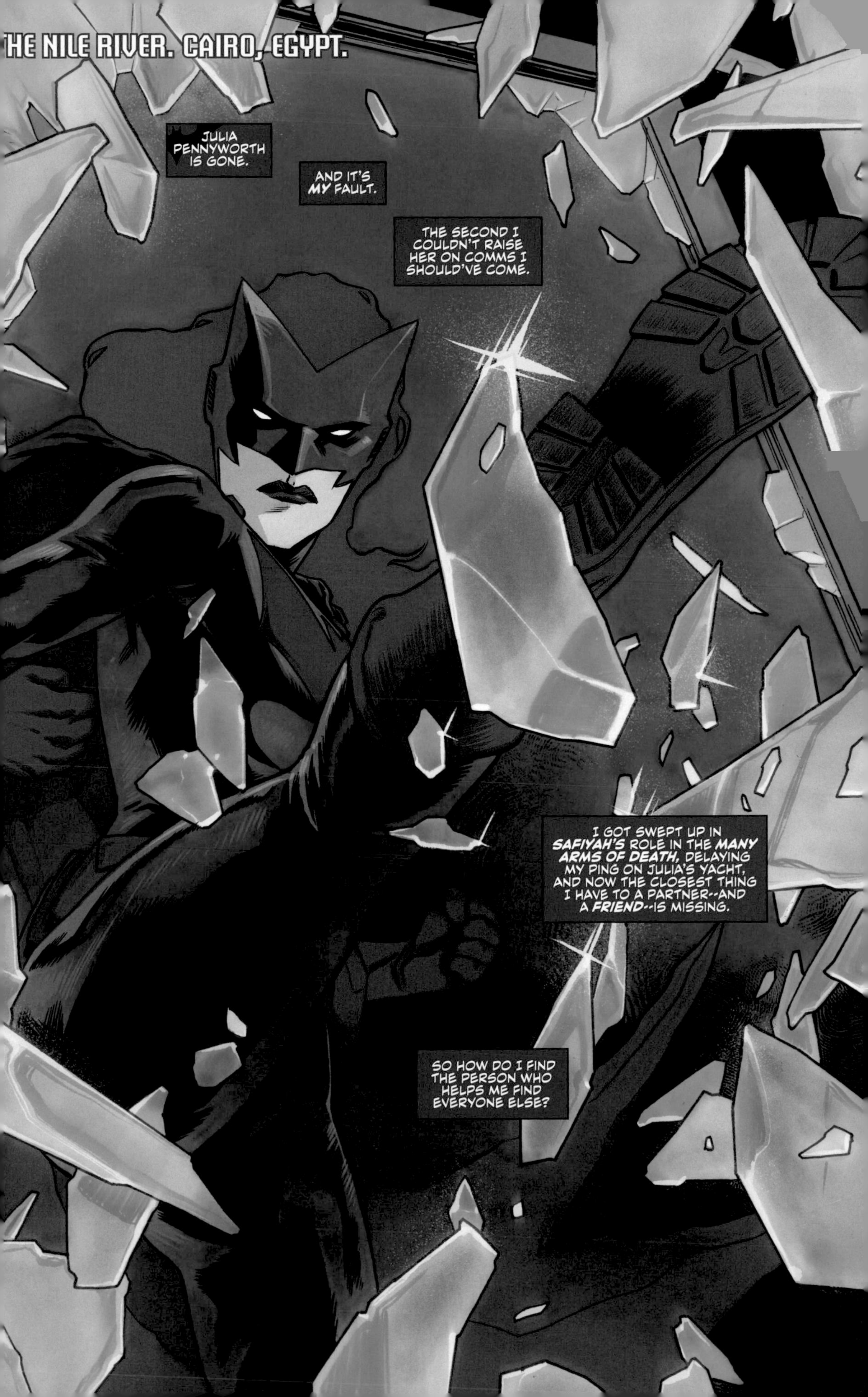
HE NILE RIVER. CAIRO, EGYPT.
JULIA PENNYWORTH IS GONE.
AND IT'S MY FAULT.
THE SECOND I COULDN'T RAISE HER ON COMMS I SHOULD'VE COME.
I GOT SWEPT UP IN SAFIYAH'S ROLE IN THE MANY ARMS OF DEATH, DELAYING MY PING ON JULIA'S YACHT, AND NOW THE CLOSEST THING I HAVE TO A PARTNER--AND A FRIEND--IS MISSING.
SO HOW DO I FIND THE PERSON WHO HELPS ME FIND EVERYONE ELSE?

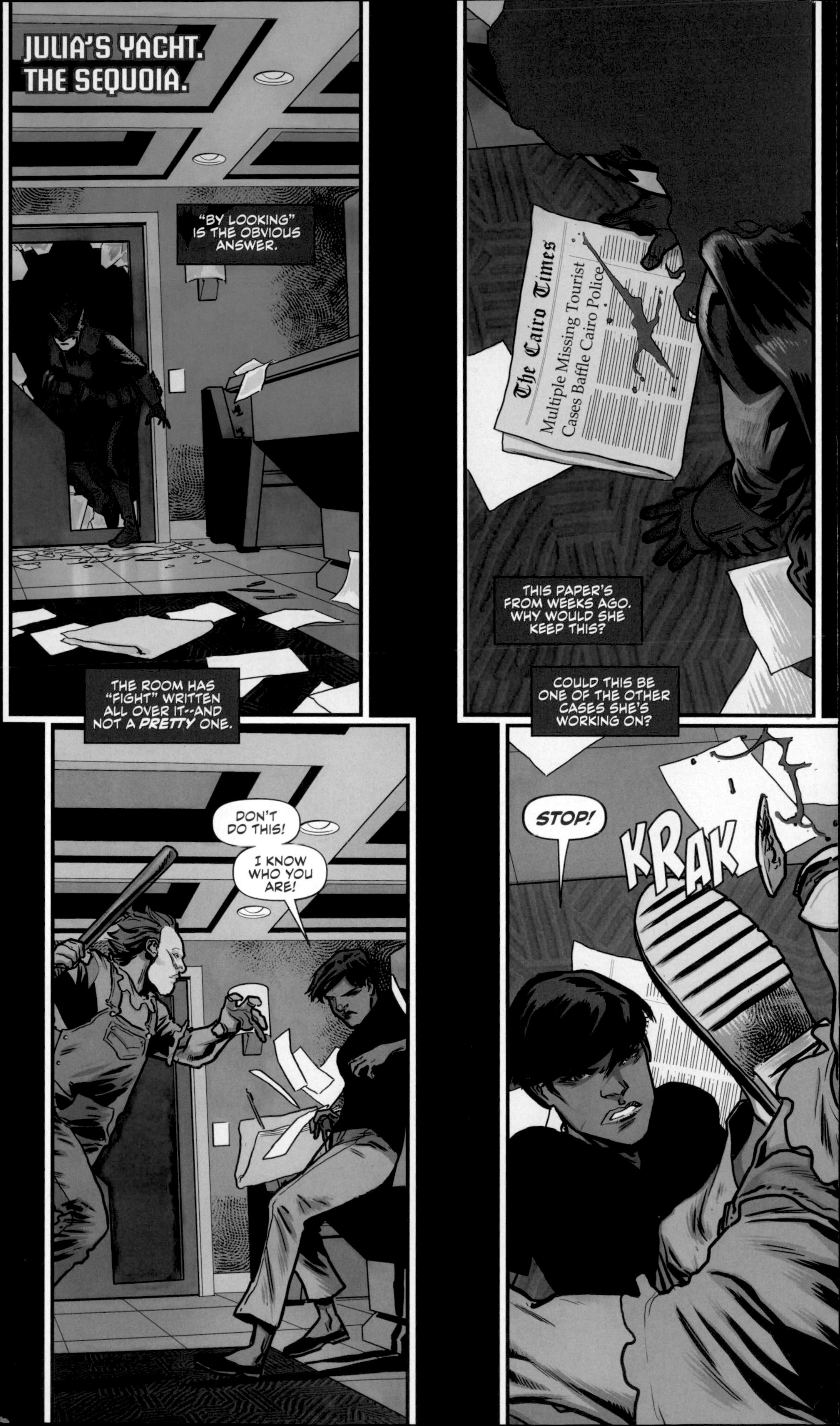
JULIA'S YACHT. THE SEQUOIA.
"BY LOOKING" IS THE OBVIOUS ANSWER.
THE ROOM HAS "FIGHT" WRITTEN ALL OVER IT--AND NOT A *PRETTY* ONE.
The Cairo Times
Multiple Missing Tourist Cases Baffle Cairo Police
THIS PAPER'S FROM WEEKS AGO. WHY WOULD SHE KEEP THIS?
COULD THIS BE ONE OF THE OTHER CASES SHE'S WORKING ON?
DON'T DO THIS!
I KNOW WHO YOU ARE!
STOP!
KRAK

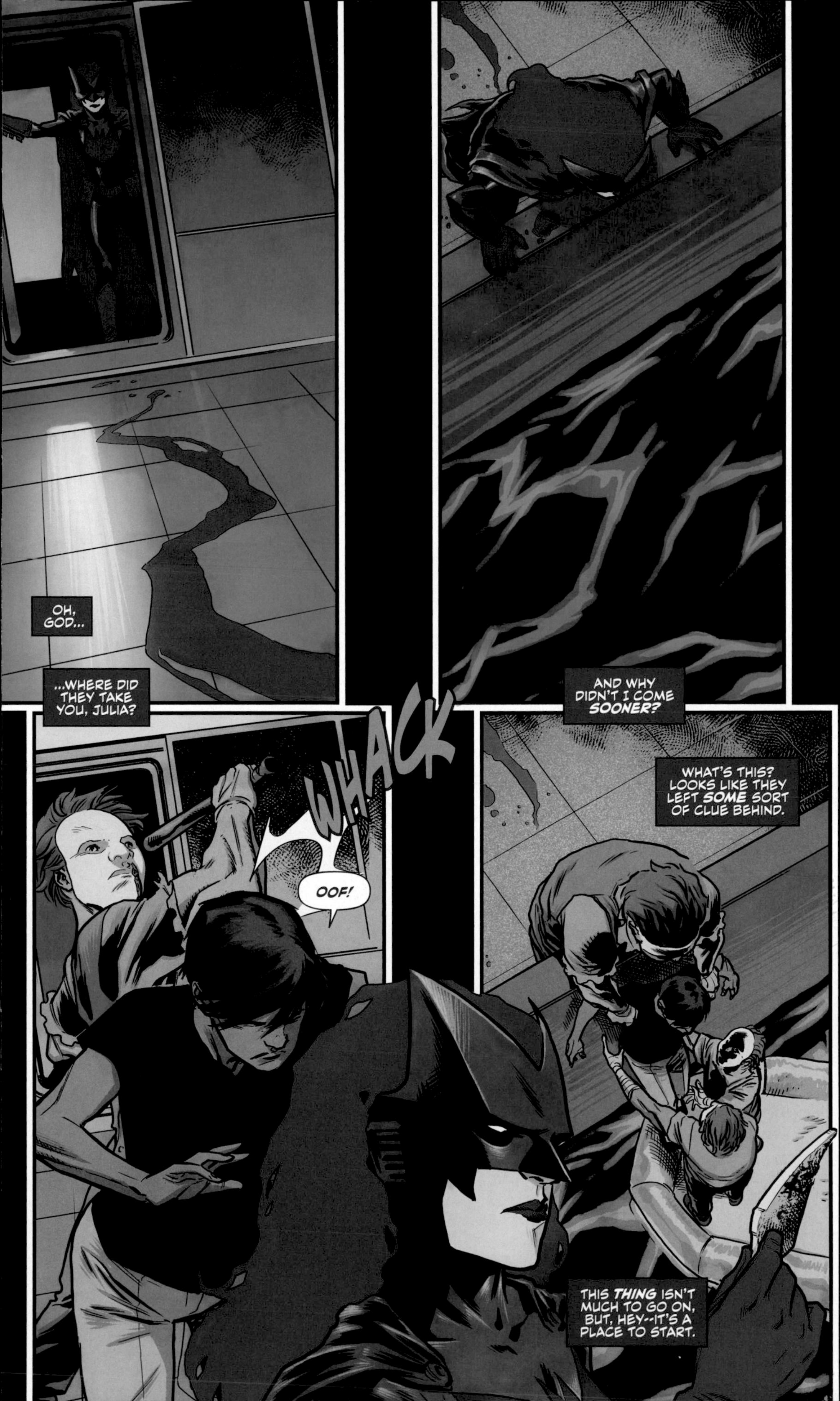
OH, GOD...
...WHERE DID THEY TAKE YOU, JULIA?
AND WHY DIDN'T I COME *SOONER?*
WHACK
OOF!
WHAT'S THIS? LOOKS LIKE THEY LEFT *SOME* SORT OF CLUE BEHIND.
THIS *THING* ISN'T MUCH TO GO ON, BUT, HEY--IT'S A PLACE TO START.

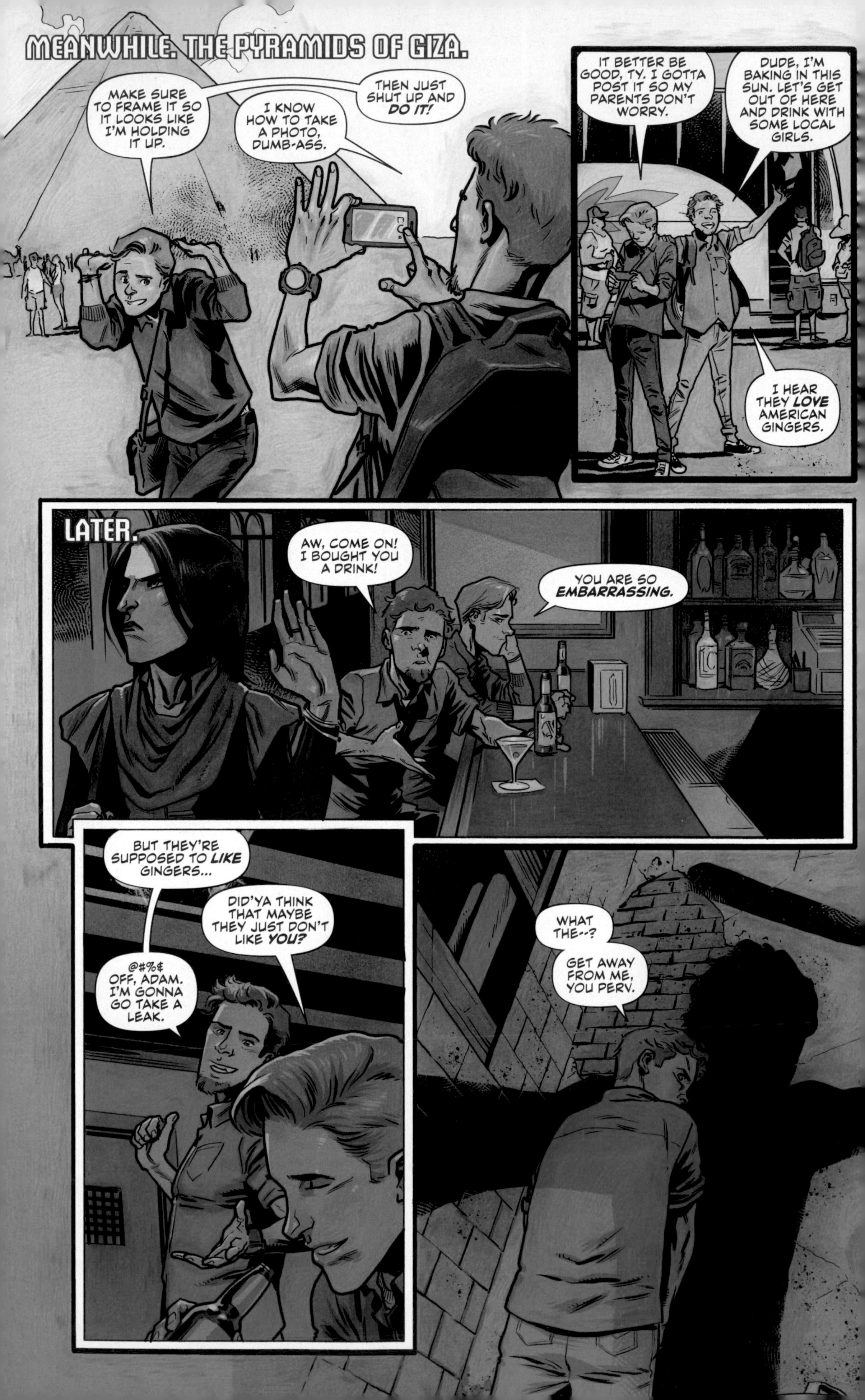
MEANWHILE. THE PYRAMIDS OF GIZA.
MAKE SURE TO FRAME IT SO IT LOOKS LIKE I'M HOLDING IT UP.
I KNOW HOW TO TAKE A PHOTO, DUMB-ASS.
THEN JUST SHUT UP AND DO IT!
IT BETTER BE GOOD, TY. I GOTTA POST IT SO MY PARENTS DON'T WORRY.
DUDE, I'M BAKING IN THIS SUN. LET'S GET OUT OF HERE AND DRINK WITH SOME LOCAL GIRLS.
I HEAR THEY LOVE AMERICAN GINGERS.
LATER.
AW, COME ON! I BOUGHT YOU A DRINK!
YOU ARE SO EMBARRASSING.
BUT THEY'RE SUPPOSED TO LIKE GINGERS...
DID'YA THINK THAT MAYBE THEY JUST DON'T LIKE YOU?
@#%$ OFF, ADAM. I'M GONNA GO TAKE A LEAK.
WHAT THE--?
GET AWAY FROM ME, YOU PERV.

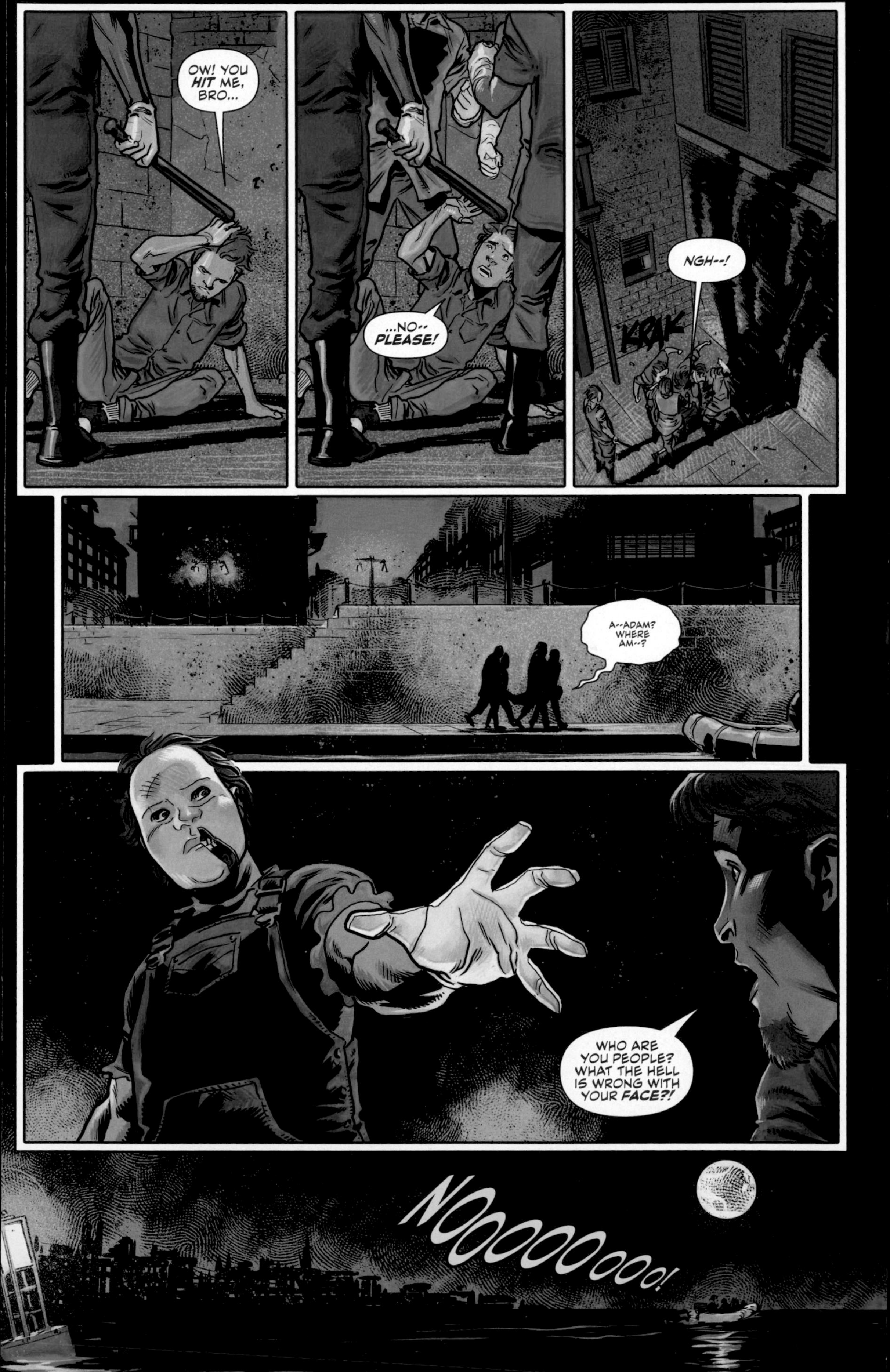
OW! YOU HIT ME, BRO...
...NO-- PLEASE!
KRAK
NGH--!
A--ADAM? WHERE AM--?
WHO ARE YOU PEOPLE? WHAT THE HELL IS WRONG WITH YOUR FACE?!
NOOOOOooo!

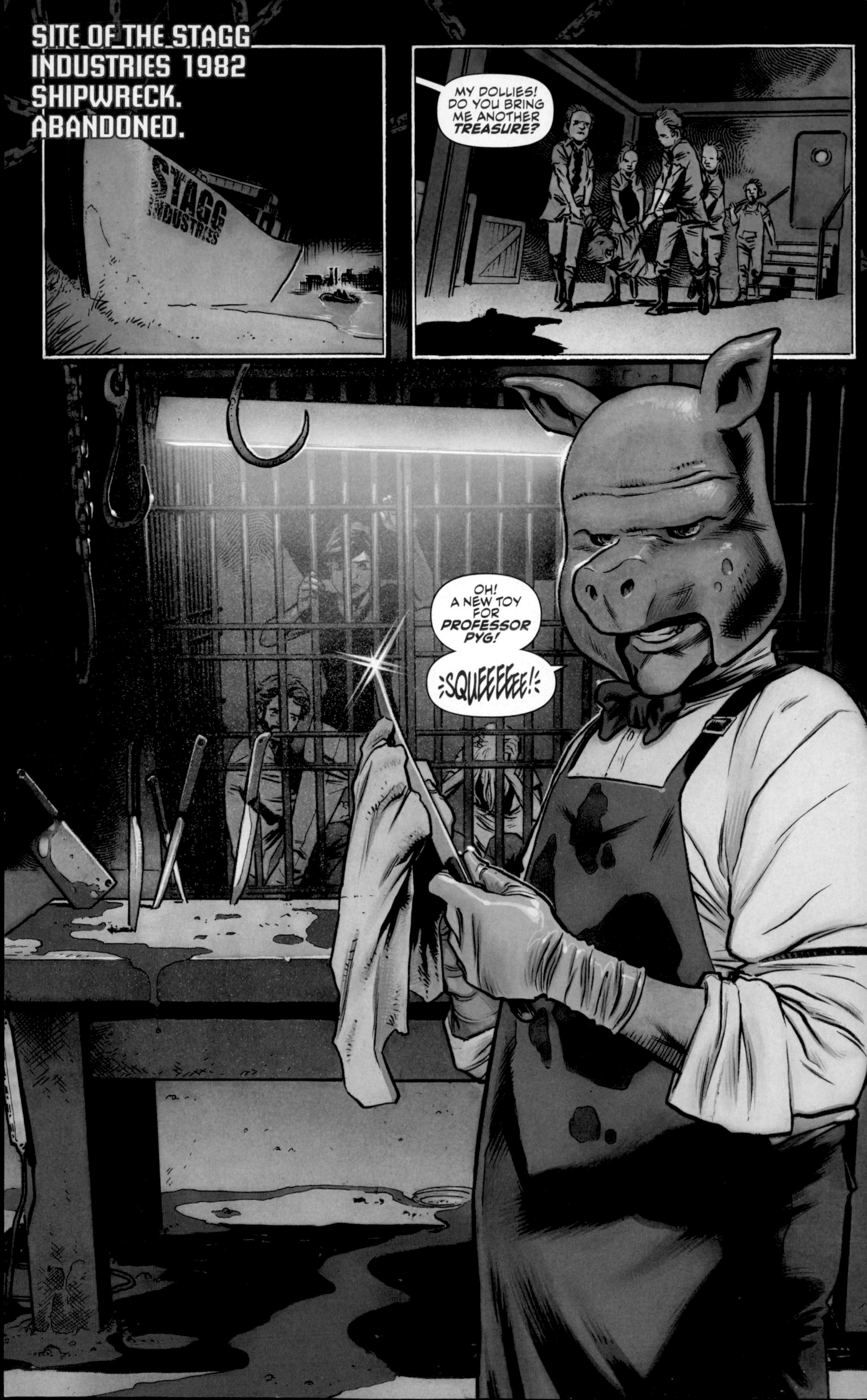
SITE OF THE STAGG INDUSTRIES 1982 SHIPWRECK. ABANDONED.
STAGG INDUSTRIES
MY DOLLIES! DO YOU BRING ME ANOTHER TREASURE?
OH! A NEW TOY FOR PROFESSOR PYG!
SQUEEEEEE!

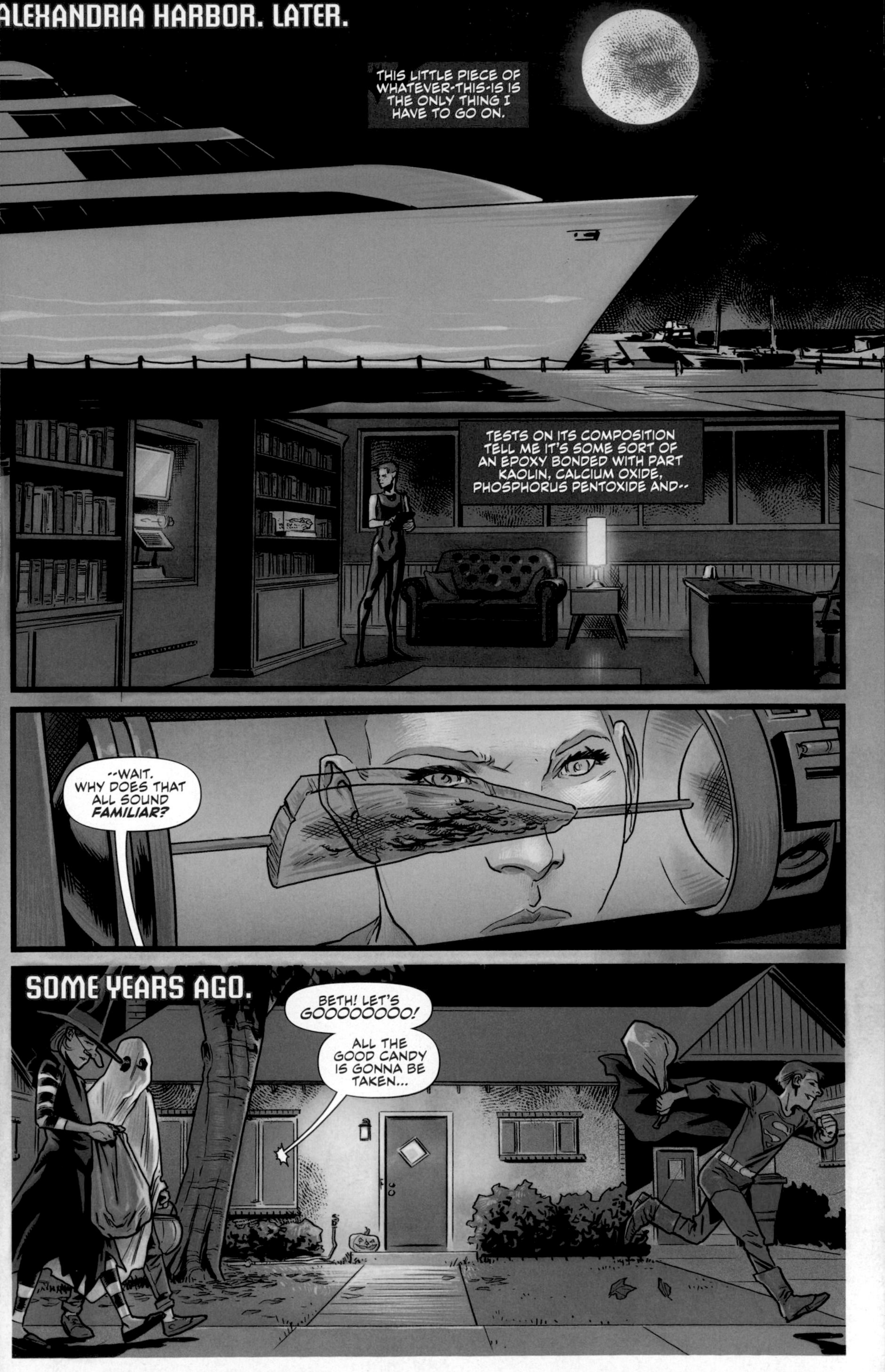
ALEXANDRIA HARBOR. LATER.
THIS LITTLE PIECE OF WHATEVER-THIS-IS IS THE ONLY THING I HAVE TO GO ON.
TESTS ON ITS COMPOSITION TELL ME IT'S SOME SORT OF AN EPOXY BONDED WITH PART KAOLIN, CALCIUM OXIDE, PHOSPHORUS PENTOXIDE AND--
--WAIT. WHY DOES THAT ALL SOUND FAMILIAR?
SOME YEARS AGO.
BETH! LET'S GOOOOOOOO!
ALL THE GOOD CANDY IS GONNA BE TAKEN...

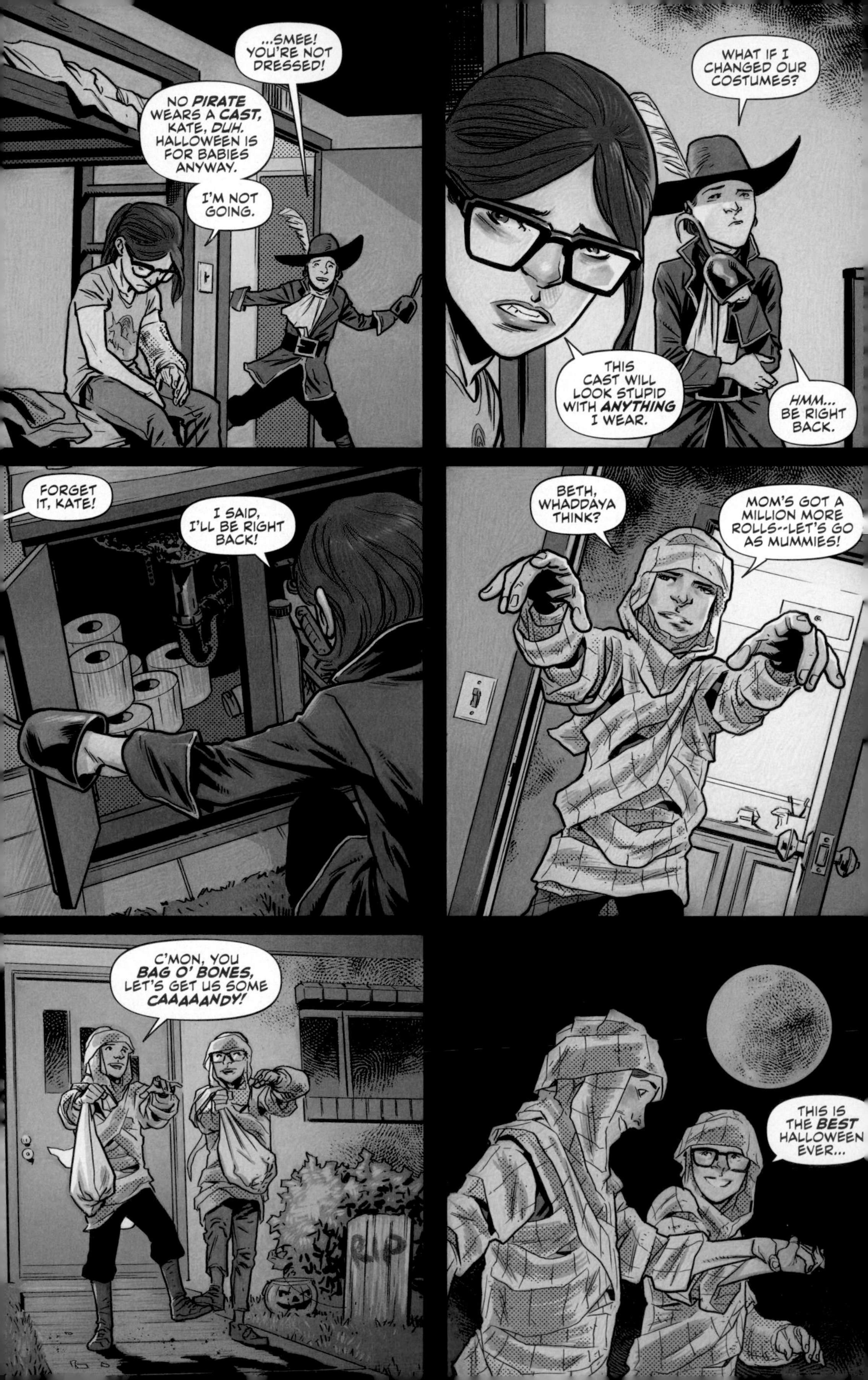
...SMEE! YOU'RE NOT DRESSED!
NO PIRATE WEARS A CAST, KATE, DUH. HALLOWEEN IS FOR BABIES ANYWAY.
I'M NOT GOING.
WHAT IF I CHANGED OUR COSTUMES?
THIS CAST WILL LOOK STUPID WITH ANYTHING I WEAR.
HMM... BE RIGHT BACK.
FORGET IT, KATE!
I SAID, I'LL BE RIGHT BACK!
BETH, WHADDAYA THINK?
MOM'S GOT A MILLION MORE ROLLS--LET'S GO AS MUMMIES!
C'MON, YOU BAG O' BONES, LET'S GET US SOME CAAAAANDY!
RIP
THIS IS THE BEST HALLOWEEN EVER...

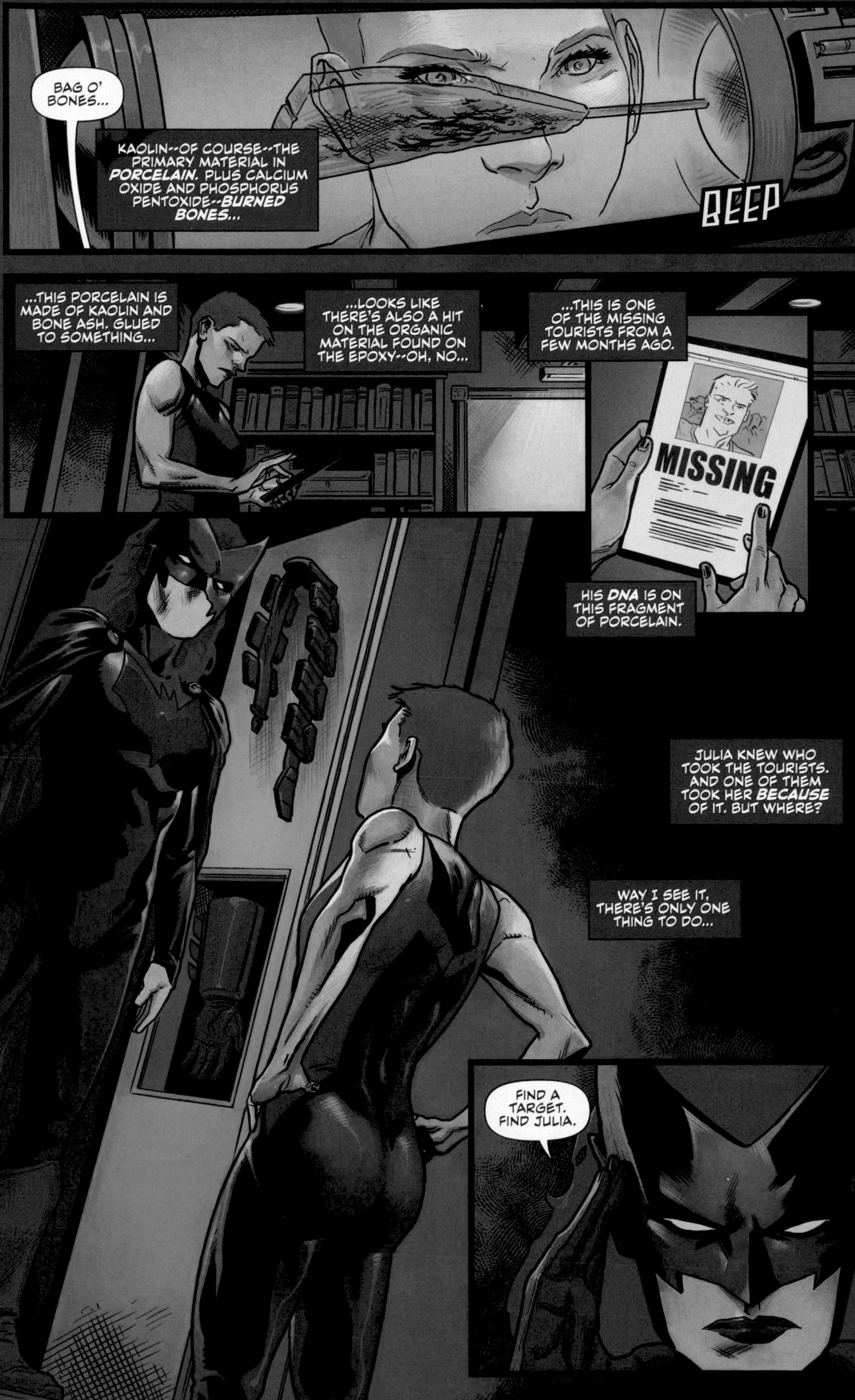
BAG O' BONES...
KAOLIN--OF COURSE--THE PRIMARY MATERIAL IN PORCELAIN. PLUS CALCIUM OXIDE AND PHOSPHORUS PENTOXIDE--BURNED BONES...
BEEP
...THIS PORCELAIN IS MADE OF KAOLIN AND BONE ASH. GLUED TO SOMETHING...
...LOOKS LIKE THERE'S ALSO A HIT ON THE ORGANIC MATERIAL FOUND ON THE EPOXY--OH, NO...
...THIS IS ONE OF THE MISSING TOURISTS FROM A FEW MONTHS AGO.
MISSING
HIS DNA IS ON THIS FRAGMENT OF PORCELAIN.
JULIA KNEW WHO TOOK THE TOURISTS. AND ONE OF THEM TOOK HER BECAUSE OF IT. BUT WHERE?
WAY I SEE IT, THERE'S ONLY ONE THING TO DO...
FIND A TARGET. FIND JULIA.

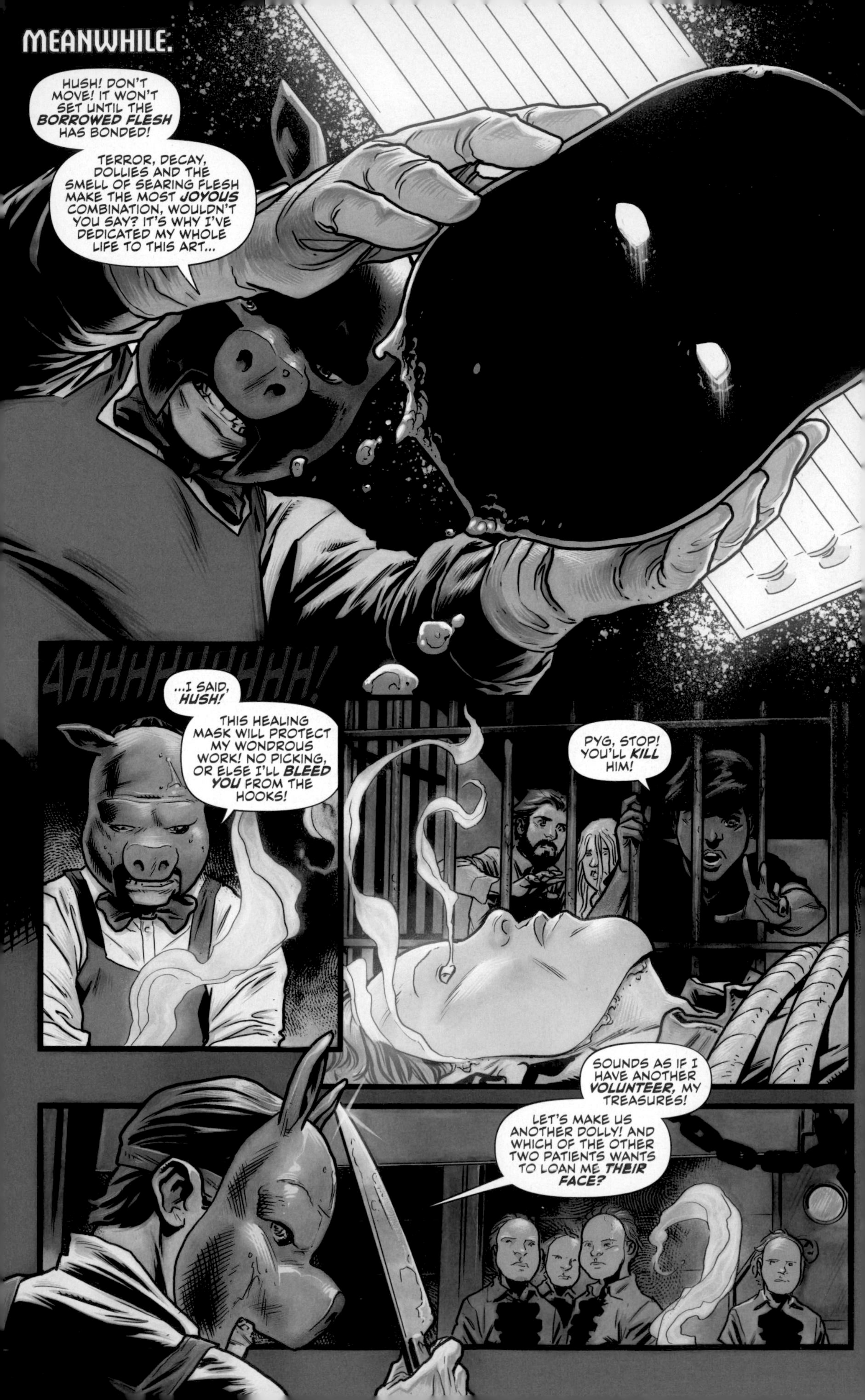
MEANWHILE.
HUSH! DON'T MOVE! IT WON'T SET UNTIL THE BORROWED FLESH HAS BONDED!
TERROR, DECAY, DOLLIES AND THE SMELL OF SEARING FLESH MAKE THE MOST JOYOUS COMBINATION, WOULDN'T YOU SAY? IT'S WHY I'VE DEDICATED MY WHOLE LIFE TO THIS ART...
AHHHHHHHHH!
...I SAID, HUSH!
THIS HEALING MASK WILL PROTECT MY WONDROUS WORK! NO PICKING, OR ELSE I'LL BLEED YOU FROM THE HOOKS!
PYG, STOP! YOU'LL KILL HIM!
SOUNDS AS IF I HAVE ANOTHER VOLUNTEER, MY TREASURES!
LET'S MAKE US ANOTHER DOLLY! AND WHICH OF THE OTHER TWO PATIENTS WANTS TO LOAN ME THEIR FACE?

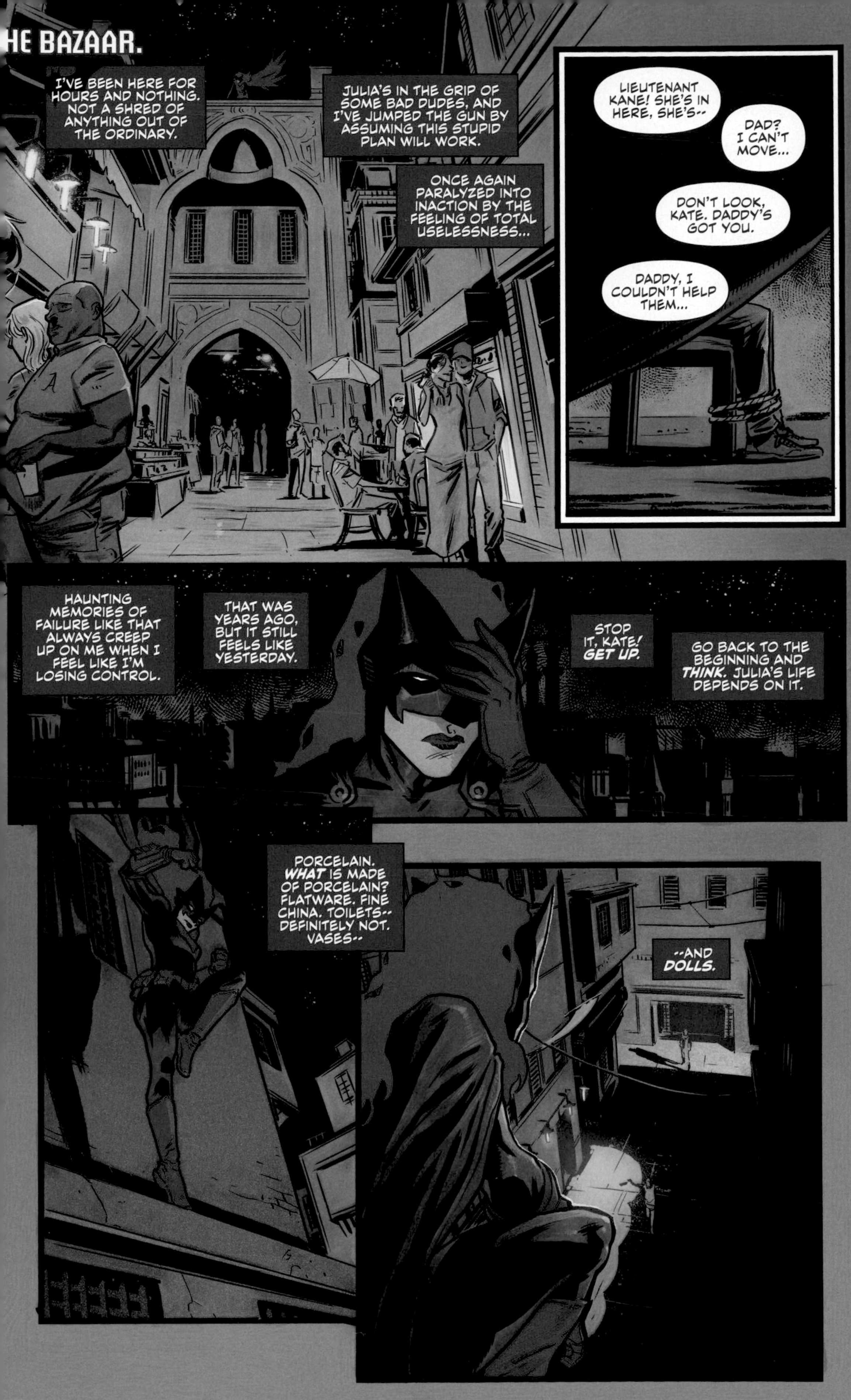

HE BAZAAR.
I'VE BEEN HERE FOR HOURS AND NOTHING. NOT A SHRED OF ANYTHING OUT OF THE ORDINARY.
JULIA'S IN THE GRIP OF SOME BAD DUDES, AND I'VE JUMPED THE GUN BY ASSUMING THIS STUPID PLAN WILL WORK.
ONCE AGAIN PARALYZED INTO INACTION BY THE FEELING OF TOTAL USELESSNESS...
LIEUTENANT KANE! SHE'S IN HERE, SHE'S--
DAD? I CAN'T MOVE...
DON'T LOOK, KATE. DADDY'S GOT YOU.
DADDY, I COULDN'T HELP THEM...
HAUNTING MEMORIES OF FAILURE LIKE THAT ALWAYS CREEP UP ON ME WHEN I FEEL LIKE I'M LOSING CONTROL.
THAT WAS YEARS AGO, BUT IT STILL FEELS LIKE YESTERDAY.
STOP IT, KATE! GET UP.
GO BACK TO THE BEGINNING AND THINK. JULIA'S LIFE DEPENDS ON IT.
PORCELAIN. WHAT IS MADE OF PORCELAIN? FLATWARE. FINE CHINA. TOILETS-- DEFINITELY NOT. VASES--
--AND DOLLS.

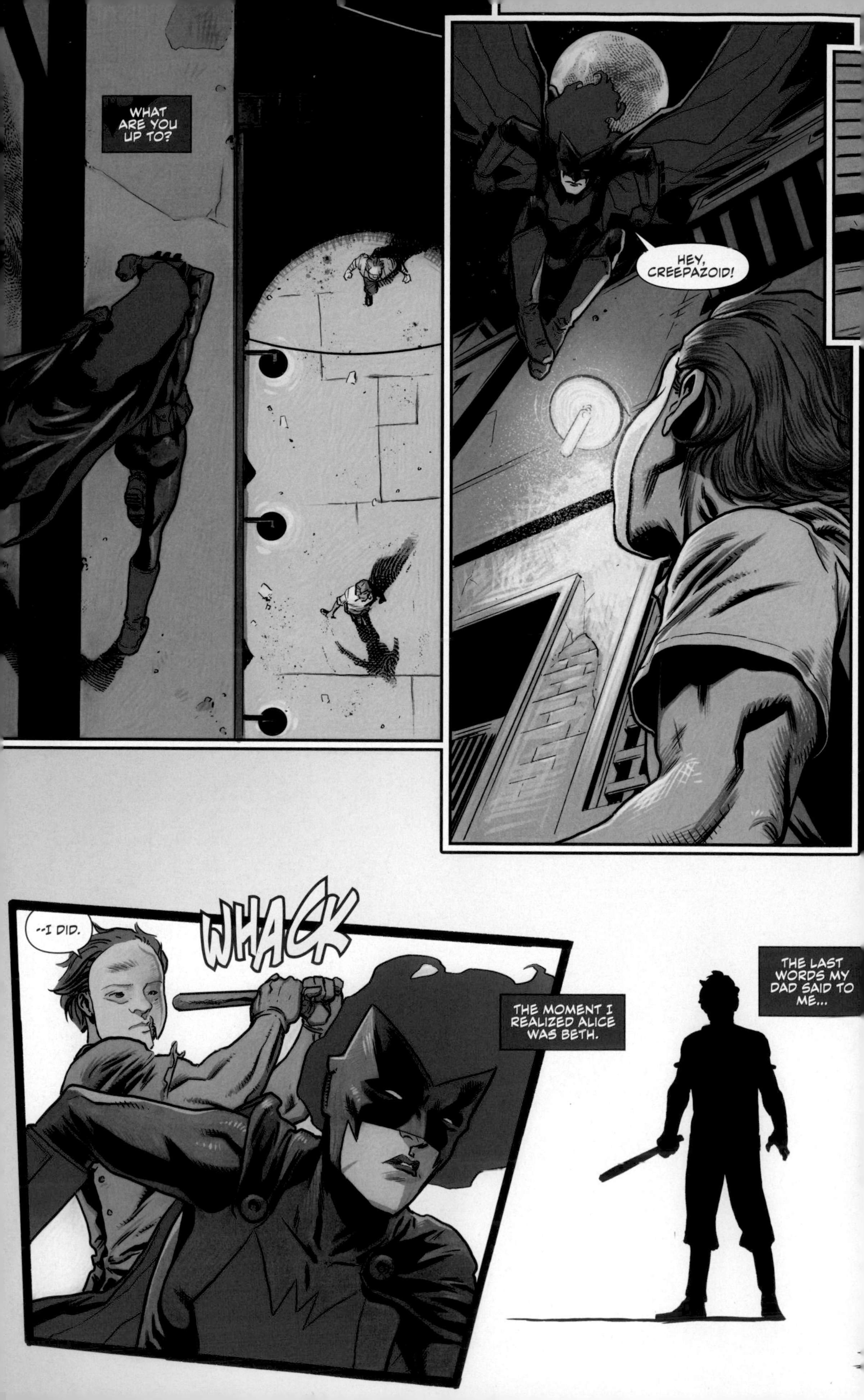

WHAT ARE YOU UP TO?
HEY, CREEPAZOID!
--I DID.
WHACK
THE MOMENT I REALIZED ALICE WAS BETH.
THE LAST WORDS MY DAD SAID TO ME...

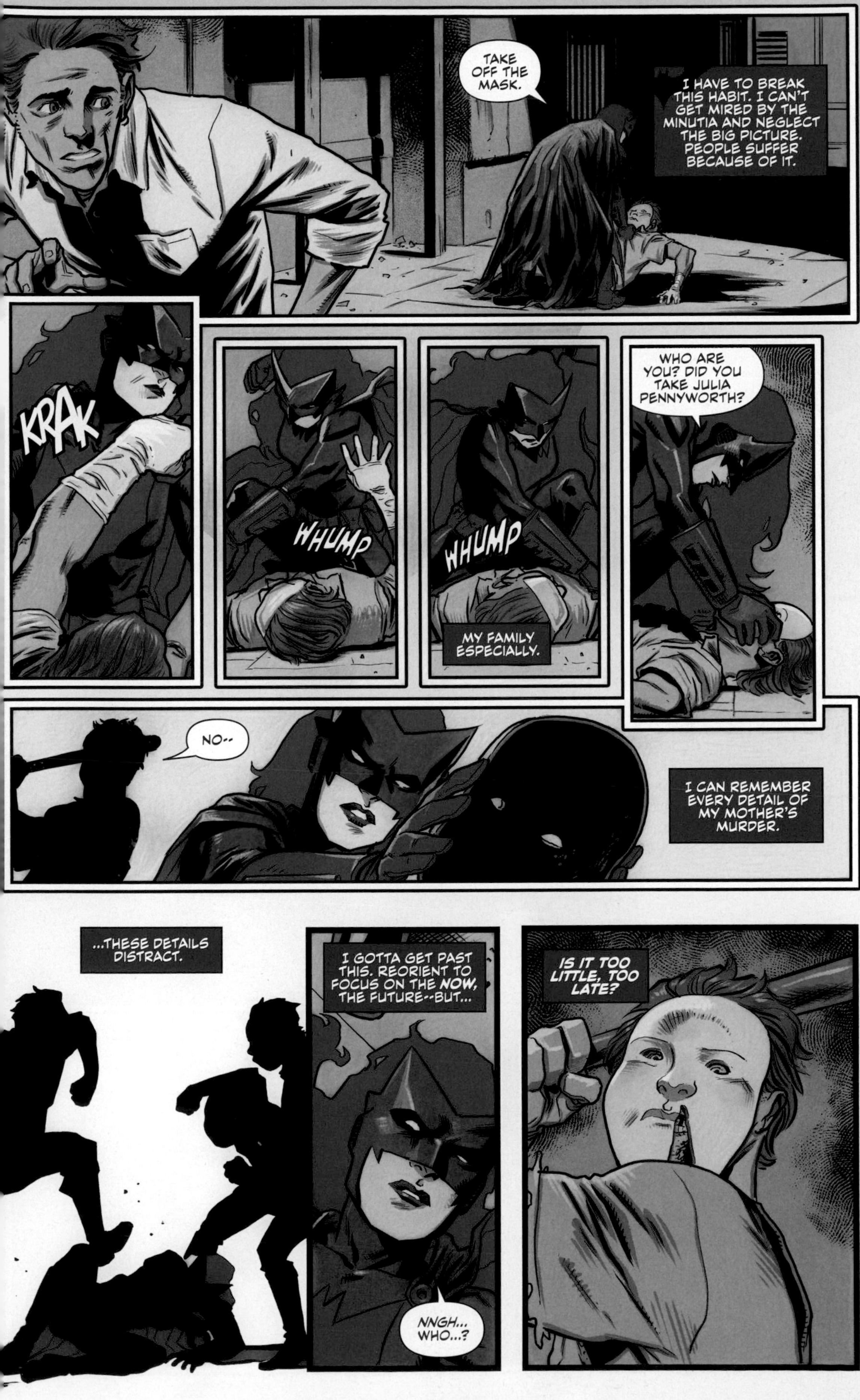

TAKE OFF THE MASK.
I HAVE TO BREAK THIS HABIT. I CAN'T GET MIRED BY THE MINUTIA AND NEGLECT THE BIG PICTURE. PEOPLE SUFFER BECAUSE OF IT.
KRAK
WHUMP
WHUMP
MY FAMILY ESPECIALLY.
WHO ARE YOU? DID YOU TAKE JULIA PENNYWORTH?
NO--
I CAN REMEMBER EVERY DETAIL OF MY MOTHER'S MURDER.
...THESE DETAILS DISTRACT.
I GOTTA GET PAST THIS. REORIENT TO FOCUS ON THE NOW, THE FUTURE--BUT...
NNGH... WHO...?
IS IT TOO LITTLE, TOO LATE?

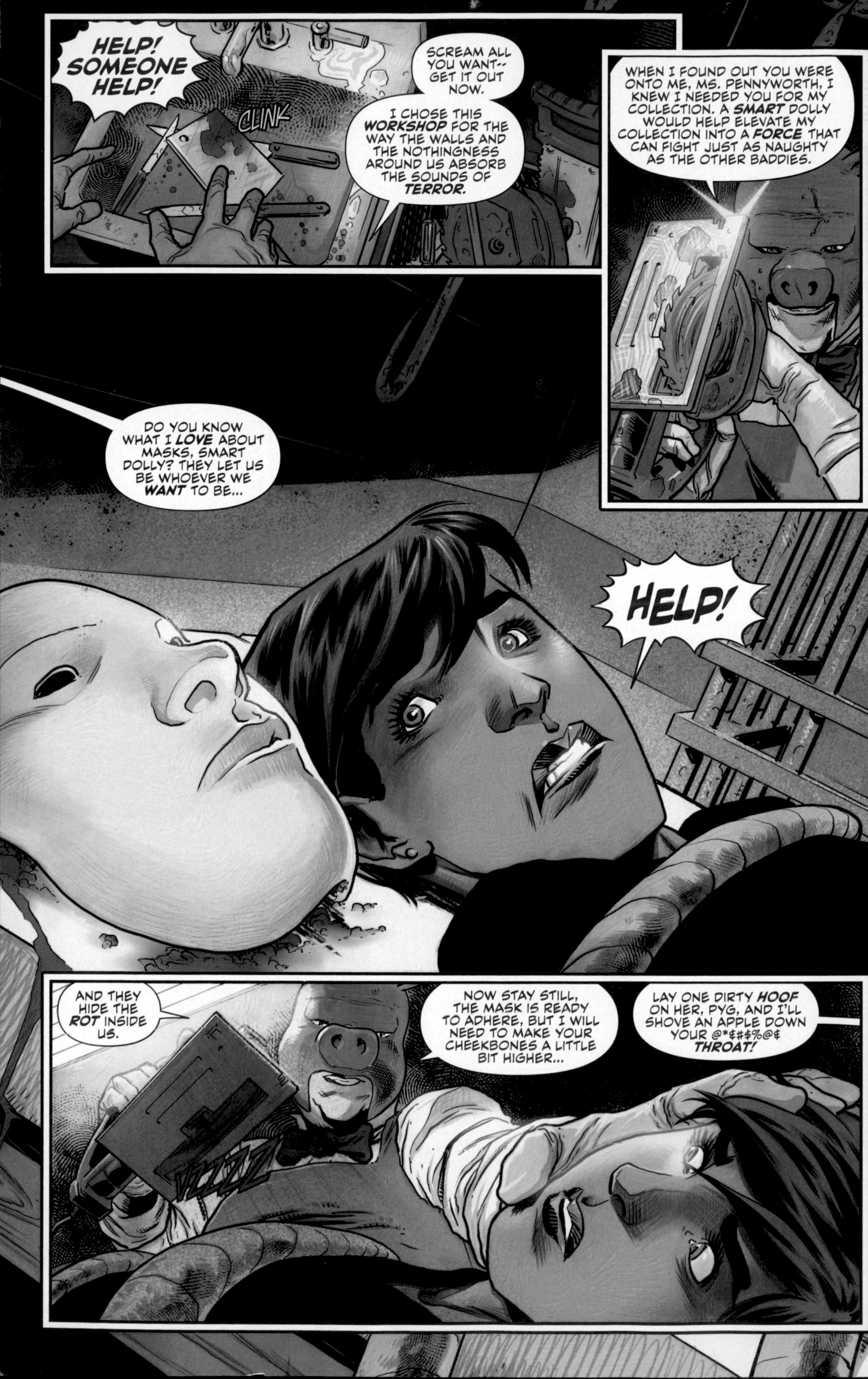
HELP! SOMEONE HELP!
CLINK
SCREAM ALL YOU WANT-- GET IT OUT NOW.
I CHOSE THIS WORKSHOP FOR THE WAY THE WALLS AND THE NOTHINGNESS AROUND US ABSORB THE SOUNDS OF TERROR.
WHEN I FOUND OUT YOU WERE ONTO ME, MS. PENNYWORTH, I KNEW I NEEDED YOU FOR MY COLLECTION. A SMART DOLLY WOULD HELP ELEVATE MY COLLECTION INTO A FORCE THAT CAN FIGHT JUST AS NAUGHTY AS THE OTHER BADDIES.
DO YOU KNOW WHAT I LOVE ABOUT MASKS, SMART DOLLY? THEY LET US BE WHOEVER WE WANT TO BE...
HELP!
AND THEY HIDE THE ROT INSIDE US.
NOW STAY STILL, THE MASK IS READY TO ADHERE, BUT I WILL NEED TO MAKE YOUR CHEEKBONES A LITTLE BIT HIGHER...
LAY ONE DIRTY HOOF ON HER, PYG, AND I'LL SHOVE AN APPLE DOWN YOUR @*$#$%@$ THROAT!

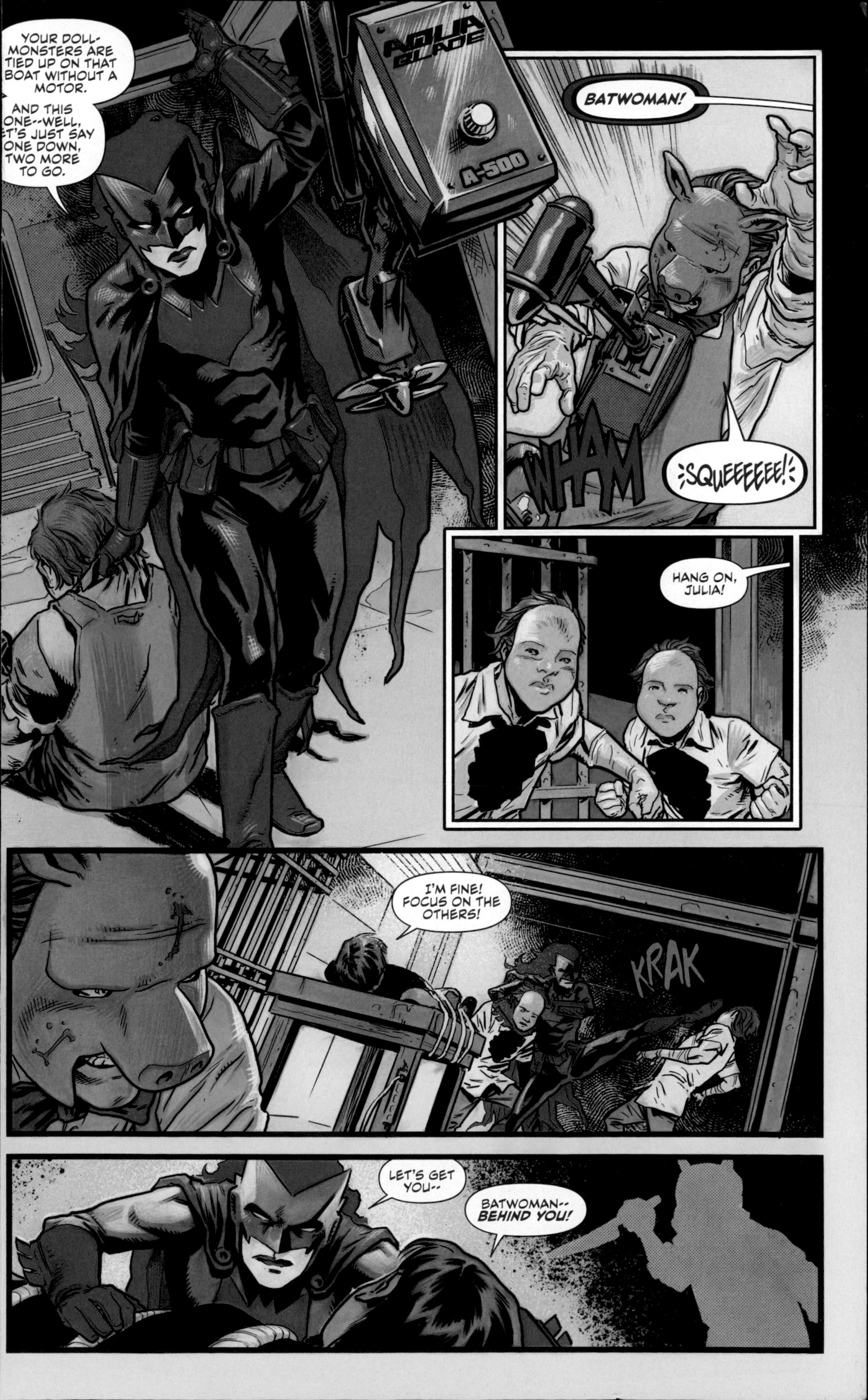
YOUR DOLL-MONSTERS ARE TIED UP ON THAT BOAT WITHOUT A MOTOR.
AND THIS ONE--WELL, LET'S JUST SAY ONE DOWN, TWO MORE TO GO.
AQUA BLADE
A-500
BATWOMAN!
WHAM
SQUEEEEEE!
HANG ON, JULIA!
I'M FINE! FOCUS ON THE OTHERS!
KRAK
LET'S GET YOU--
BATWOMAN-- BEHIND YOU!

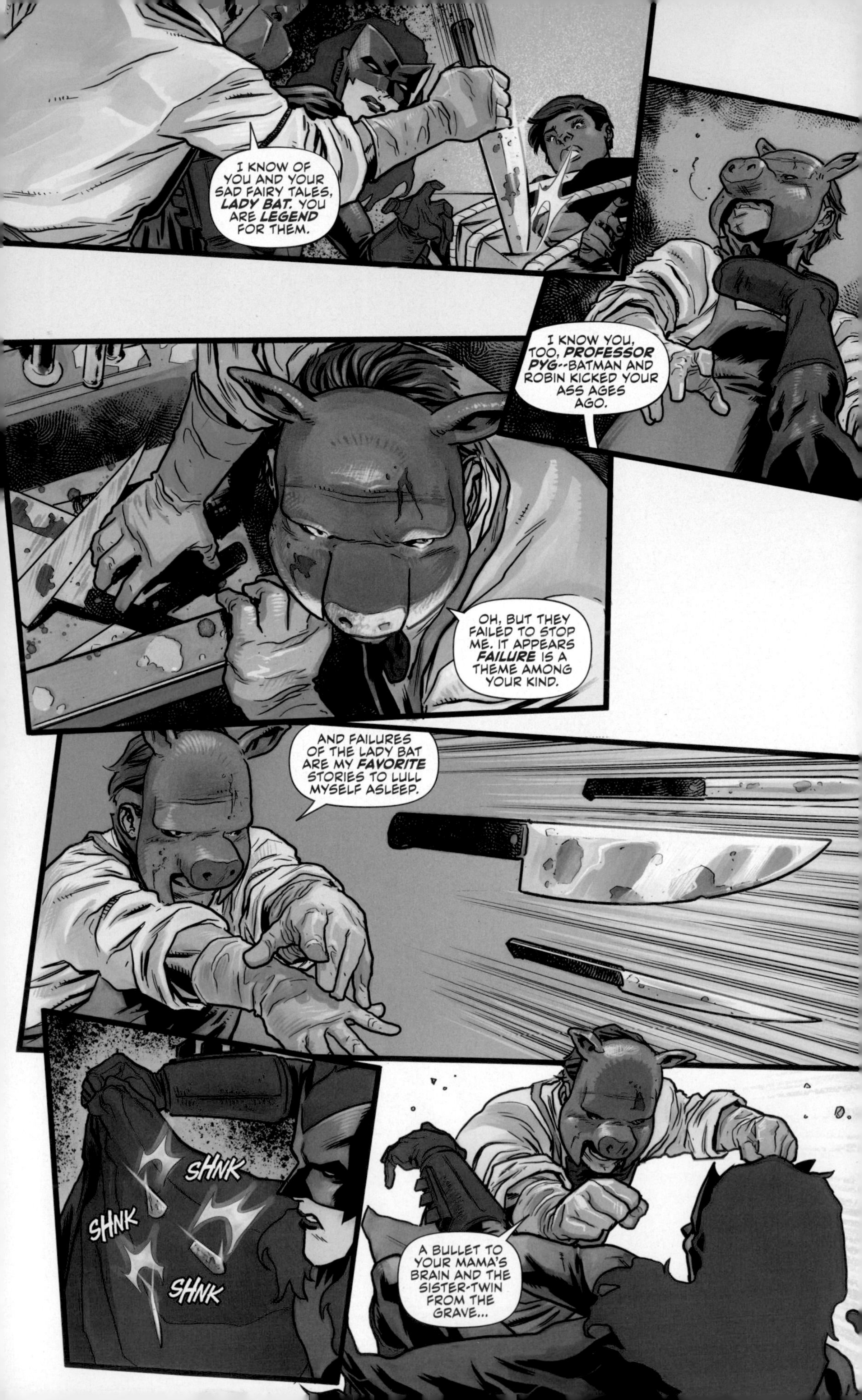
I KNOW OF YOU AND YOUR SAD FAIRY TALES, LADY BAT. YOU ARE LEGEND FOR THEM.
I KNOW YOU, TOO, PROFESSOR PYG--BATMAN AND ROBIN KICKED YOUR ASS AGES AGO.
OH, BUT THEY FAILED TO STOP ME. IT APPEARS FAILURE IS A THEME AMONG YOUR KIND.
AND FAILURES OF THE LADY BAT ARE MY FAVORITE STORIES TO LULL MYSELF ASLEEP.
SHNK
SHNK
SHNK
A BULLET TO YOUR MAMA'S BRAIN AND THE SISTER-TWIN FROM THE GRAVE...

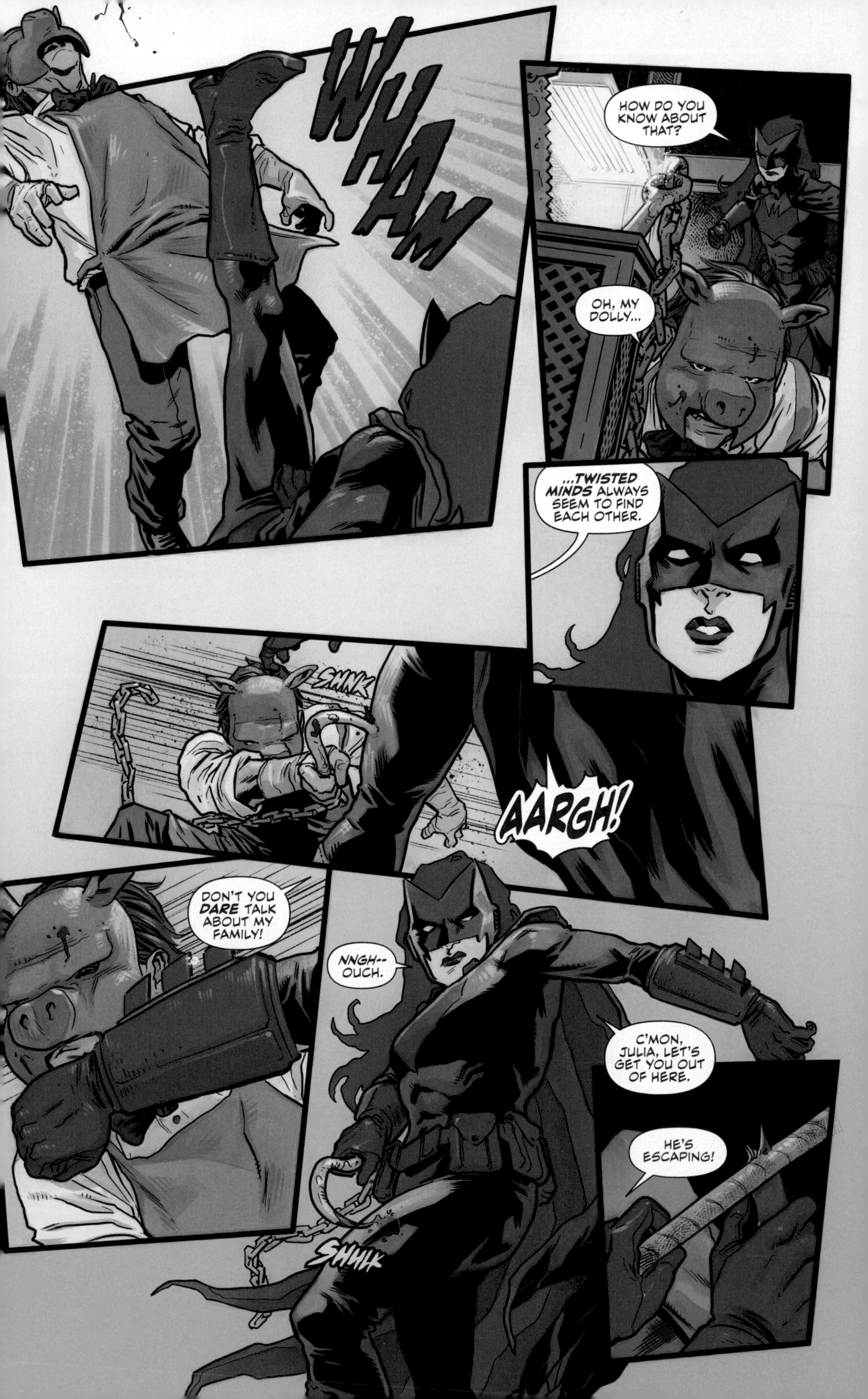
WHAM
HOW DO YOU KNOW ABOUT THAT?
OH, MY DOLLY...
...TWISTED MINDS ALWAYS SEEM TO FIND EACH OTHER.
SHNK
AARGH!
DON'T YOU DARE TALK ABOUT MY FAMILY!
NNGH-- OUCH.
C'MON, JULIA, LET'S GET YOU OUT OF HERE.
HE'S ESCAPING!
SHUNK

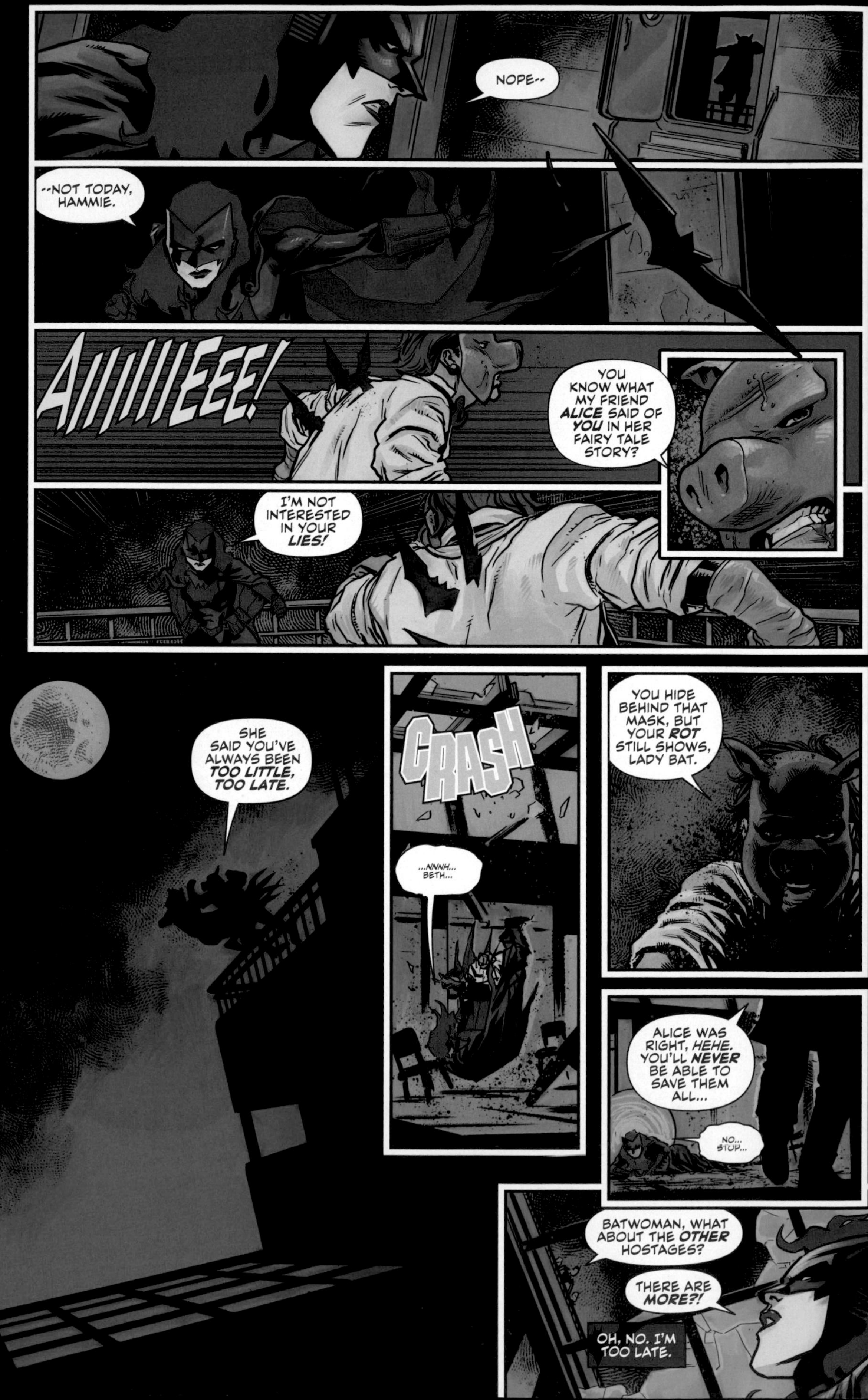
NOPE--
--NOT TODAY, HAMMIE.
AIIIIIIEEE!
YOU KNOW WHAT MY FRIEND ALICE SAID OF YOU IN HER FAIRY TALE STORY?
I'M NOT INTERESTED IN YOUR LIES!
SHE SAID YOU'VE ALWAYS BEEN TOO LITTLE, TOO LATE.
CRASH
...NNNH... BETH...
YOU HIDE BEHIND THAT MASK, BUT YOUR ROT STILL SHOWS, LADY BAT.
ALICE WAS RIGHT, HEHE. YOU'LL NEVER BE ABLE TO SAVE THEM ALL...
NO... STOP...
BATWOMAN, WHAT ABOUT THE OTHER HOSTAGES?
THERE ARE MORE?!
OH, NO. I'M TOO LATE.

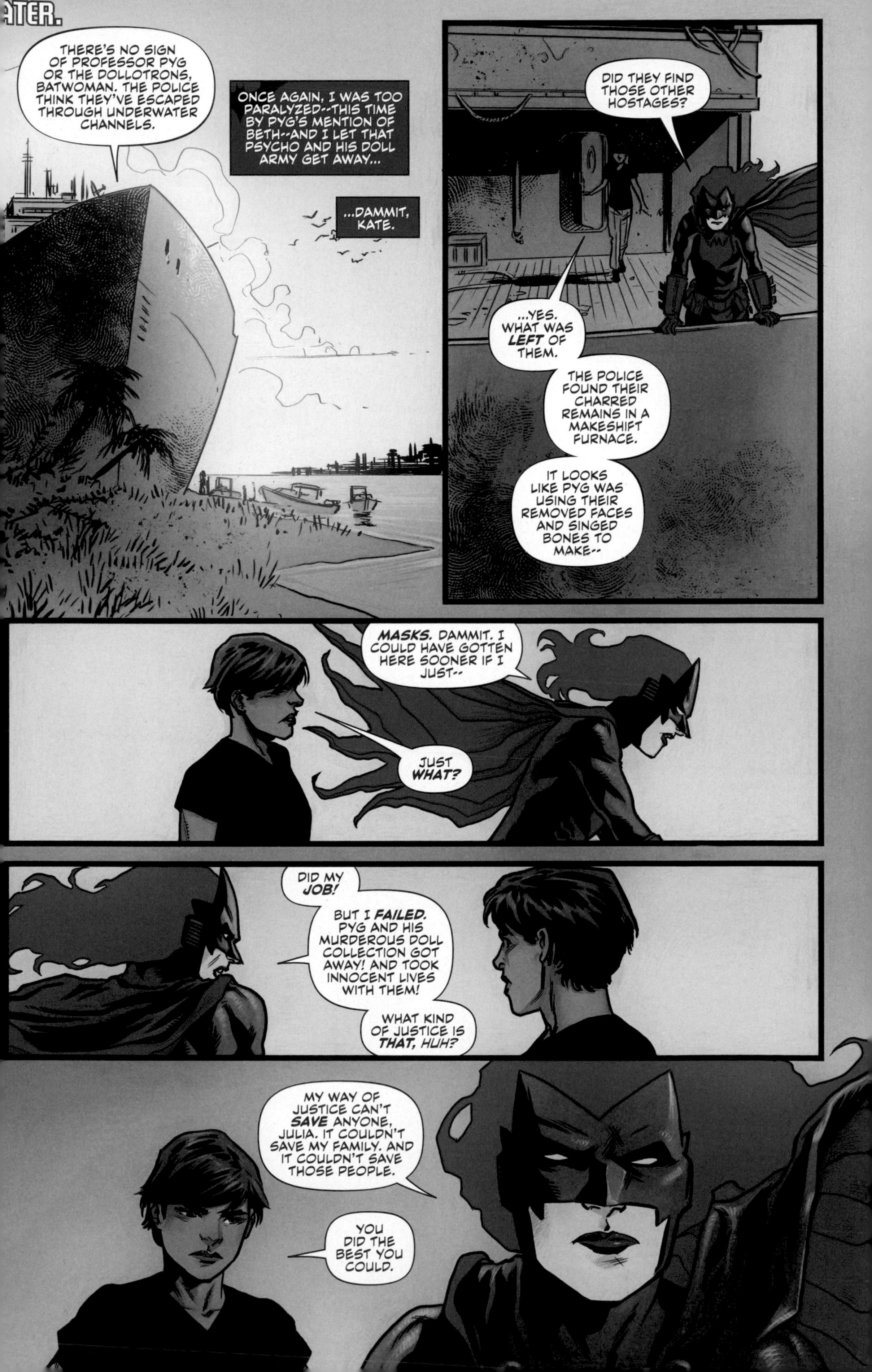

ATER.
THERE'S NO SIGN OF PROFESSOR PYG OR THE DOLLOTRONS, BATWOMAN. THE POLICE THINK THEY'VE ESCAPED THROUGH UNDERWATER CHANNELS.
ONCE AGAIN, I WAS TOO PARALYZED--THIS TIME BY PYG'S MENTION OF BETH--AND I LET THAT PSYCHO AND HIS DOLL ARMY GET AWAY...
...DAMMIT, KATE.
DID THEY FIND THOSE OTHER HOSTAGES?
...YES. WHAT WAS LEFT OF THEM.
THE POLICE FOUND THEIR CHARRED REMAINS IN A MAKESHIFT FURNACE.
IT LOOKS LIKE PYG WAS USING THEIR REMOVED FACES AND SINGED BONES TO MAKE--
MASKS. DAMMIT. I COULD HAVE GOTTEN HERE SOONER IF I JUST--
JUST WHAT?
DID MY JOB!
BUT I FAILED. PYG AND HIS MURDEROUS DOLL COLLECTION GOT AWAY! AND TOOK INNOCENT LIVES WITH THEM!
WHAT KIND OF JUSTICE IS THAT, HUH?
MY WAY OF JUSTICE CAN'T SAVE ANYONE, JULIA. IT COULDN'T SAVE MY FAMILY. AND IT COULDN'T SAVE THOSE PEOPLE.
YOU DID THE BEST YOU COULD.

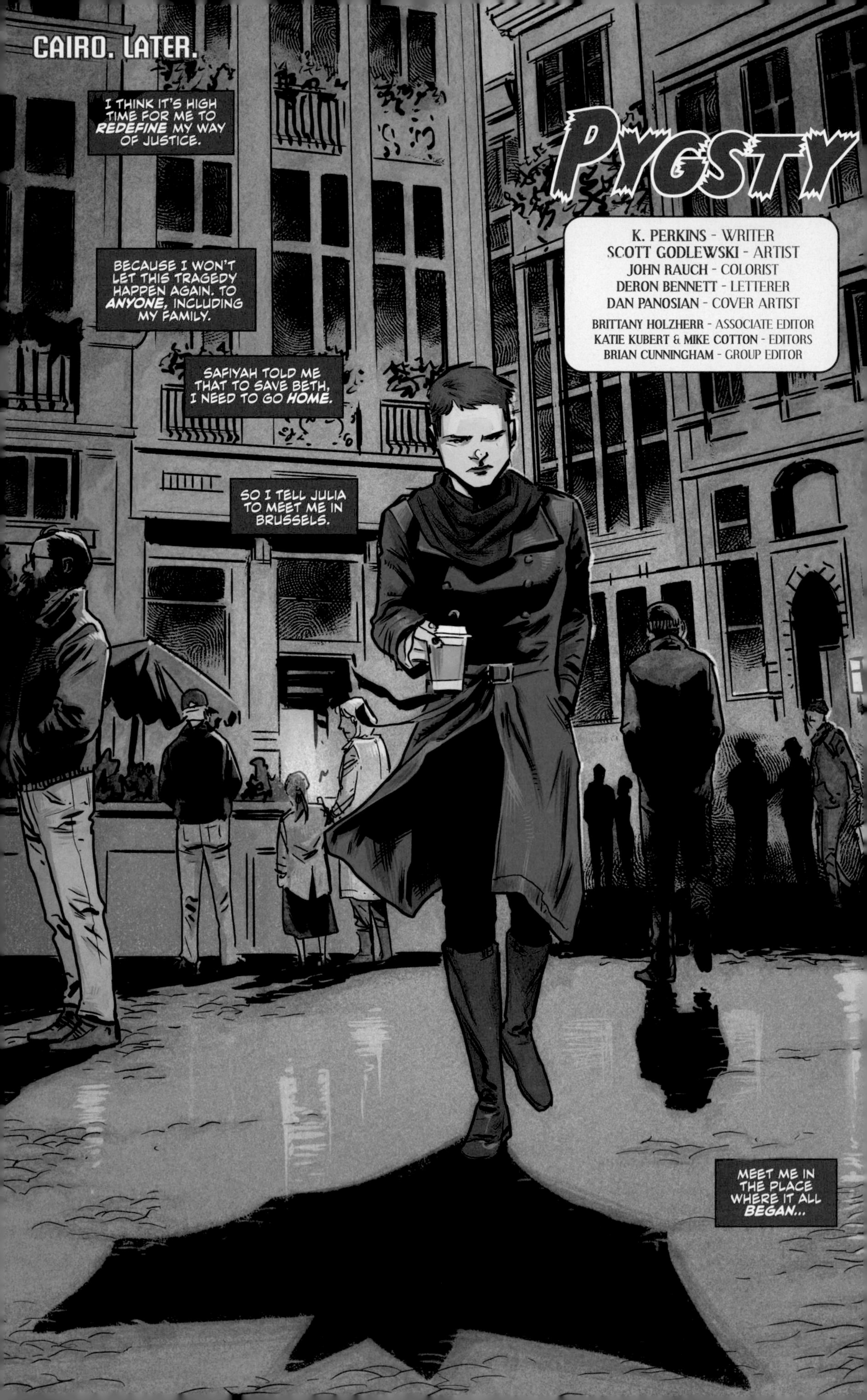
CAIRO. LATER.
I THINK IT'S HIGH TIME FOR ME TO REDEFINE MY WAY OF JUSTICE.
BECAUSE I WON'T LET THIS TRAGEDY HAPPEN AGAIN. TO ANYONE, INCLUDING MY FAMILY.
SAFIYAH TOLD ME THAT TO SAVE BETH, I NEED TO GO HOME.
SO I TELL JULIA TO MEET ME IN BRUSSELS.
PYGSTY
K. PERKINS - WRITER
SCOTT GODLEWSKI - ARTIST
JOHN RAUCH - COLORIST
DERON BENNETT - LETTERER
DAN PANOSIAN - COVER ARTIST
BRITTANY HOLZHERR - ASSOCIATE EDITOR
KATIE KUBERT & MIKE COTTON - EDITORS
BRIAN CUNNINGHAM - GROUP EDITOR
MEET ME IN THE PLACE WHERE IT ALL BEGAN...

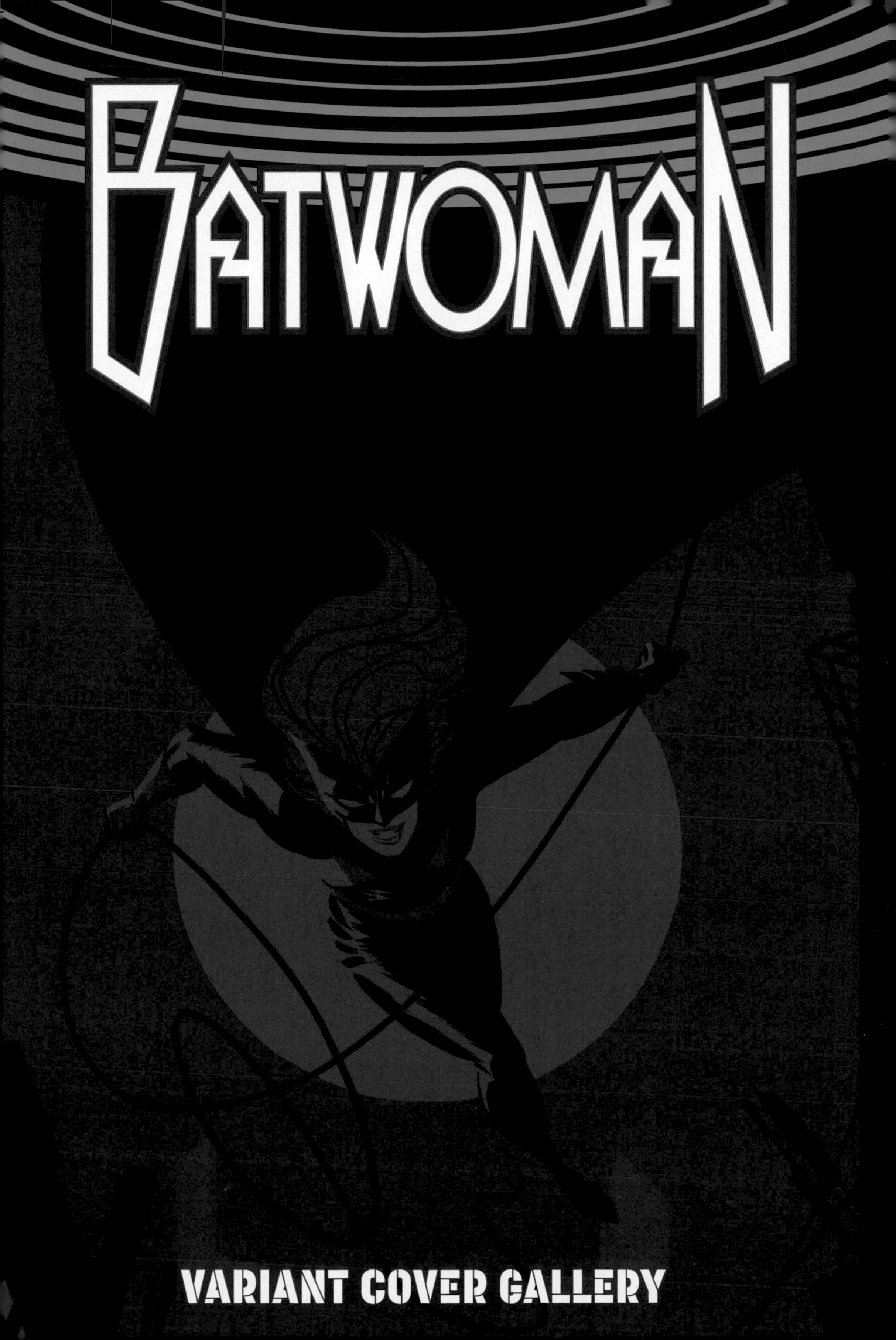
BATWOMAN
VARIANT COVER GALLERY

BATWOMAN #7 variant cover by Robbi Rodriguez

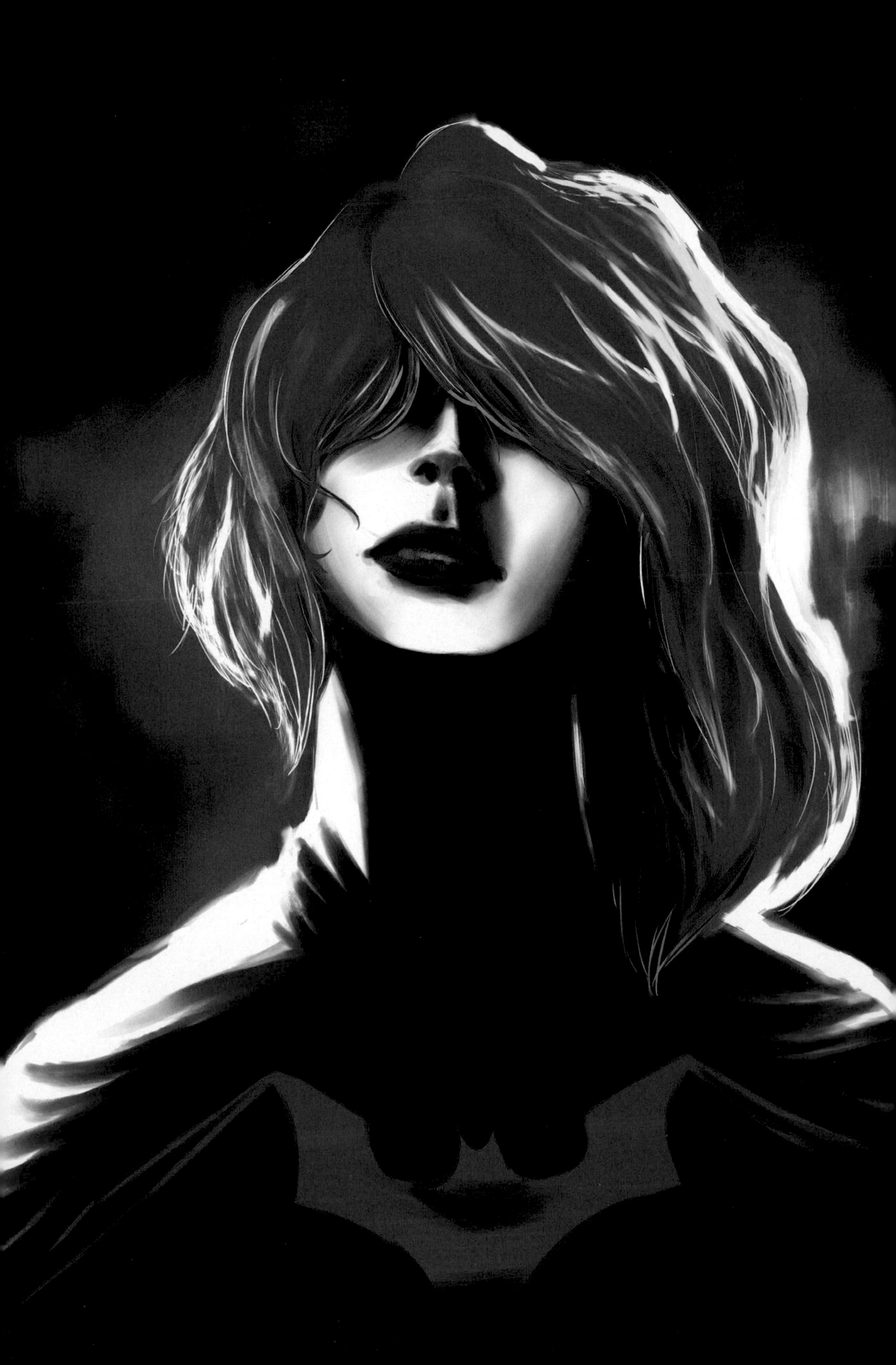

BATWOMAN #8 variant cover by Michael Cho

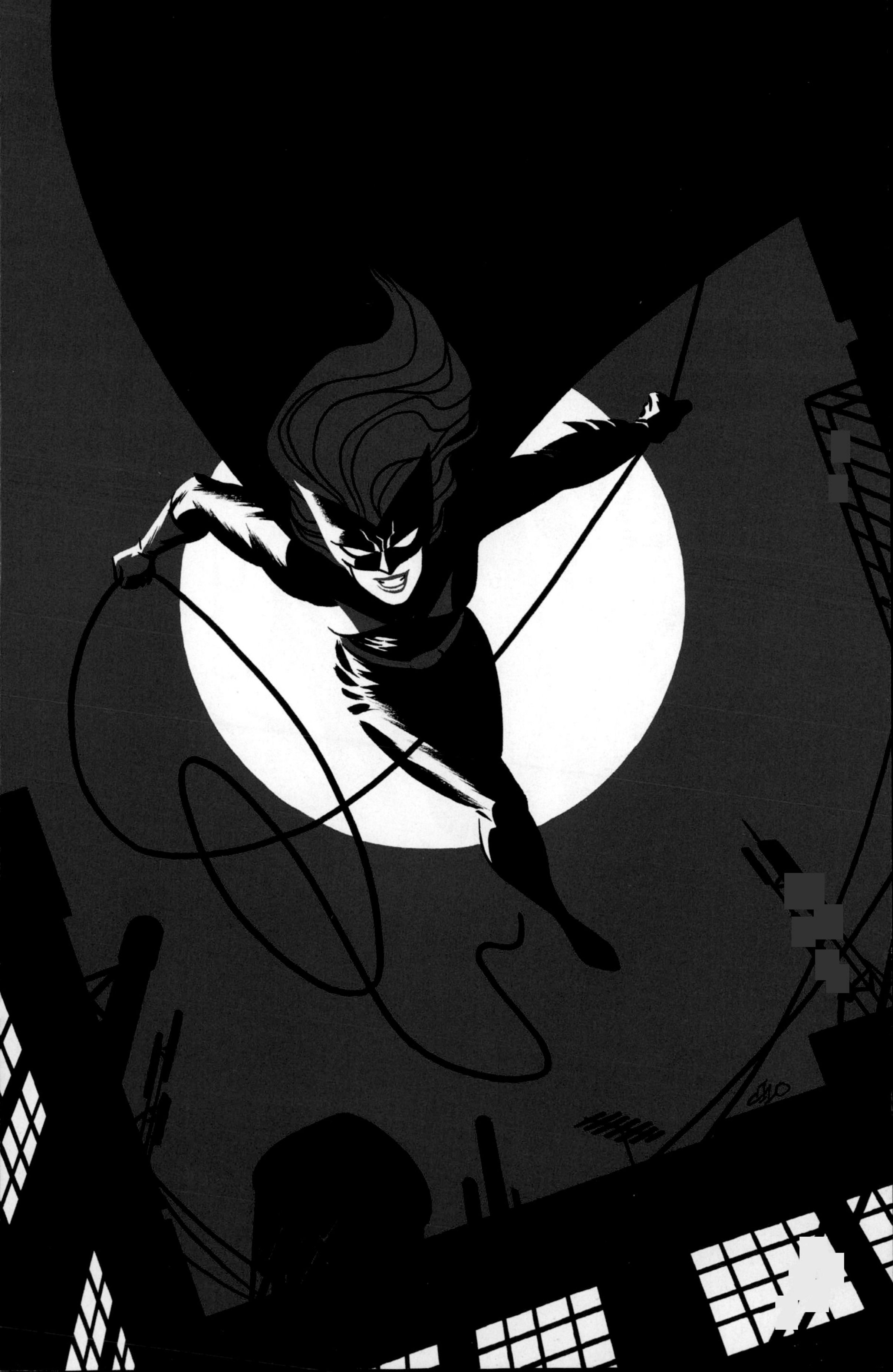

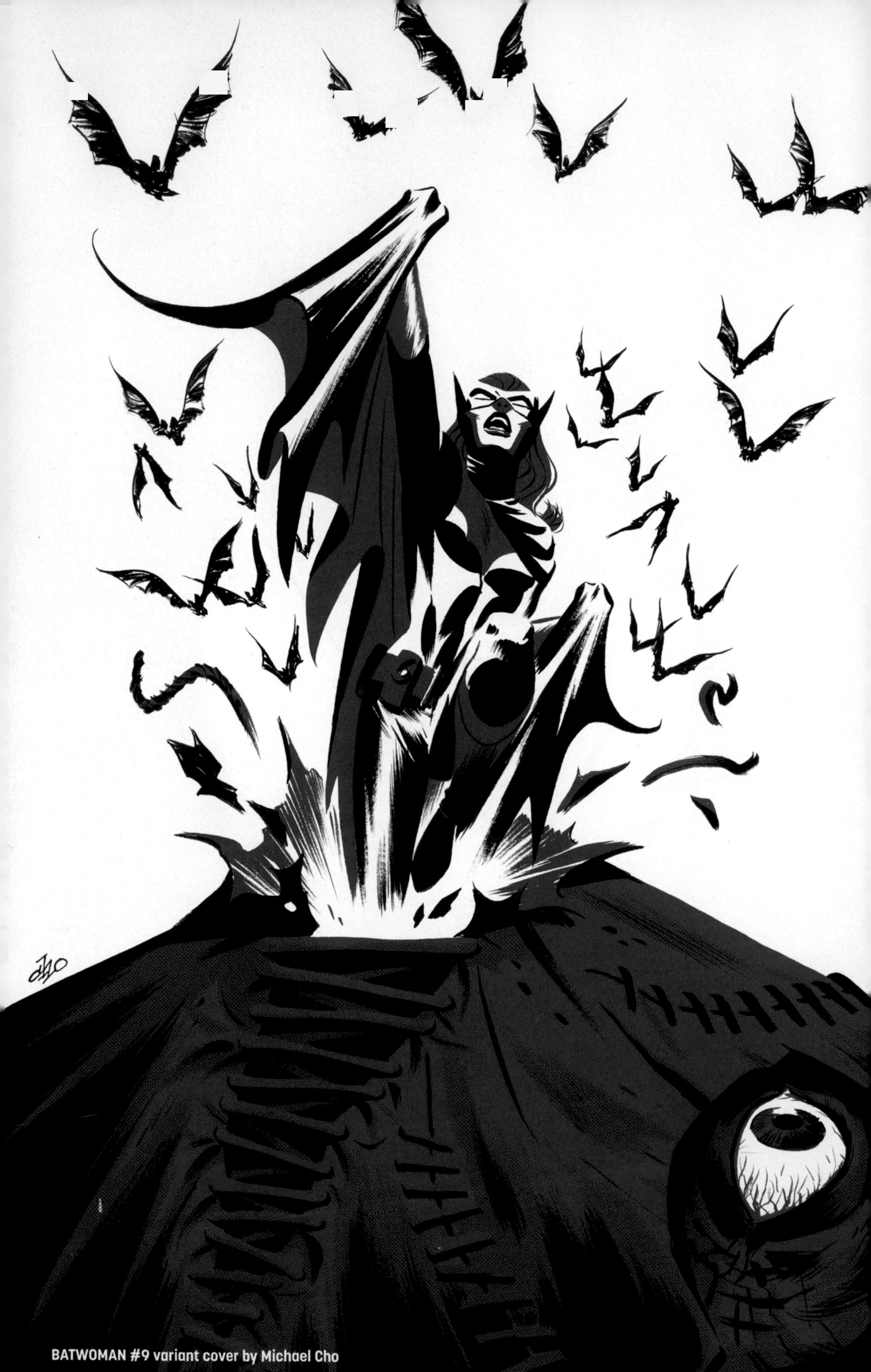

BATWOMAN #9 variant cover by Michael Cho

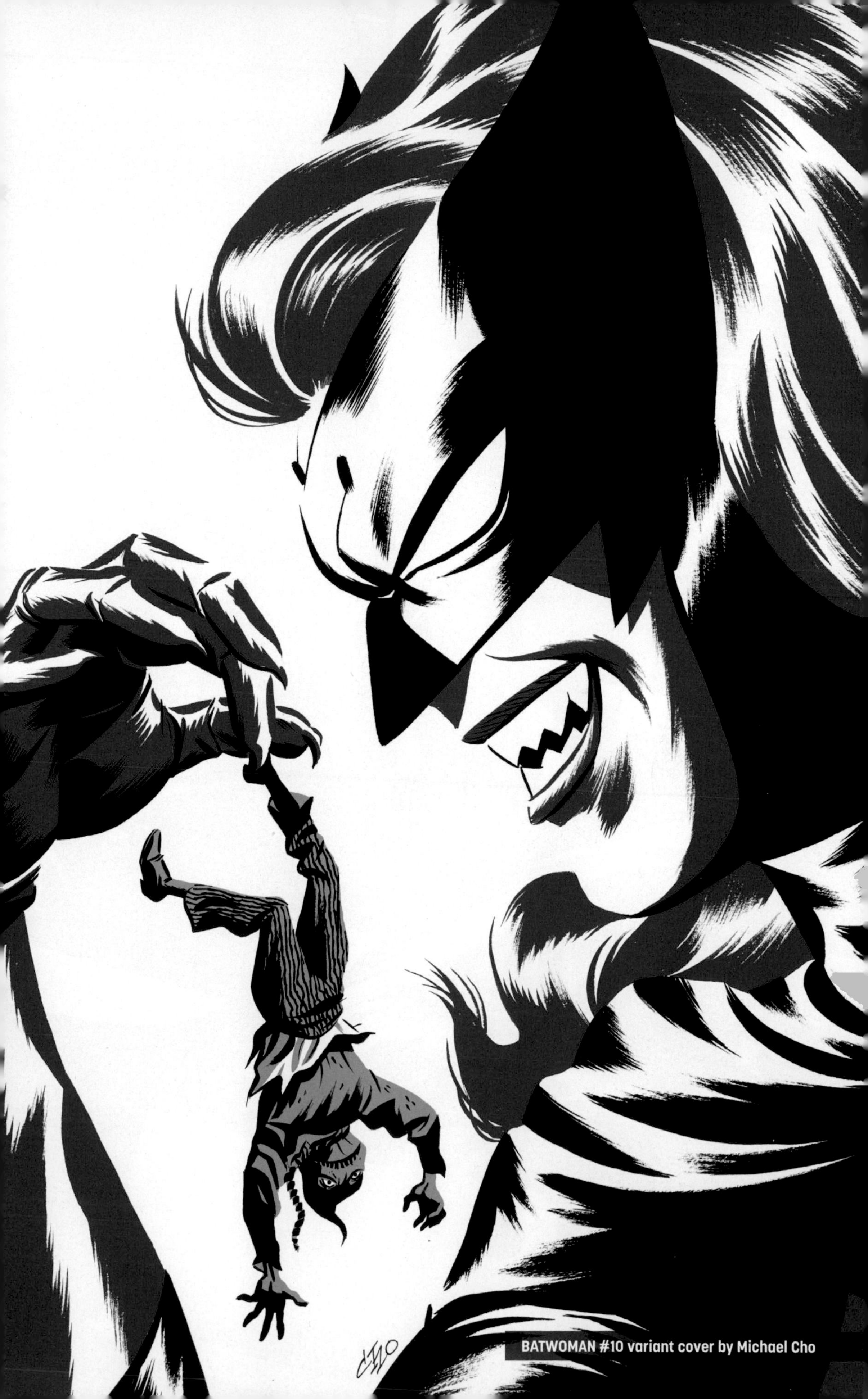

BATWOMAN #10 variant cover by Michael Cho

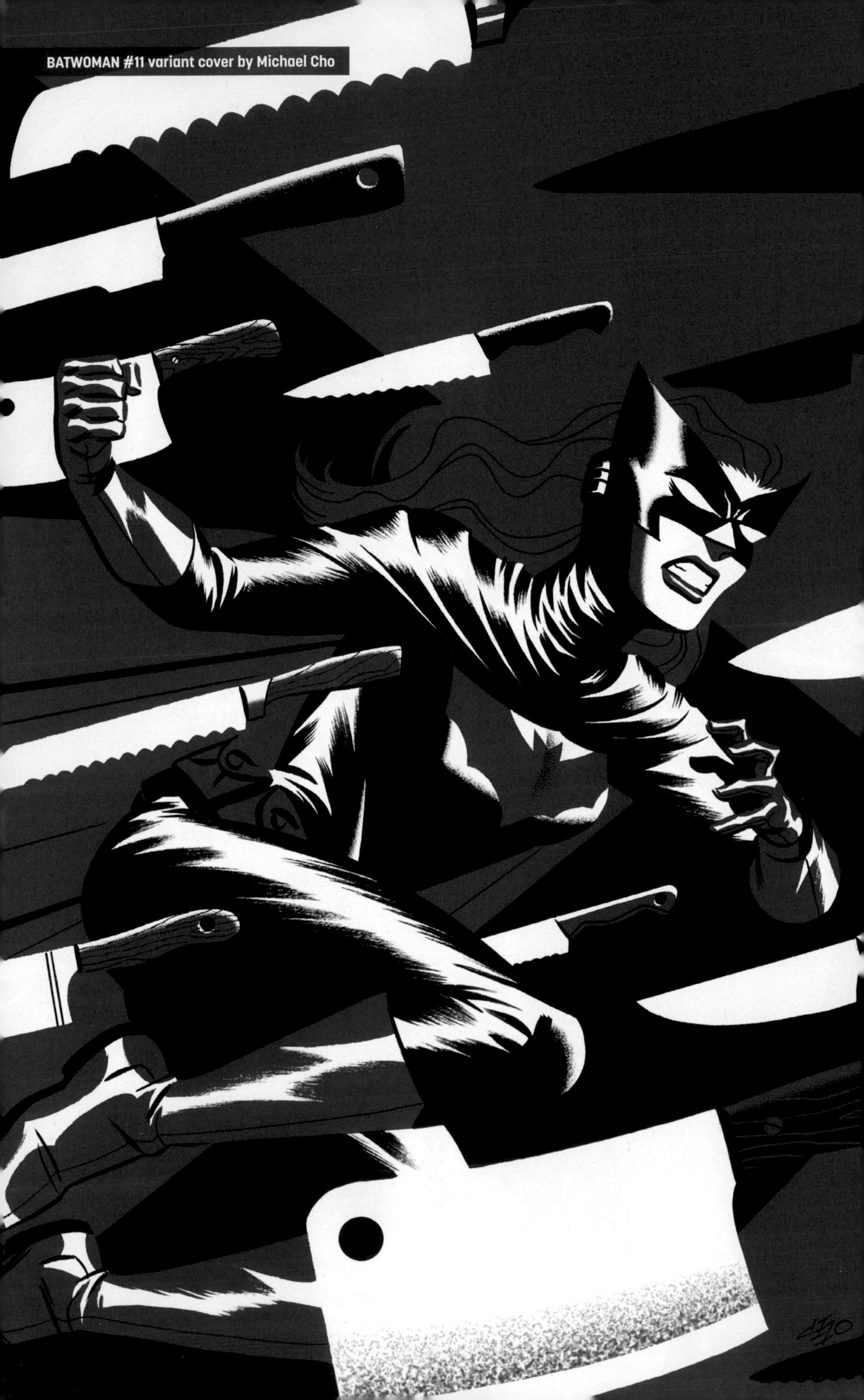

BATWOMAN #11 variant cover by Michael Cho

BATWOMAN #8 and #9 cover sketches by Fernando Blanco

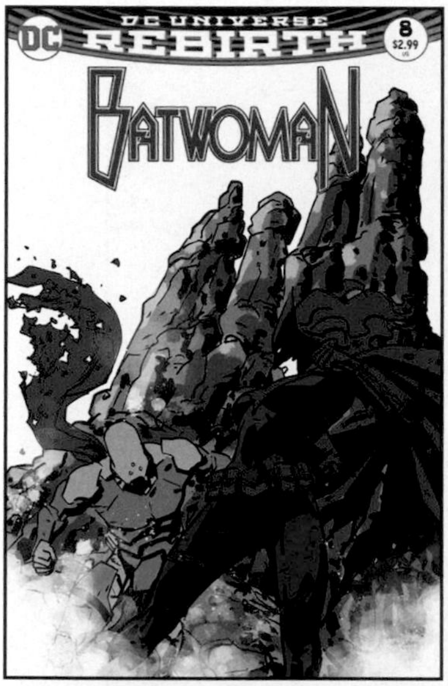
DC UNIVERSE
REBIRTH
8
$2.99
BATWOMAN

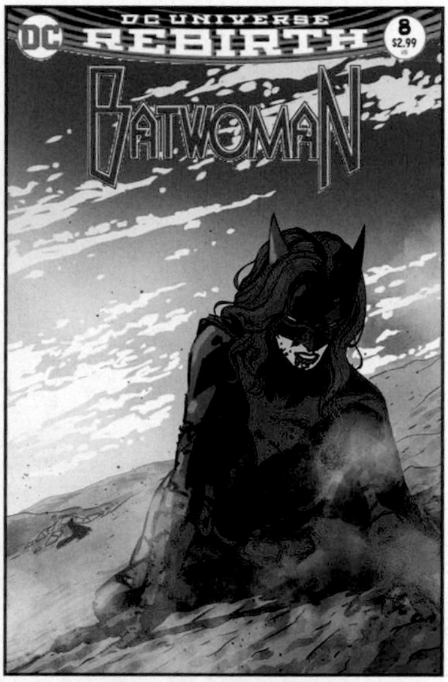
DC UNIVERSE
REBIRTH
8
$2.99
BATWOMAN

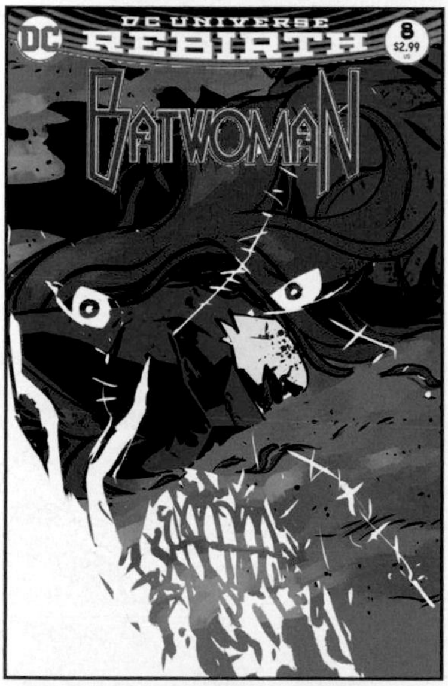
DC UNIVERSE
REBIRTH
8
$2.99
BATWOMAN

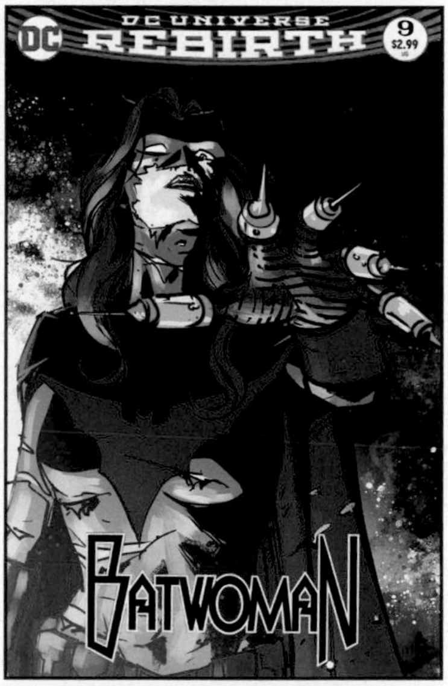
DC UNIVERSE
REBIRTH
9
$2.99
BATWOMAN

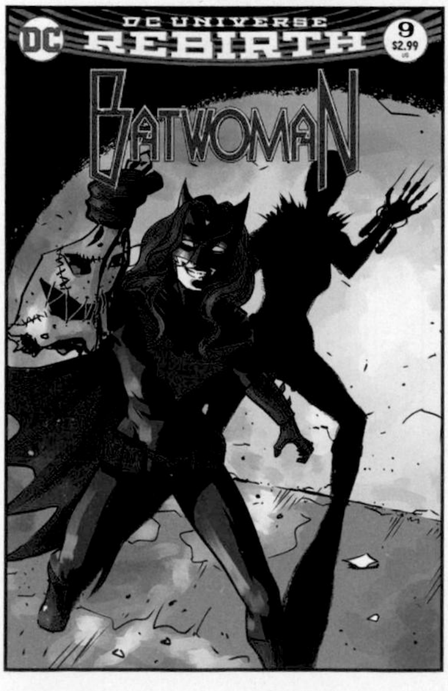
DC UNIVERSE
REBIRTH
9
$2.99
BATWOMAN

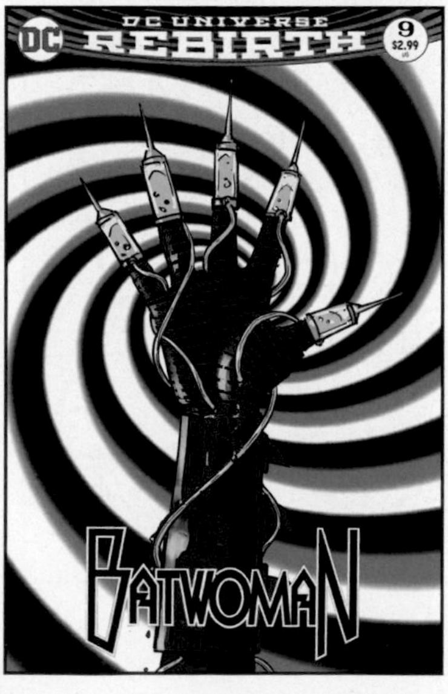
DC UNIVERSE
REBIRTH
9
$2.99
BATWOMAN

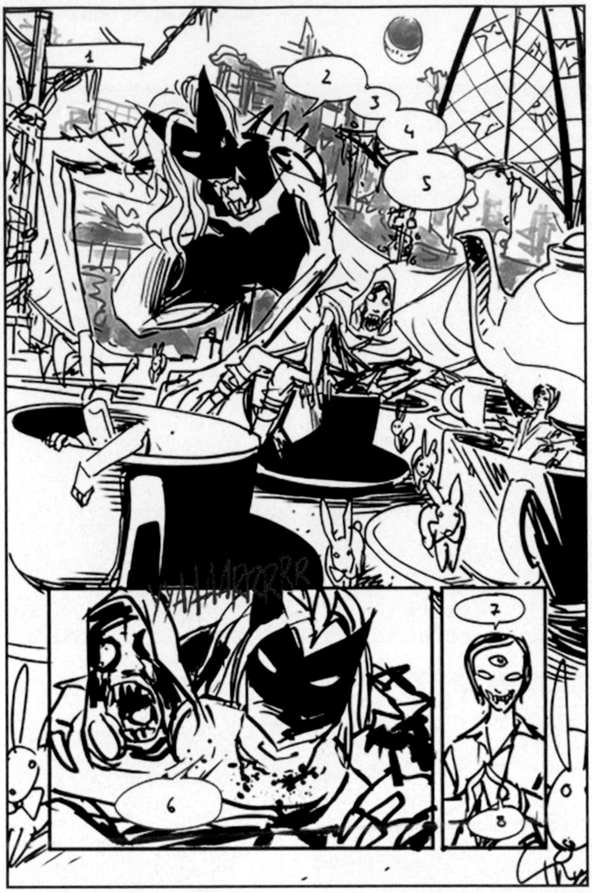

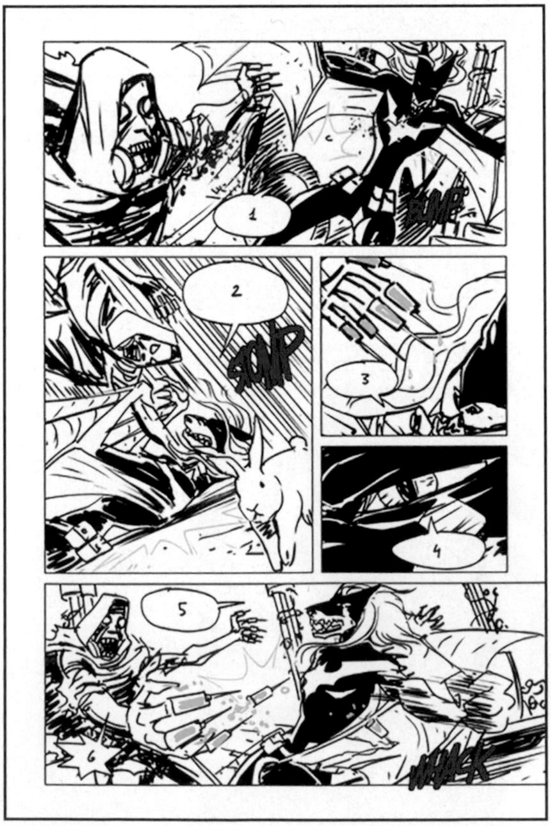

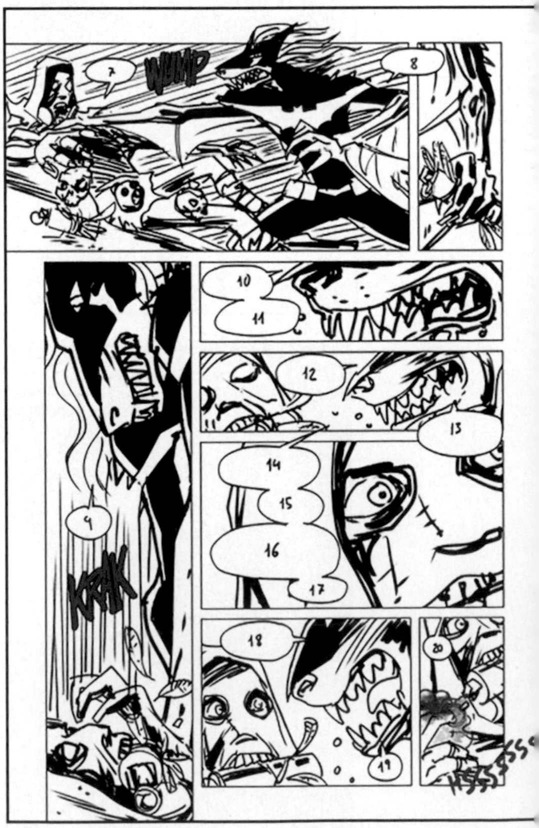
WUMP
KRAK

Thumbnail layouts for BATWOMAN #10 pages 1-3 by Fernando Blanco

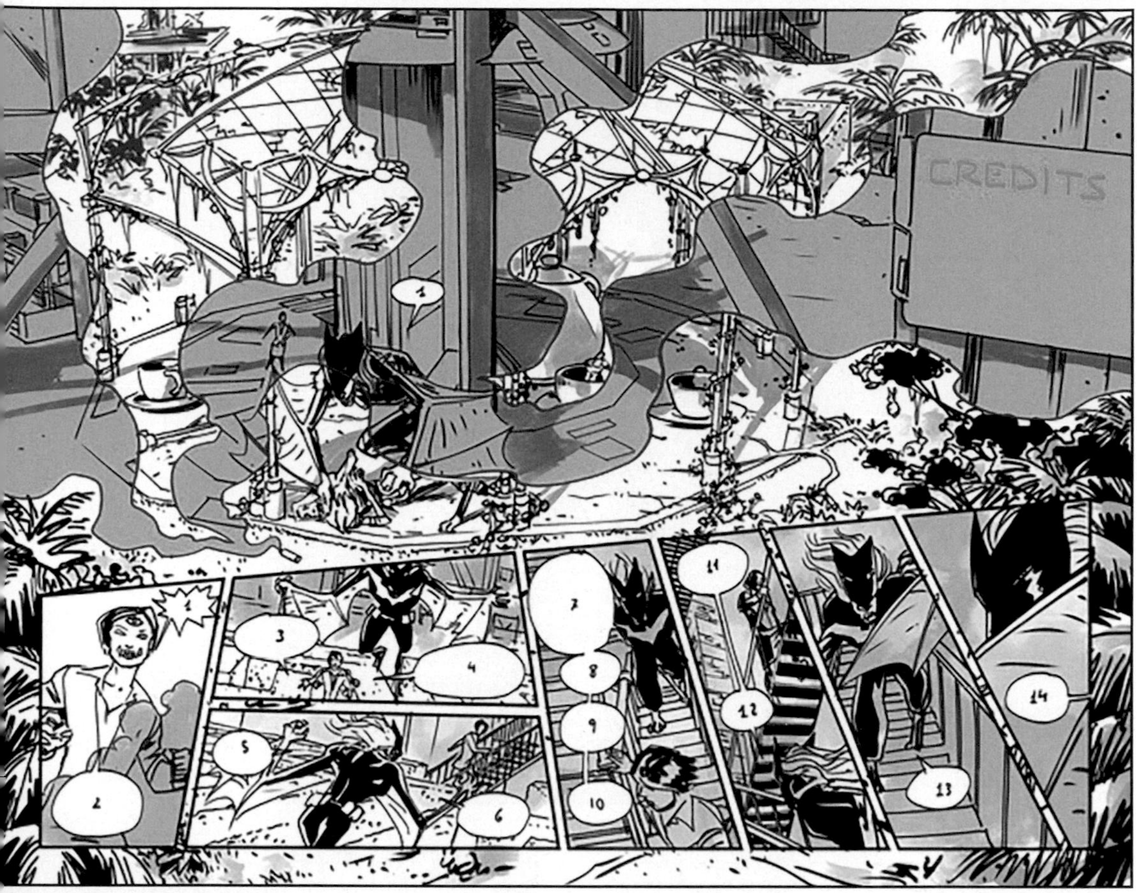
CREDITS

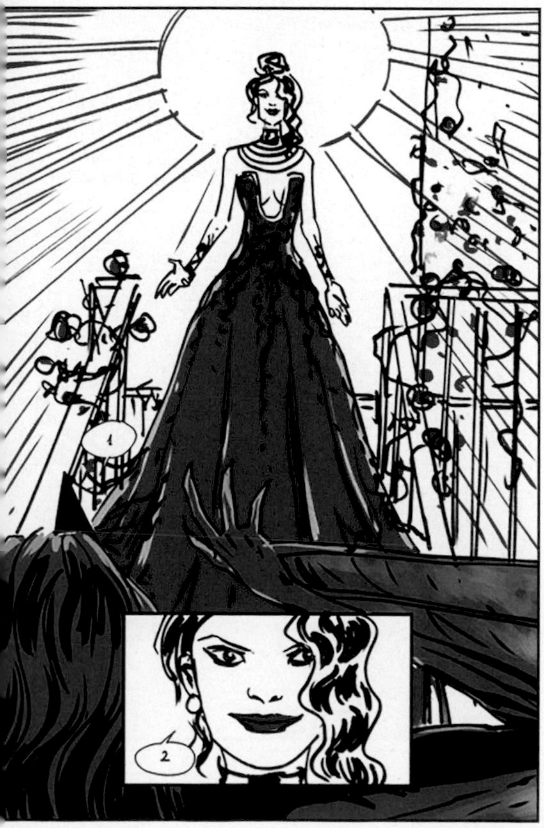

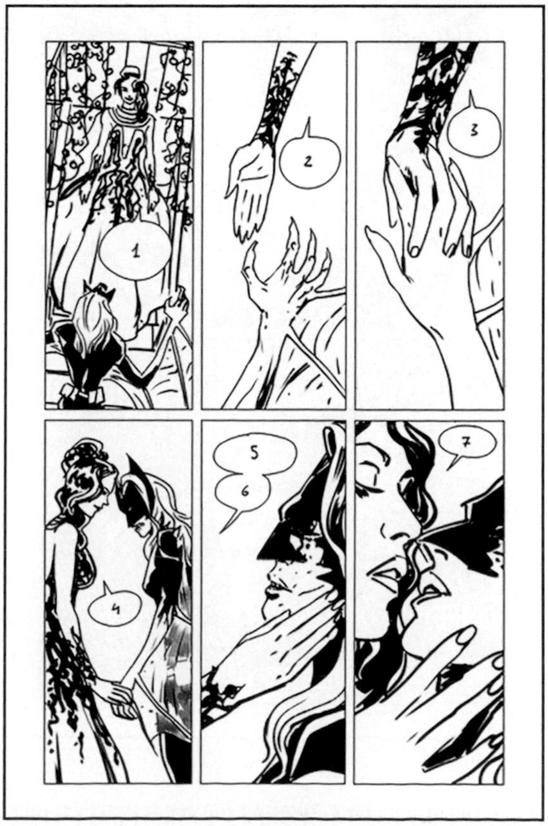

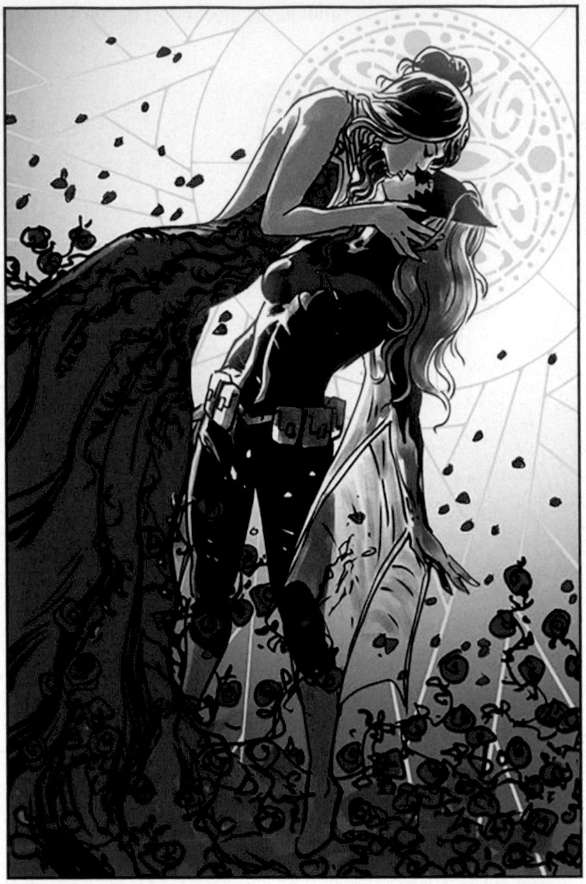

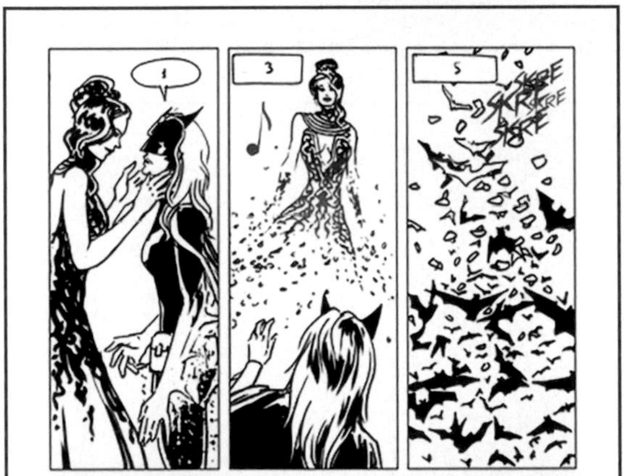
CRRRK
BOOOM

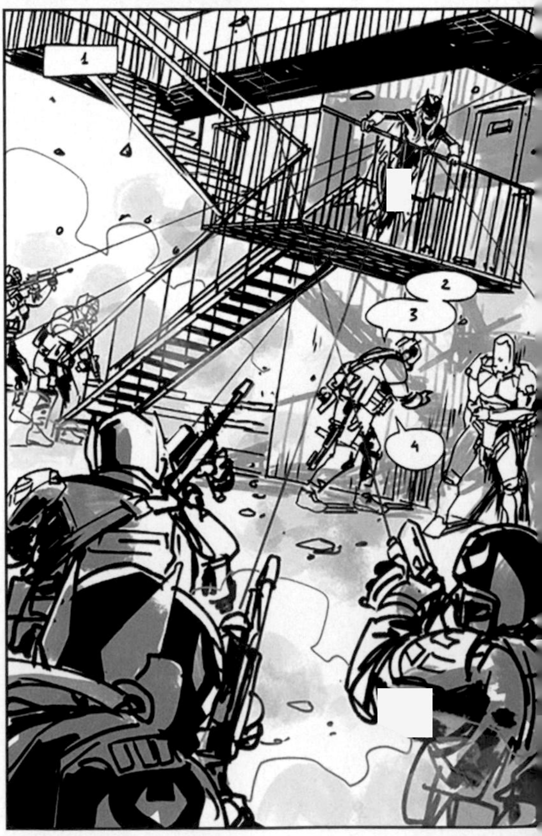

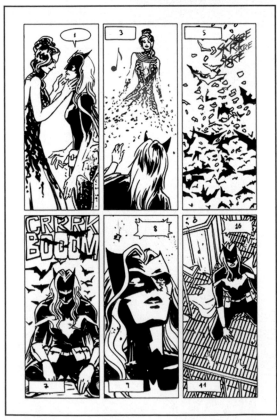

Thumbnail layouts for BATWOMAN #10 pages 8-10 by Fernando Blanco

Thumbnail layouts for BATWOMAN #10 pages 11-13 by Fernando Blanco

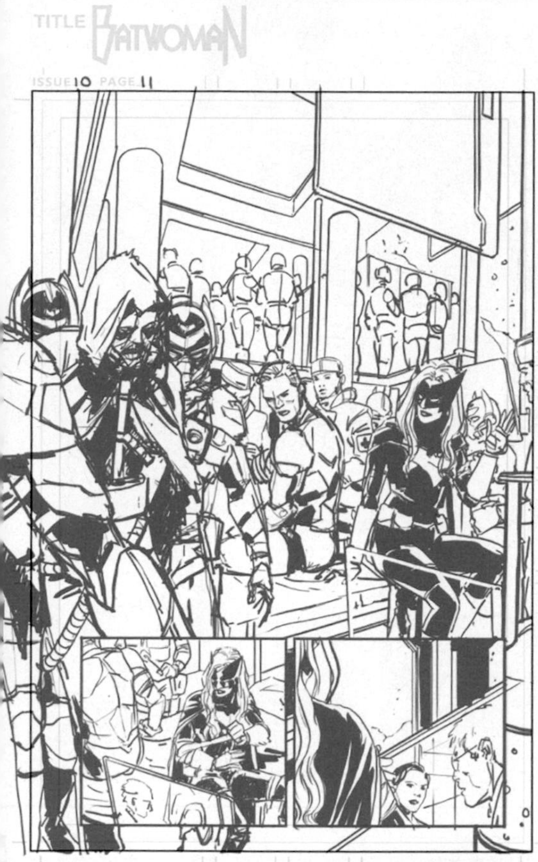
TITLE BATWOMAN
ISSUE 10 PAGE 11

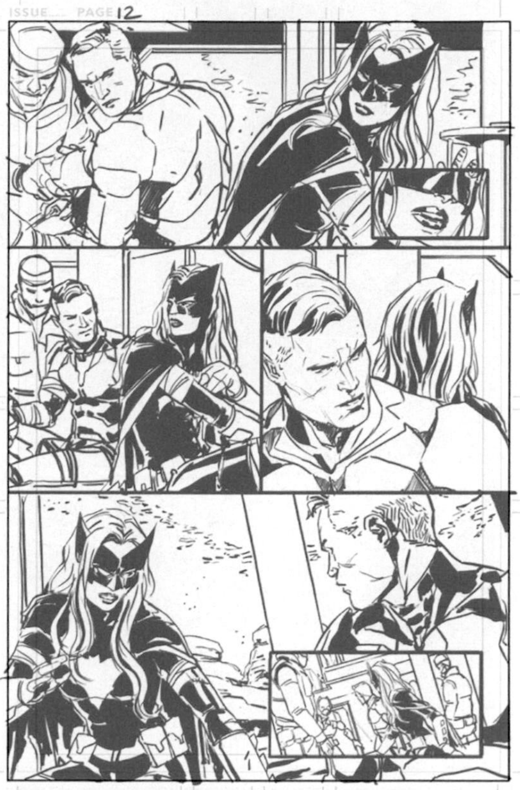
ISSUE PAGE 12

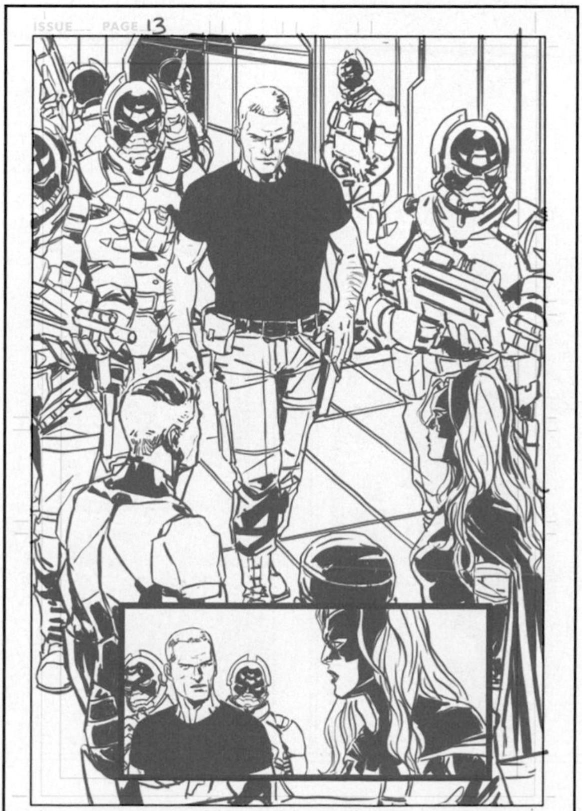
ISSUE PAGE 13

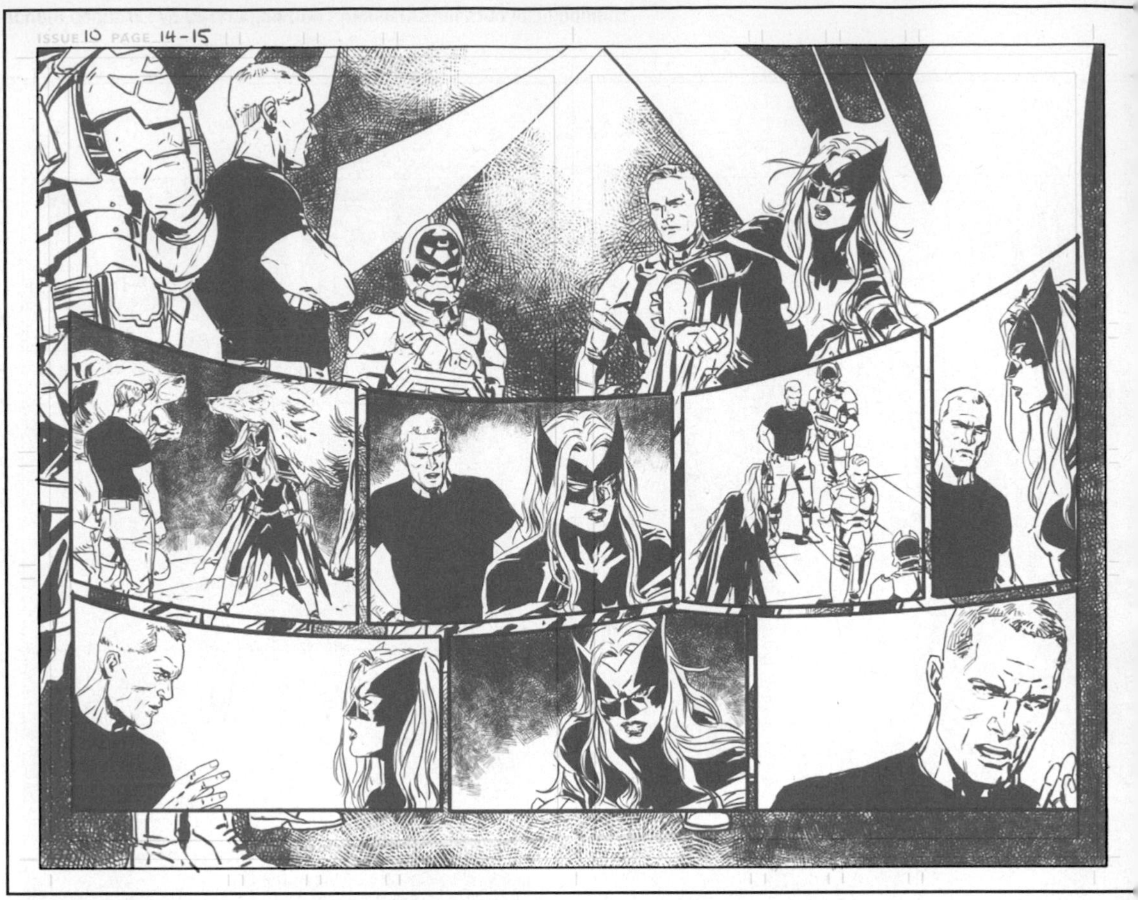
ISSUE 10 PAGE 14-15

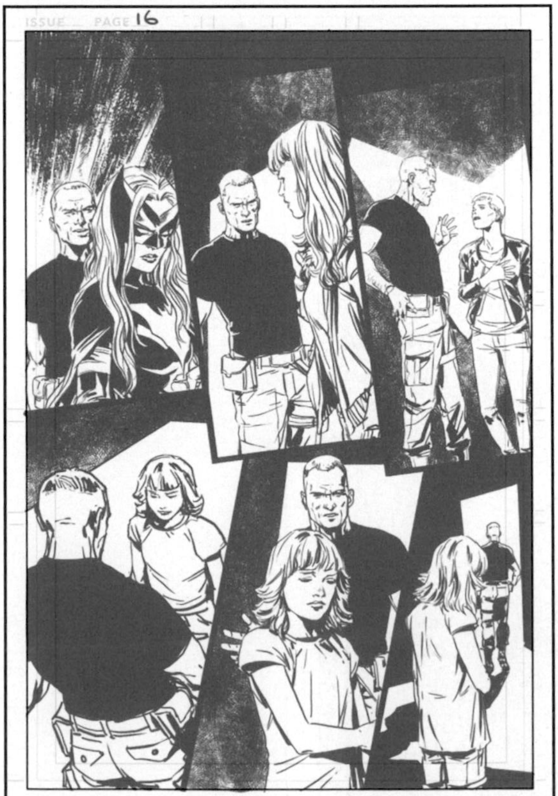
ISSUE PAGE 16

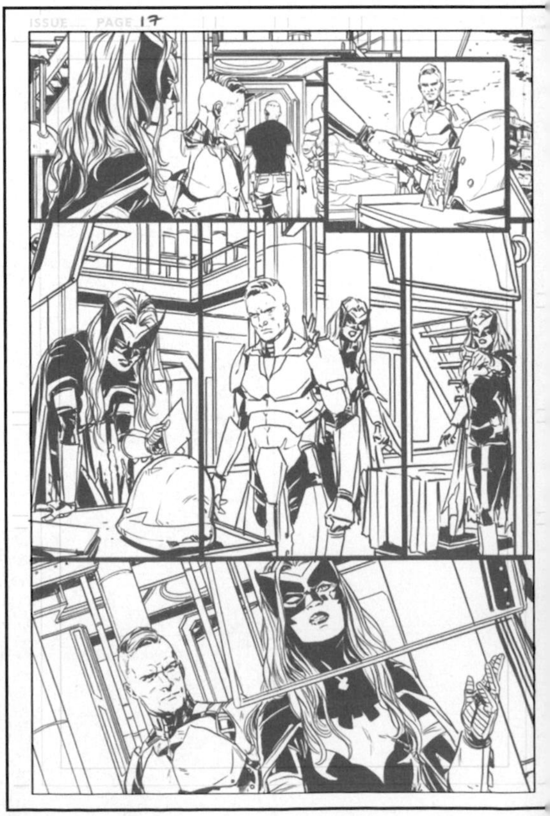
ISSUE PAGE 17

Thumbnail layouts for BATWOMAN #10 pages 14-17 by Fernando Blanco

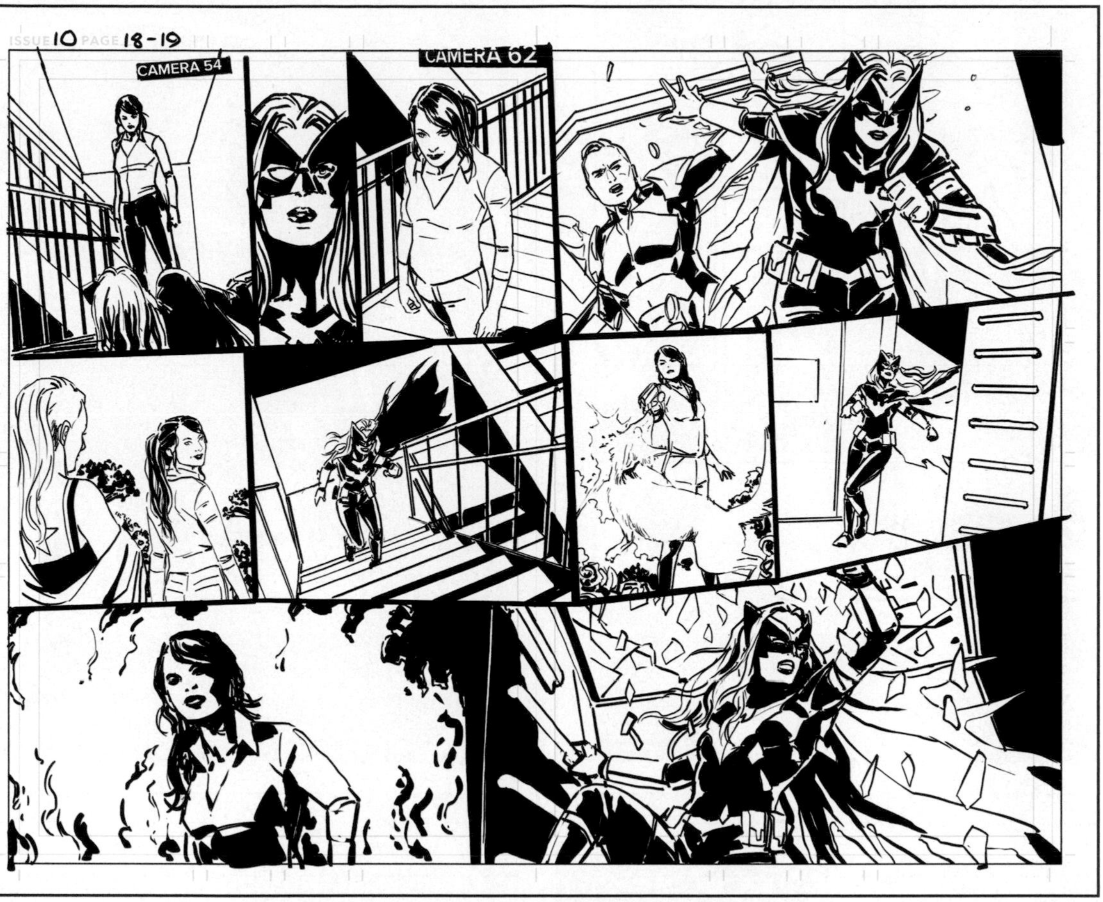
ISSUE 10 PAGE 18-19
CAMERA 54
CAMERA 62

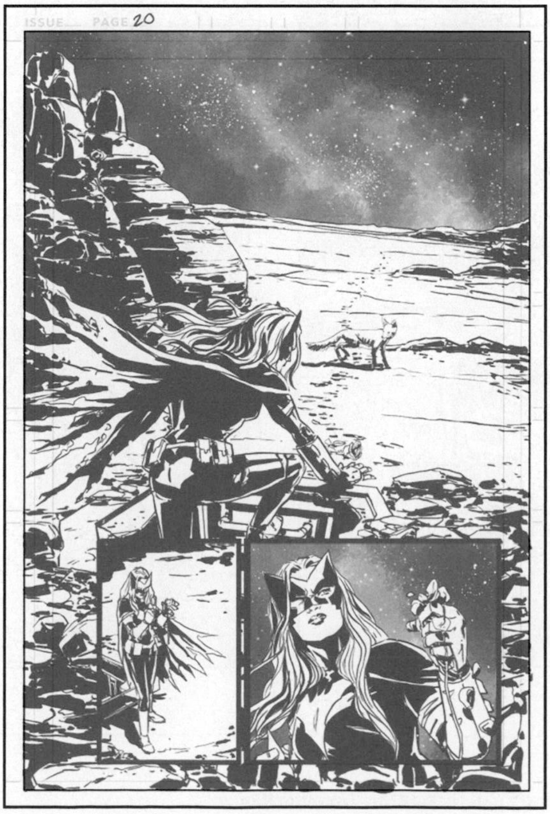
ISSUE PAGE 20

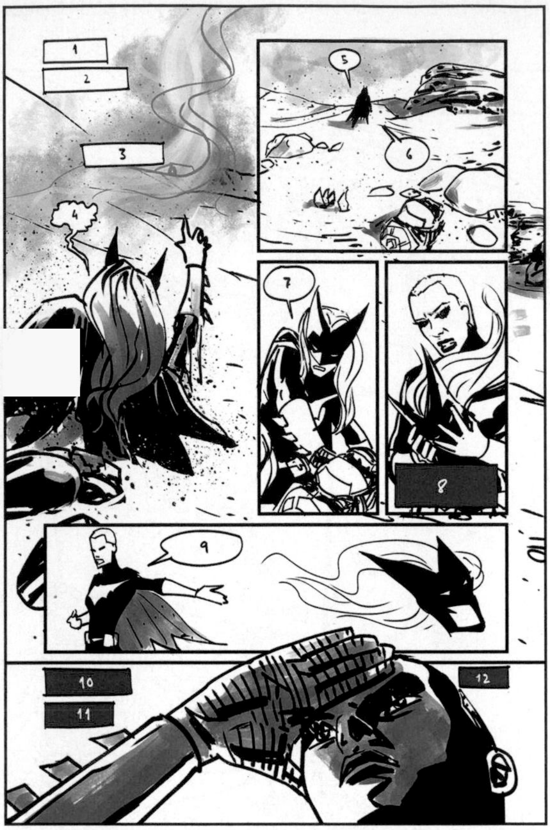

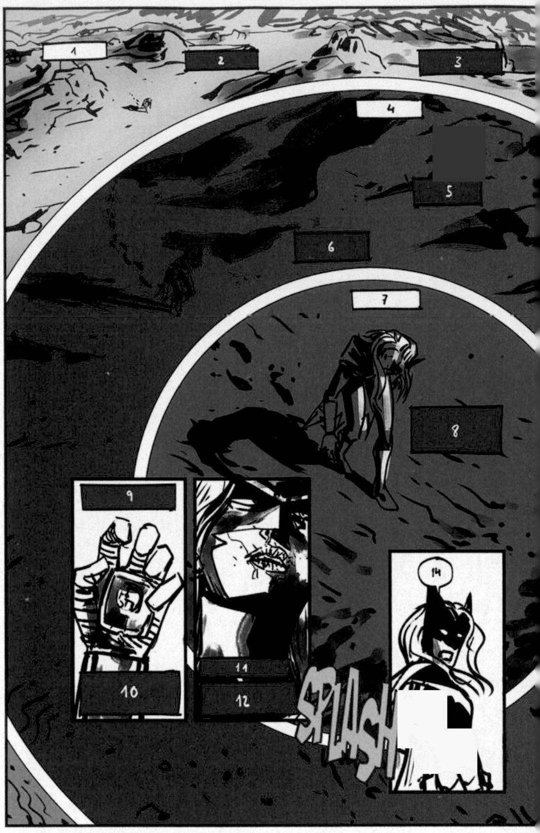
SPLASH

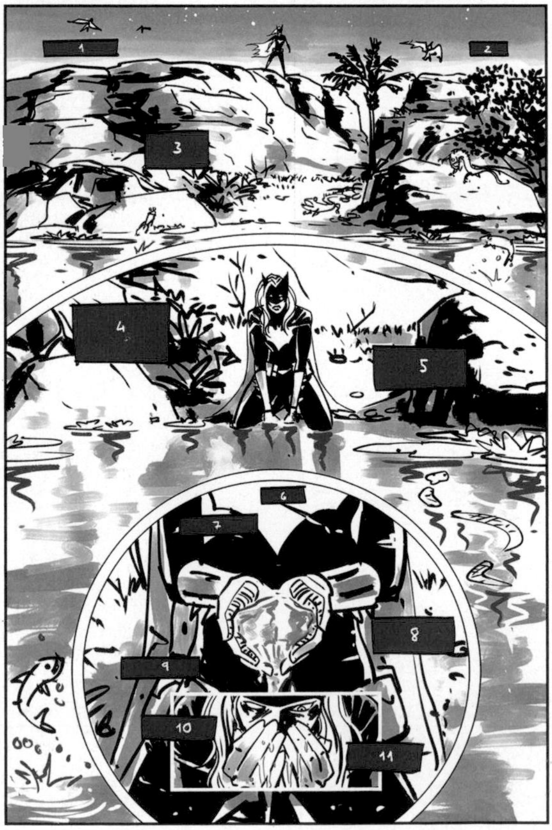

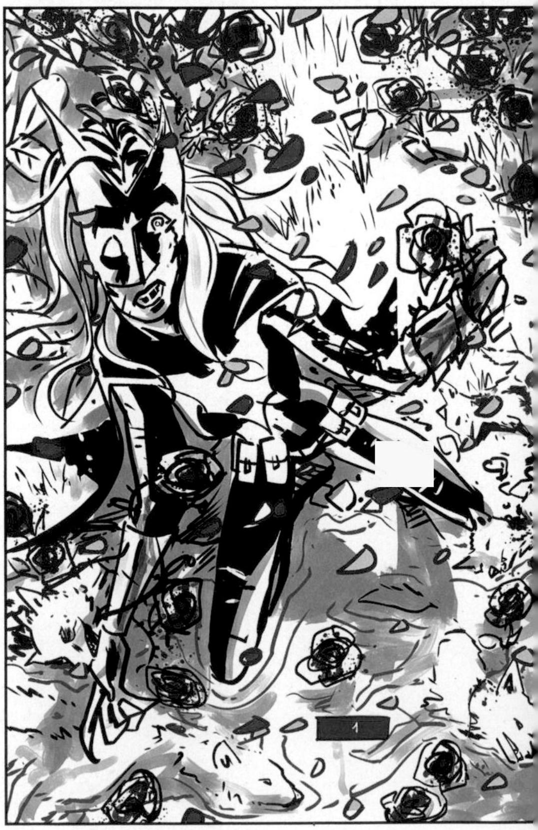

Thumbnail layouts for BATWOMAN #7 pages 15-18 by Fernando Blanco